A Celebration of Poets

Pennsylvania
Grades 4-6
Fall 2009

creativeCOMMUNICATION
A CELEBRATION OF TODAY'S WRITERS

A Celebration of Poets
Pennsylvania
Grades 4-6
Fall 2009

An anthology compiled by Creative Communication, Inc.

Published by:

creativeCOMMUNICATION
A CELEBRATION OF TODAY'S WRITERS

1488 NORTH 200 WEST • LOGAN, UTAH 84341
TEL. 435-713-4411 • WWW.POETICPOWER.COM

Authors are responsible for the originality of the writing submitted.

All rights reserved. No part of this book may be reproduced or transmitted in any form or by any means, electronic or mechanical without written permission of the author and publisher.

Copyright © 2010 by Creative Communication, Inc.
Printed in the United States of America

ISBN: 978-1-60050-313-9

FOREWORD

In today's world there are many things that compete for our attention. From the far reaching influence of the media, to the voices we hear from those around us, it is often difficult to decide where to commit our energies and focus. The poets in this book listened to an inner voice; a voice that can be the loudest of the many voices in our world, but to pay attention to this voice takes self-control. The effect of these words may not be far reaching, but to even make a small difference in the world is a positive thing.

Each year I receive hundreds of letters, calls, and emails from parents, teachers, and students who share stories of success; stories, where being a published writer provided the catalyst to a different attitude toward school, education and life. We are pleased to provide you with this book and hope that what these writers have shared makes a small but meaningful difference in your world.

Thomas Worthen, Ph.D.
Editor
Creative Communication

WRITING CONTESTS!

Enter our next POETRY contest!

Enter our next ESSAY contest!

Why should I enter?
Win prizes and get published! Each year thousands of dollars in prizes are awarded throughout North America. The top writers in each division receive a monetary award and a free book that includes their published poem or essay. Entries of merit are also selected to be published in our anthology.

Who may enter?
There are four divisions in the poetry contest. The poetry divisions are grades K-3, 4-6, 7-9, and 10-12. There are three divisions in the essay contest. The essay divisions are grades 3-6, 7-9, and 10-12.

What is needed to enter the contest?
To enter the poetry contest send in one original poem, 21 lines or less. To enter the essay contest send in one original non-fiction essay, 250 words or less, on any topic. Please submit each poem and essay with a title, and the following information clearly printed: the writer's name, current grade, home address (optional), school name, school address, teacher's name and teacher's email address (optional). Contact information will only be used to provide information about the contest. For complete contest information go to www.poeticpower.com.

How do I enter?

Enter a poem online at:
www.poeticpower.com
or
Mail your poem to:
  Poetry Contest
  1488 North 200 West
  Logan, UT 84341

Enter an essay online at:
www.studentessaycontest.com
or
Mail your essay to:
  Essay Contest
  1488 North 200 West
  Logan, UT 84341

When is the deadline?
Poetry contest deadlines are August 18th, December 2nd and April 5th. Essay contest deadlines are July 15th, October 19th, and February 17th. Students can enter one poem and one essay for each spring, summer, and fall contest deadline.

Are there benefits for my school?
Yes. We award $15,000 each year in grants to help with Language Arts programs. Schools qualify to apply for a grant by having 15 or more accepted entries.

Are there benefits for my teacher?
Yes. Teachers with five or more students published receive a free anthology that includes their students' writing.

For more information please go to our website at **www.poeticpower.com**, email us at editor@poeticpower.com or call 435-713-4411.

TABLE OF CONTENTS

POETIC ACHIEVEMENT HONOR SCHOOLS 1

LANGUAGE ARTS GRANT RECIPIENTS 5

GRADES 4-5-6 HIGH MERIT POEMS 7

INDEX 137

Fall 2009 Poetic Achievement Honor Schools

Teachers who had fifteen or more poets accepted to be published

The following schools are recognized as receiving a "Poetic Achievement Award." This award is given to schools who have a large number of entries of which over fifty percent are accepted for publication. With hundreds of schools entering our contest, only a small percent of these schools are honored with this award. The purpose of this award is to recognize schools with excellent Language Arts programs. This award qualifies these schools to receive a complimentary copy of this anthology. In addition, these schools are eligible to apply for a Creative Communication Language Arts Grant. Grants of two hundred and fifty dollars each are awarded to further develop writing in our schools.

Anne Frank School
Philadelphia
    Christine M. Schuler*

Cambria Heights Middle School
Patton
    Laura Wargo*

Central Elementary School
Perryopolis
    Janet Frescura
    Mary Kay Toth

Chichester Middle School
Boothwyn
    Susan O. Fitzgerald*

Clearview Elementary School
Bethlehem
    Amy M. Kravetz*

Colonial Elementary School
Plymouth Meeting
    Roe Overcash*

East Union Intermediate Center
Russellton
    Cheryl Cisek*
    Paula Pellafone*
    Donna Vokish*

Fairview Elementary School
Midland
    Mrs. Bobin
    Donna Harn
    Rose Onuska*

Foster Elementary School
Pittsburgh
    Mary Hopkins*
    Lora Lutz

Hamilton Elementary School
Lancaster
    Peg Aulisio
    Lori Irvin*
    William E. Way*

Hillcrest Elementary School
Holland
    Kelly Weiss*

Holy Child Academy
    Drexel Hill
        Michelle M. Dugan*
        Patricia McDaniel*
        Barbara Sherwood

Holy Martyrs Elementary School
    Oreland
        Eugenie McClintock*

Holy Rosary School
    Duryea
        Lisa Casey*

Hopewell Memorial Jr High School
    Aliquippa
        Dawn Gailey*

Immaculate Conception School
    Pittsburgh
        Mrs. Attwood
        Sr. Teresa Baldi
        Mrs. Guy

Interboro GATE Program
    Prospect Park
        Joyce Faragasso*

Jefferson Elementary School
    Pittsburgh
        Joy Buettner
        Mrs. Stack

Lincoln Elementary School
    Gettysburg
        Debra J. Kinard*

McKinley Elementary School
    Elkins Park
        Mr. Beam
        Miss Bunjun*
        Dennis Donnelly
        Mrs. Hartzell
        Mrs. Hazelwood
        Miss Livingood
        Marsha Marcy*
        Mrs. McGettigan

McKinley Elementary School (cont.)
    Elkins Park
        Miss Murphy
        Natalie Pawell*
        Joanne Stoll
        Lynne Wilkins

Middle Smithfield Elementary School
    East Stroudsburg
        Barbara Dahl*

Moravian Academy Middle School
    Bethlehem
        Christine Masick
        Cindy Siegfried*

Nazareth Area Intermediate School
    Nazareth
        Mrs. Post*

Notre Dame School
    Hermitage
        Olga Metro*

Our Lady of Ransom School
    Philadelphia
        Lorraine Cole*

Pennridge North Middle School
    Perkasie
        Mrs. P. Ritchie*
        Melissa D. Young*

Pocopson Elementary School
    West Chester
        David Lichter
        Kristie Spina

Ross Elementary School
    Pittsburgh
        Maddy Gillingham
        Karen Jones*

Saint Theresa School
    New Cumberland
        Vikki DeBastiani
        Rhonda Houseman

Ss Simon and Jude Elementary School
    Pittsburgh
        Mrs. Scully*

St Andrew's School
    Johnstown
        Sharon Kaufman*

St Anselm School
    Philadelphia
        Mrs. P. Erwin
        Ruth McIntyre
        Freda M. Tait*

St Hilary of Poitiers School
    Rydal
        Patricia Sermarini*

St Jerome Elementary School
    Philadelphia
        Luba Kwoczak*

St Joan of Arc School
    South Park
        Kathy Moeslein*

St Joseph School
    Mechanicsburg
        Mrs. Connolly
        Louise M. Dolson*
        Rosanna Ellis
        Barbara Jessick*
        Marie C. Vassey

St Maria Goretti School
    Hatfield
        Joanne Ryan*

St Sebastian Elementary School
    Pittsburgh
        Susan L. Slifkin*

The American Academy
    Philadelphia
        Dr. Sharon Traver*

Trinity Middle School
    Washington
        Denise R. Cummins*
        Francesca Lounder

Watsontown Elementary School
    Watsontown
        Jodie Danowsky
        Becky Geiger
        Jenn Harer
        Alison Newman
        Dana Pick
        Eric Rockey
        Marcia Saam*

West Allegheny Middle School
    Imperial
        Mary Damratoski*
        Deana Mack*
        Susan Martin
        Anita Miller

Wickersham Elementary School
    Lancaster
        Rachel Tadlock*

Wissahickon Charter School
    Philadelphia
        Leslie S. Leff*

Language Arts Grant Recipients 2009-2010

After receiving a "Poetic Achievement Award" schools are encouraged to apply for a Creative Communication Language Arts Grant. The following is a list of schools who received a two hundred and fifty dollar grant for the 2009-2010 school year.

Arrowhead Union High School, Hartland, WI
Blessed Sacrament School, Seminole, FL
Booneville Jr High School, Booneville, AR
Buckhannon-Upshur Middle School, Buckhannon, WV
Campbell High School, Ewa Beach, HI
Chickahominy Middle School, Mechanicsville, VA
Clarkston Jr High School, Clarkston, MI
Covenant Life School, Gaithersburg, MD
CW Rice Middle School, Northumberland, PA
Eason Elementary School, Waukee, IA
East Elementary School, Kodiak, AK
Florence M Gaudineer Middle School, Springfield, NJ
Foxborough Regional Charter School, Foxborough, MA
Gideon High School, Gideon, MO
Holy Child Academy, Drexel Hill, PA
Home Choice Academy, Vancouver, WA
Jeff Davis Elementary School, Biloxi, MS
Lower Alloways Creek Elementary School, Salem, NJ
Maple Wood Elementary School, Somersworth, NH
Mary Walter Elementary School, Bealeton, VA
Mater Dei High School, Evansville, IN
Mercy High School, Farmington Hills, MI
Monroeville Elementary School, Monroeville, OH
Nautilus Middle School, Miami Beach, FL
Our Lady Star of the Sea School, Grosse Pointe Woods, MI
Overton High School, Memphis, TN
Pond Road Middle School, Robbinsville, NJ
Providence Hall Charter School, Herriman, UT
Reuben Johnson Elementary School, McKinney, TX
Rivelon Elementary School, Orangeburg, SC
Rose Hill Elementary School, Omaha, NE

Language Arts Grant Winners cont.

Runnels School, Baton Rouge, LA
Santa Fe Springs Christian School, Santa Fe Springs, CA
Serra Catholic High School, Mckeesport, PA
Shadowlawn Elementary School, Green Cove Springs, FL
Spectrum Elementary School, Gilbert, AZ
St Edmund Parish School, Oak Park, IL
St Joseph Institute for the Deaf, Chesterfield, MO
St Joseph Regional Jr High School, Manchester, NH
St Mary of Czestochowa School, Middletown, CT
St Monica Elementary School, Garfield Heights, OH
St Vincent De Paul Elementary School, Cape Girardeau, MO
Stevensville Middle School, Stevensville, MD
Tashua School, Trumbull, CT
The New York Institute for Special Education, Bronx, NY
The Selwyn School, Denton, TX
Tonganoxie Middle School, Tonganoxie, KS
Westside Academy, Prince George, BC
Willa Cather Elementary School, Omaha, NE
Willow Hill Elementary School, Traverse City, MI

Grades 4-5-6 Top Ten Winners

List of Top Ten Winners for Grades 4-6; listed alphabetically

Hailey Benesh, Grade 6
T J Walker Middle School, Sturgeon Bay, WI

Anne Cebula, Grade 6
Intermediate School 239 Mark Twain for the Gifted & Talented, Brooklyn, NY

Zari Gordon, Grade 5
Walker Elementary School, Evanston, IL

Helena Green, Grade 5
Hopewell Elementary School, Hopewell, NJ

Kristin Kachel, Grade 6
Discovery Canyon Campus, Colorado Springs, CO

Carrie Mannino, Grade 5
The Ellis School, Pittsburgh, PA

Mariah Reynolds, Grade 4
School for Creative and Performing Arts, Cincinnati, OH

Jeremy Stepansky, Grade 5
Hillside Elementary School, Montclair, NJ

Anne-Katherine Tallent, Grade 5
Providence Academy, Johnson City, TN

Claudia Zhang, Grade 6
Rolling Ridge Elementary School, Chino Hills, CA

All Top Ten Poems can be read at www.poeticpower.com

Note: The Top Ten poems were finalized through an online voting system. Creative Communication's judges first picked out the top poems. These poems were then posted online. The final step involved thousands of students and teachers who registered as the online judges and voted for the Top Ten poems. We hope you enjoy these selections.

Summer
Summer
It is nice and hot,
I swim in the cool water,
Summer is so fun!
Ashlee Camarote, Grade 5
Russell Elementary School

The Winter Day
It is snowing,
And the hot cocoa is flowing.
There is a sled,
That looks like a snow bed.
Ally Kelly, Grade 4
Sacred Heart School

Hiking in the Woods
Lots of grass growing wild,
Also flowers in bunches and piles.
People hiking behind all the trees,
And all the tall weeds blowing in the breeze.
Maria DiSanti, Grade 4
Sacred Heart School

Snow Days
S now days!
N eighborhood on the run
O n slippery ice to skate!
W hole bunch of snow.
Mya Brener, Grade 4
McKinley Elementary School

Grandparents Are…
Helpful whenever you need it.
Making you feel joyful when you are sad.
Giving you almost whatever you want.
Very loyal to your happiness.
Allura Kistler, Grade 6
Moravian Academy Middle School

My Dog
My dog is fun, my dog is cute.
He fell down the laundry chute.
He came back up and looked around.
And there he saw a bone on the ground.
Maya Cannon, Grade 5
East Union Intermediate Center

Cats
Cats are cute and peaceful.
They purr when you are kind.
Some cats feel unbelievable
And some cats are hard to find.
Hannah Brennan, Grade 4
St Joseph School

Joy
Joy is a baby crying for the first time after it is born.
Joy is all your family gathered together for a Thanksgiving feast.
Joy is peace for the whole entire world.
Joy is shiny gold just like the North Star up in the sky.
Joy tastes like chunky, chewy, chocolate chip cookies right out of the oven.
Joy smells like the sweet aroma of newly bloomed flowers.
Joy sounds like the ding-dong of the church bells after a wedding.
Joy feels smooth like my baby blanket against my skin.
Joy looks like a shiny gold penny lying on the road.
Joy makes me dance under the moonlit sky on a starry night.
Joy is waking up and finding presents underneath the tree on Christmas morning.
Joy is helping those who cannot help themselves.
Megan Wurst, Grade 6
West Allegheny Middle School

Calmness
Calmness is a still lake with no ripples
Calmness is a dim light in a dark room
Calmness is a slow and quiet song
Calmness is lavender like a lilac
Calmness tastes like a piece of candy that isn't too sweet or too tart
Calmness smells like a bouquet of sweet smelling lilacs
Calmness sounds like waves crashing on the shore
Calmness feels like a cozy blanket on a chilly night
Calmness looks like a soothing scene of a meadow filled with flowers
Calmness makes me want to sit down and relax
Calmness smiles at you and gives you a warm feeling inside
Calmness is like a relaxing day at the beach
Pryclynn Campbell, Grade 6
West Allegheny Middle School

Happiness
Happiness is the Pittsburgh Steelers winning the Super Bowl
Happiness is a soft, warm blanket from your mom
Happiness is a person winning one million dollars in the lottery
Happiness is a lavender flower in full bloom
Happiness tastes like an ice cream cone on a hot summer day
Happiness smells like a bouquet of flowers given to you after an achievement
Happiness sounds like tons of chirping birds singing a song in the morning
Happiness feels like a pillow that is soft and fuzzy
Happiness looks like the beach on a summer day
Happiness makes me want to burst out laughing for no reason
Happiness is a tree that bends over to give you shade
Happiness is a smiley face that smiles every second of the day
Karly Krisovenski, Grade 6
West Allegheny Middle School

Happy
Happy is yellow
It sounds like you're cheering on the Fourth of July
It smells like roses
It tastes like mint ice cream with caramel, whip cream, and a cherry on top
It looks like a peaceful, newborn baby
Happy feels like you're lying in a bed of flowers
Lance Jarman, Grade 4
Anne Frank School

High Merit Poems – Grades 4, 5 and 6

Chocolate Chip Cookies
Melts in your mouth when
the warm creamy chocolate
hits your tongue,
Chewy or crunchy,
Whichever kind you want.
Chocolate chip cookies are
Yum yum yum.
Isabella DeLuca, Grade 6
Hillcrest Elementary School

The Benchwarmer and the Superstar
Benchwarmer
Mad, sad
Sobbing, sleeping, sitting
Bench, strikeout, home run, hitter
Batting, pitching, fielding
Slugger, awesome
Superstar
Trevor Gardiner, Grade 5
Pocopson Elementary School

Girl/Boy
Girl
pretty, soft
singing, dancing, giggling
dolls, ribbons, trucks, snakes
running, throwing, jumping
handsome, tough
Boy
Jacob Spirnock, Grade 5
East Union Intermediate Center

Black/White
Black
Ebony, sable
Creeping, howling, sneaking
Coal, ink, clean, light
Illuminating, cooling, shining
Powerful, pretty
White
Mia Friedel, Grade 4
Jefferson Elementary School

Fall Is Here
Fall is here
Let's all give a cheer
It's just four months away
From the year.
Fall is like the wind between my ears
Like the blue blossoms on the pier,
It is like the breezy windy days in the fall.
Lindsay Rachko, Grade 6
Holy Rosary School

Piano
I play the piano and it is very fun,
I am always sad when the song is done.
I love playing all the notes,
All the sharps and flats in all the songs.

I try to play all the rests,
As I always try my best!
I don't press any keys,
As I play the silent beats.
Clare Marchese, Grade 4
Sacred Heart School

Halloween
Halloween, it is a scary sight
It is so scary
And dark.
You don't know
If anything is out there
But, it is fun
Because we Trick or Treat
You always know that
Halloween is the scariest time of the year!
Hayley Lytle, Grade 4
W R Croman Elementary School

Christmas
C hrist
H oliday
R eindeer
I cicles
S anta
T rees
M istletoe
A ngels
S now
Hailey Donson, Grade 6
St Joseph School

Fall Walk
Fall
Flaming red and orange leaves
Walking, screaming, and running around
The wind sounds as loud as an opera singer.
Autumn
Christine Garis, Grade 6
Pennridge North Middle School

Colors
Pink is pretty.
Blue is pity.
Green is a tree.
When it is clear you can see.
Yellow is the sun that shines in the sky.
Now it's time to say bye-bye.
Samantha Haniman, Grade 4
McKinley Elementary School

Friends/Bullies
Friends
humorous, kind
caring, loving, trusting
heavenly, courageous, bullets, untrustful
hurting, punching, disliked
mean, horrible
Bullies
Lauren DuPlessis, Grade 5
St Sebastian Elementary School

Friends/Bullies
Friends
caring, peaceful
helping, trusted, loving
heavenly, enthusiastic, mean, heartless
unloved, hated, careless
evil, distrustful
Bullies
Kelsey Locante, Grade 5
St Sebastian Elementary School

Cats/Dogs
Cats
Cuddly, energetic
Meowing, playing, crouching
Cat beds, dog houses
Barking, wagging, helping
Paws, tails
Dogs
Devon Conroy, Grade 5
McKinley Elementary School

Friends/Bullies
Friends
nice, caring
loving, trusted, liked
hero, ally, villain, teenagers
unloved, hated, unwilling
careless, mean
Bullies
Ryan Haag, Grade 5
St Sebastian Elementary School

Friends/Bullies
Friends
helpful, grateful
giving, willing, supporting
sports, school, playground, leader
taunting, excluding, taking
hateful, heartless
Bullies
Mark Faller, Grade 5
St Sebastian Elementary School

A Dream
As I stick
the needle through
the fine fabric of silk
I suddenly pierce my finger
and crimson blood spurts out.
I ignore what has happened
and keep on sewing
as I finish my last stitch
the clock chimes midnight…
I wake up
to my mother's
soft and reassuring voice
realizing all was but a dream
I hold out my finger
and see the mark
of blood, now dry
I know it is not a dream,
or was it?
Chenlang Gao, Grade 5
Lincoln Elementary School

Sky
The sky is blue
That is true

The sky is high
Where birds fly

The sky has clouds
They make thunder that's loud

From the sky it rains
It rains so bad it's insane

When the sky is clear
The sun is near

To the sky
I say "Good-Bye"
Steven Ennis, Grade 6
St Joan of Arc School

November
During this fall there will come a November
This month I will remember
It will have its ups and downs
Whether it's Thanksgiving or school
Either way November is cool
You may argue if you feel so compelled
As for this month I hope it goes well
My aunt will wear her turkey gown
If you ask me, that is a down
But November will come to an end
I told you it would turn and bend
Michael Pigoni, Grade 6
Hopewell Memorial Jr High School

Darkness
Darkness is released
Blackening every corner
Every cave and hole
Engulfing all that's in view
Misty shrouds of black in sight
Run, Run, Run…or else!
Fear can be found everywhere
You can't escape it
No more thoughts, just fear remains
A shout, or is it a scream?
Stay calm, and don't fret
You hear another loud scream
Your ears ring so loud
You can't bear it any longer
You hope it's almost over
Gasp! Light has appeared
All worry has left your thoughts
You now feel relaxed
You now hear a voice…"Wake up!"
Your eyes open, it's over!
Malek Khalifa, Grade 6
Ross Elementary School

Rain
Drip, drop, drip, drop
Rain falls on top
Of my head.
Shouldn't I dread
The rain?
Instead I gain happiness
As I sing.
I'll dance in puddles,
Let all the mud fall
On my boots.
While you may be inside,
On a magic day like this
Looking for the sun
I know where it is.
It's in my heart,
And in my feet,
As they dance in puddles,
As I sing in the rain.
All alone, but still happy
I sing in the rain.
Emma Kobb, Grade 6
Chichester Middle School

Thanksgiving Is…
Spending time with my family.
Sun bathing on the beach.
Playing Frisbee with my uncle.
Swimming in the ocean with my dad.
Playing games.
Laughing at my grandpa's jokes.
Murphy DiRosa, Grade 6
Moravian Academy Middle School

Winter
Winter is my favorite season
Sledding and skiing are the reason.

Don't forget forts, and snowball fights,
Hot chocolate and cookies by the fire light.

Oh, look at the time!
It's almost nine!

This winter day is done,
But tomorrow I'll have more fun!
Lindsey Marshall, Grade 5
Foster Elementary School

What Is Green?
Green is Christmas
With the tree so bright.
Green misbehaves
Please don't fight.
Green is clever yet very smart.
Green are the leaves in a big pile.
Green reminds me of kids with a big smile.
Green will trick you into so many things,
Sometimes he pretends he's a king.
Green is a shamrock, and St. Patrick's Day.
It's my favorite that's all I have to say!
Erin Przybylinski, Grade 6
St Hilary of Poitiers School

Rambo
Once I saw Rambo.
He was hiding all in camo.
He is really tough.
And looks quite rough.
He also wears a belt of ammo.
One day he hit a buck.
While driving a Dodge truck.
It had such a large rack.
Rambo couldn't carry him on his back.
Maybe next time, he'll have more luck,
And hit a duck!
Nicholas Hooper, Grade 4
Burgettstown Elementary Center

My Dog Izzy
I have a dog named Izzy
She's silver and white
She sleeps in my bed
And kicks me all night.

She loves to be cuddled
And her belly to be scratched
She's the best dog ever
And can never be matched!
Julie Stillwagon, Grade 5
East Union Intermediate Center

Creative World

The golden green grass is waving, like hands in the wind
The aqua stream is flowing with glee.
Cuddly animals are free as can be.

My family is caring, like the heavens
My friends are perfect as can be.
You can see that my buddies are fair, sweet, and kind.

Cassidy Cumming, Grade 4
Fairview Elementary School

Fall

Orange, red, and yellow stars fall down from the trees
Lightly drifting away, in the light autumn breeze.
Flame colored leaves cover the streets,
Hoping to find a wind to ride, that smells oh so sweet.
Birds chirping, bugs buzzing all know fall is here,
Why oh why does this magnificent fall
Come only once a year?

Victoria Le, Grade 6
Pennridge North Middle School

Fall

Fall is a beautiful scene.
Fall looks like a rainbow broke apart on the trees.
Red, yellow, orange, brown, green.
"*SWISH*" as the wind flutters through the rainbow trees.
Animals trying to get through the maze of leaves.
Fall is as lovely and cute as a newborn puppy.
Fall is a lovely scene.

Trevor Facer, Grade 6
Pennridge North Middle School

Thanksgiving Is…

Playing in the big Ping-Pong tournament.
Giving out weird awards like the trencherman.
Eating Mom's cranberry chutney she always forgets.
Looking over little baby cousins.
Stuffing your face with food.
Celebrating your sister and your grandpa's birthdays.

Noah Ruebeck, Grade 6
Moravian Academy Middle School

Thanksgiving

Thanksgiving is
Eating turkey with gravy
Making mashed potatoes and stuffing
Baking pumpkin and apple pie
Playing with my cousins
Having a blast while talking with my family!

Ashley Ender, Grade 6
Moravian Academy Middle School

Sleepy Old Fred

There once was a kid named Fred,
That loved his own comfortable bed.
He would sleep all day,
And not go out and play.
Whenever he got up, he was as weak as lead.

Theodore Chesson, Grade 4
Sacred Heart School

Grandparents Are…

Getting fed every morning.
Helping me with hard projects.
Listening to history lessons every two seconds.
Learning about the good old times.
Being loved and thought of.

Lance O'Rourke, Grade 6
Moravian Academy Middle School

Thanksgiving Night

I can see my scampering cousins going toward the dinner table.
I hear my family chortling at the decorative dinner table.
I smell the heavenly apple pie baking in the warm oven.
I taste the mountain of whip cream dancing on my tongue.
I feel the toasty fireplace, sitting with my loving family.

Daniel Green, Grade 4
Colonial Elementary School

Goodbye

I feel like someone's gone, someone that I love
She was there for me every second
But now she's gone to a better place
I just wanted to say goodbye.

Lizzie Gladden, Grade 4
Jefferson Elementary School

Blue

I am laying on the ground looking at the blue sky,
While eating a piece of grandma's blueberry pie,
I think of the blue fish in the blue sea,
Suddenly I see a blue flower occupied by a bee.

Grace Tipton, Grade 4
Sacred Heart School

Thanksgiving Is…

Watching and playing football with friends and family.
Eating turkey till you're about to throw up.
Sleeping in because you have no school.
Visiting family all over New Jersey.

Vivek Katara, Grade 6
Moravian Academy Middle School

Ocean

Crystal, beautiful
Waves crash against rocky shores
to erase footprints

Emily Goldfarb, Grade 4
McKinley Elementary School

Jaguar/Feline
Jaguar
Cat and large
Fast, sneaky, and quiet
Awesome, neat, interesting, and colorful
Feline
Parkar Kopchik, Grade 4
West Branch Area Elementary School

Christmas
Jesus Christ is born
Carolers run door to door
Santa's on his way
Wrapping presents before dark
Christmas time's finally here!
Julia Violi, Grade 5
Holy Martyrs Elementary School

Halloween
spooky
creepy, scary
trick-or-treating
a day of candy
costumes
Emmanuel N. Torres, Grade 5
Hamilton Elementary School

Christmas
I see Christmas lights
I taste sweet hot chocolate
I feel white, cold snow
Jesus is born on Christmas
My family loves Christmas
Nolan Debes, Grade 5
Holy Martyrs Elementary School

Carlos Ruiz
Chooch is his nickname
Awesome catcher behind plate
Star Phillies player
The NLCS winner
Caught last pitch of World Series
Evan McFadden, Grade 5
Holy Martyrs Elementary School

December
December is an awesome season.
But not for those that are wheezin'
It is such a lovely sight
But the snow fills our hearts with fright
We also start all of the sneezin'.
Alyssa Buck, Grade 4
West Branch Area Elementary School

Excitement
Excitement is an ocherus orange like an energetic sun in June on a summer day,
  outside playing a board game with my family.

Excitement looks like your first precious pleasant puppy
  playing proudly at the park in August.

It tastes like a chocolaty chunky warm brownie
  melting in my mouth on the 4th of July.

Excitement smells like a delightful daisy
  daring itself to bloom out in spring.

Excitement sounds like luscious laughter coming from my family and I,
  cooling down in the house on a summer day.

It feels like jumping all around, and spreading the joy to everyone.
Ashley Carabajal, Grade 6
Our Lady of Ransom School

Holidays
I see a beaming Christmas tree sparkling with light
It smells like the forest as I sit in my house
I hear my family laughing as they walk up the pathway
They are so happy and excited for the family party
I taste the cookies my mom baked in the kitchen
My favorites are the yummy Reese Cup cookies
I look at many things in the mall as we go to shop
Gifts to be bought and given to make others happy
I see the church beaming like the sun with the nativity scene, a star on top
Family and friends inside lighting candles and sharing peace
Ring-a-ding-ding the Church bells ring as we walk up the aisle
Christmas Eve mass gives us a reason to smile
I feel just how lucky I am to have a great family
The holidays are a time of joy
A time to be thankful for all we have.
Mike Metzger, Grade 6
St Jerome Elementary School

Astonishment
Astonishment is someone walking into their surprise party and seeing everyone jump out
Astonishment is the bewilderment of an animal finding out it's being hunted
Astonishment is the amazement of a question answered
Astonishment is blanched with shock like someone's face after a secret has been shared
Astonishment tastes like the bitter sweetness of Sour Patch Kids at the movie theaters
Astonishment smells like a whiff of pepper that was stronger than you thought
Astonishment sounds like an extra foot thudding on the floor, louder than the last
Astonishment feels like thinking there's another step and having your foot fall
  through the air only to find there's not another step
Astonishment looks like the expression of someone gullible enough to believe the
  generous amount of mischievous merciless gossip
Astonishment makes me wonder and rethink what I had set in stone in my mind
Astonishment sneaks up on someone unexpectedly making them jump
Astonishment is that shriek behind your back that makes you twirl around to investigate
Keri Watters, Grade 6
West Allegheny Middle School

High Merit Poems – Grades 4, 5 and 6

Today Was a Nerf Day
Five lives total
Get hit by a bullet
Lose one life
Bang!

Bullets whizzing past my ear,
The excitement builds,
As you get ready to shoot,
The enemy nearby,

Bang! Bang! Bang! Bang!
Went your pistol,
B-B-B-B-B-B
Went your machine gun,

Bullets stick to your sweater,
One more life,
You sneak up on him,
Bang! Total darkness for him,

You won,
Mission accomplished,
Held on to your life,
Today is a nerf day.
Rudy Mikus Berzins, Grade 6
Pennridge North Middle School

Blue
Blue is the color of Blue Jays feathers.
A whistle, a flower, a warm winter's night.

The sadness of a death
Or a baby being born.

Blueberries are sweet
Just like icey pops.

Blue is a soft song you sing
Like a blanket that snuggles with you.

Blue is the Earth's sky
Or the seas that pulls you in.

Eyes of girls and boys sparkle
With the magic color blue

Shirts, cups, pens, and dresses
Wear the color Blue.

Blue is a feeling
That stays with you and
Makes you feel secure
Elizabeth Brazukas, Grade 6
St Hilary of Poitiers School

Honey Creeper
H awaii is its habitat
O rnithologists study it
N eat in color
E ager in flight
Y oungsters leave soon

C ool to watch if you can find them
R ainforest species
E xcited to defend nest
E nthusiastic to eat nectar
P lumage is colorful
E xtinction is feared
R are
Steven Salivonchik, Grade 6
Nazareth Area Intermediate School

Autumn
The cold crisp air there is no heat
The crunch of leaves beneath my feet
There's apple pie so warm and tasty
Much better than a store bought pastry
The smell of cooking in the air
While I'm munching on a pear
My parents are watching the news
And kids play tag without their shoes
Yes, autumn is a great season
And there is many more a reason
But now it's time for me to go
So now I will say good-bye
And don't forget the apple pie
Kyle Schoener, Grade 5
McKinley Elementary School

As the Storm Goes, He Is…
As the storm goes,
His tears come down as rain,
From all the hurt and pain.

His voice booms as thunder,
As he yells his disappointment,
From all the disobeying.
He shouts from hearing,
All the lies from people below.

As his mouth opens, he strikes lightning.
He is the one who is,
Way up above.
Jada Jefferson, Grade 6
Chichester Middle School

Dolphins
Dolphins are friendly,
Playful in the blue ocean,
Helpful to sailors.
Hunter Russell, Grade 5
East Union Intermediate Center

Evil/Good
Evil
Scared, horror
Creeping, haunted, wicked
Frightening, hurting, saving, winner
Defending, useful, wonderful
Faster, awesome
Good
John Tracey, Grade 5
McKinley Elementary School

Friends/Bullies
Friends
Helpful, witty
Sharing, caring, amusing
Love, loyal, evil, disaster
Stealing, deadly, gloomy
Fighting, angry
Bullies
Jayna Ray Harding, Grade 5
St Sebastian Elementary School

Friends/Bullies
Friends
Flawless, pure
Loving, calming, smiling
Pals, leaders, enemies, criminals
Harming, disliking, upsetting
Hurtful, danger
Bullies
Sarah Hefferin, Grade 5
St Sebastian Elementary School

Friends/Bullies
Friends
kind, sincere
supporting, concerned, forgiving
pal, buddy, foe, intimidator
annoying, harassing, teasing
cruel, harmful
Bullies
Jonathon Lutz, Grade 5
St Sebastian Elementary School

Halloween/Christmas
Halloween
Night, spooky
Creeping, listening, scaring
Candy, witches, presents, snow
Giving, singing, laughing
Decorations, family
Christmas
Rachel Soveral, Grade 5
McKinley Elementary School

Flowers/Lilies
Flowers
Red, orange
Swaying, opening, growing
One of a kind
Lilies
Jenna Cowder, Grade 4
West Branch Area Elementary School

Earth
One planet of life
The one of friendship and faith
The one of true trust
With the sea mountains and plains
Also animals and plants
Juliana Mosser, Grade 5
Central Elementary School

Latitude and Longitude Lines
The latitude lines
Run from the east to the west
The longitude lines
Run from the north to the south
They help us use the map best
Sarah Stiffy, Grade 5
Central Elementary School

Gettysburg
Brave men and brothers
Rebels and Federals
Fought against each other
The North won, the South lost
In a town called Gettysburg.
Daniel Babyak, Grade 5
Central Elementary School

Bad Cat
Once there was a bad cat with a hat.
He played with his hat on the mat.
He ran in the tar very far.
The cat with his hat,
ran into the street and now he's flat.
Ryan Stocku, Grade 5
Indian Lane Elementary School

Phillies Game
Clamoring home crowd
Topnotch players zing home runs
Yummy ball park franks
Soft pretzels and greasy fries
Dancing Philly Phanatic
Gregory McGrath, Grade 5
Holy Martyrs Elementary School

Friendship
Friendship is a blossoming flower during springtime.
Friendship is a new puppy on Christmas morning.
Friendship is a big win for the Penguins at the Stanley Cup.
Friendship is neon pink on a race car zooming around the track.
Friendship tastes like fresh baked cookies out of the sizzling oven.
Friendship smells like fresh cut flowers on your 50th Anniversary.
Friendship sounds like a newborns laugh, giggle, giggle, giggle!
Friendship feels like a fuzzy flannel quilt on a blustery winter day.
Friendship looks like a baby just learning to talk, warm and satisfying.
Friendship makes me feel like I got a new car on my 16th birthday.
Friendship is the warm feeling when you know you're loved.
Christina George, Grade 6
West Allegheny Middle School

Friendship
Friendship is like a dog cuddling with you on a cold winter day.
Friendship is painting your nails with your friends.
Friendship is putting a smile on somebody's face.
Friendship is yellow like the summer sun shining on you and your friends.
Friendship tastes like a sweet piece of candy.
Friendship smells like a hot cup of hot chocolate.
Friendship sounds like the hush whisper of telling secrets.
Friendship feels like a warm blanket fresh from the dryer.
Friendship looks like puppies playing with each other.
Friendship makes me laugh, cry, and smile.
Friendship is friends playing and laughing together.
Paige Davis, Grade 6
West Allegheny Middle School

Love
Love is a newborn puppy you saw for the very first time
Love is a dream come true for everyone racing in Hankey Farms
Love is a smile on a child's face Christmas morning
Love is a big beautiful blushing pink heart
Love tastes like a large explosion of chewy heart candy entering your mouth
Love smells like a large cinnamon roll on a tiny blue plate
Love sounds like the thump, thump of someone's heart
Love feels like a steaming hot creamy chocolaty cup of cocoa on an icy winter day
Love looks like a pair of doves huddling together in a tree
Love makes me feel cared for and loved
Love is an important part of life
Zoe McDaniel, Grade 6
West Allegheny Middle School

Crazy
Crazy is checkered
It sounds like a person talking to himself
It smells like you taking out the trash in the morning
It tastes like a Whopper with one beef patty and a veggie burger put together
It looks like a car driving the wrong way on a one-way road
Crazy feels like you're doing what the man next to you tells you to do
but nobody see him but you
Johnathan Wilson, Grade 4
Anne Frank School

Chores

I despise doing chores
Especially cleaning the floors.
When I clean my room
I sit around in gloom.
Swish, swish, swish, goes the mop
When the water hits the bucket it goes, Plop!
I try to get them done as fast as a rabbit
But doing them slow is just a habit.
I wish someone would help me out
So I wouldn't sit around and pout.
When I get close to being done
I can't wait to go out and have fun!
Finally, I can leave my house
I leave as fast as a cat chasing a mouse!

Brigid McMullen, Grade 6
St Jerome Elementary School

Bald Eagles

Gracefully fly through the skies
Show us your majestic power
You fight for what's right
In the end you're the symbol of our nation

Many people underestimate your power
Once you disperse our pride does the same
You hold the arrows and olive branch with devotion
Your eyes are for watching down on us

A true leader in our fight for victory
You gaze on us with your wisdom
As you swish through the sky, people marvel
You're our shining star; show us the way

Frank Marricone, Grade 6
St Jerome Elementary School

My Zoo

In my yard I have a zoo,
Lions, elephants, and monkeys too
I have a seal that runs in a wheel,
I have a giraffe that loves to laugh,
and I have beaver that's friends with a retriever

In my yard I have a zoo,
Tigers, sharks, and penguins too
I have a whale that likes to read mail,
I have a polar bear that loves solitaire,
and I have a frog that is able to jog

But the most amazing animal I have is…
My brother!

Amy Johnson, Grade 6
Bedford Middle School

Winter Snow

As the first snowflakes hit the ground
We watch at the window without a sound.
As they gracefully glide down from the sky
We try to catch them as they fly by.

With laughter and fun, this day will be filled.
Sledding down a hill, then a snowman we will build.
Making snow angels is something we will try.
Soon snowballs will be flying like birds in the sky.

Blinding white snow brings smiles to young and old.
A picture perfect day of fun to behold.
Wintry, white weather with whirling winds blowing.
This is my favorite kind of day, when it's snowing.

Jessica Scalen, Grade 6
St Jerome Elementary School

Polluted River

The river flowed really fast,
With greenish water roaring past,
Polluted as the river may be,
Ducks and geese swim with glee.

People help to clean it out.
They want to help without a doubt.
If there's trash in a river nearby,
Help clean it, it's as easy as pie.

A bike, a bag, a shopping cart,
Get them out, let's do our part.
If we all help in small, little ways,
All the trash will be gone in a matter of days.

Zachary Sorbello, Grade 6
St Jerome Elementary School

I Will Be a Firefighter

I will be a firefighter
When the bell rings I will go rescue people from the glow.

The bright orange glow of the blazing fire
I raise the ladder, I climb higher.

I tell the people, "Do not fear"
My crew is here

The fire is out, my job is done
Until the bell rings again, and then I run.

To make this world a whole lot brighter
I will be a firefighter.

Tristan Coble, Grade 4
Fairview Elementary School

Gold

Gold is the color of winning
like when you get 100 steps in reading
or when you win a spelling bee
Gold makes you feel good
about yourself.
Jonah Saleem, Grade 4
Wissahickon Charter School

The First Day of School

On the first day of school your crayons
are up to the tip of your box.
Your pencils are sharpened perfectly.
Your glue stick is not even used.
Your scissors are so keen.
Zoe Nikolos, Grade 5
Russell Elementary School

Precipitation/Snow

Precipitation,
Soft, water,
It's like stars,
Cold, white,
Snow.
Bryan Archambo, Grade 5
Russell Elementary School

Cupcake

Treat
Sweet, sprinkles,
They are delicious,
Tasty, soft,
Cupcake.
Matt Landis, Grade 5
Russell Elementary School

Fishing

Sitting by the pond,
Patiently waiting for fish,
Watching many trout.
Rod bends, jerks violently.
Finally you've caught a fish.
Andrew Imredy, Grade 5
Holy Martyrs Elementary School

Halloween

Halloween
scary stuff
lots of costumes
Halloween, trick-or-treat
Boo!
Alexis Figueroa, Grade 5
Hamilton Elementary School

Cheesecake

C heesecake, cheesecake I love cheesecake,
H ow I love it so,
E at it, eat it I like to…
E at it,
S weet and tasty and very creamy,
E at all the cheesecake and the…
C rust outside goes with the cream,
A te it finished it,
K eeps me distracted for a few minutes but not for long 'cause I like to…
E at, eat, eat.
Eric Lang, Grade 4
Shady Grove Elementary School

Sadness

Sadness is a huge storm of teardrops
Sadness is a hole in your heart that will never be filled
Sadness is a pool of sorrow
Sadness tastes like soggy sandwiches on a cloudy day
Sadness smells like the odor of not making the team
Sadness sounds like cars that crash into each other
Sadness feels like a heavy load on my back
Sadness looks like a dog left alone
Sadness makes me feel like a box of toys that have never been played with
Sadness is the beating of a lonely heart
Kara Hamilton, Grade 6
West Allegheny Middle School

Courage

Courage is the sudden urge to never give up.
Courage is not taking the easy way out.
Courage is telling the truth in the worst situation.
Courage is orange like the fire in your eyes as you take on your enemy.
Courage tastes as good as ice cream.
Courage smells like a new car.
Courage feels like cold hard steel.
Courage looks like the happiest sight for sore eyes.
Courage makes me fired up.
Courage is all these reasons put together.
Connor Roese, Grade 6
West Allegheny Middle School

Halloween Fright

Halloween is like a room with no doors,
No windows, no way out.
Everywhere you go you hear shrieks as loud as a fire truck.
You see vampires, witches, goblins and ghosts coming out to get you!
They hear your heart pounding.
They know you're weak and afraid.
You feel their cold hard hands.
Hands as cold as the Arctic.
Halloween is like a dream.
The only thing keeping you from waking up is — you!
Sylvie Cherry, Grade 5
McKinley Elementary School

High Merit Poems – Grades 4, 5 and 6

The Great Snowman
There was a snowman that was great.
He had a friend who was named Kate.
Snowman and Kate were wishing,
That they could go ice fishing.
But the snowman didn't have any bait.
Curtis Rowles, Grade 4
West Branch Area Elementary School

The Snake and the Rake!
There once was a school girl named Jill
She lived on top of a big hill.
One day she saw a snake
So she hit it with a rake.
She ran home and told her father, Bill.
Madysen Turner, Grade 4
West Branch Area Elementary School

Chicken Fingers
Hot and tangy taste
Delicious meaty goodness
Garlicky and crisp
Fried in seasoned bread crumb mix
Finger lickin' sizzling treat
Sean Mahoney, Grade 5
Holy Martyrs Elementary School

Winter
snow falling, putting heavy coats
on, putting on mittens, sledding

snowmen, igloos, snowball fights,
and snowboarding
Tanner Melvin, Grade 5
Hamilton Elementary School

Fall/Colorful
Fall
Colorful, pretty
Windy, hibernation, frosty
Excited, lovely, exquisite, terrific
Colorful
E.J. Muriceak, Grade 4
All Saints Catholic School

Ocean City, NJ
Waves gently crashing
Soft, fluffy sand between toes.
Taste the salty surf
Swooping seagulls getting food
Yellow, blue and red beach chairs.
Emily Mancini, Grade 5
Holy Martyrs Elementary School

If I Were in Charge of the World*
If I were in charge of the world
I'd cancel having brothers, bedtimes,
And people getting hit by hurricanes and losing their homes.

If I were in charge of the world
There would be more doctors to take care of people, more cute and cuddly animals,
There would also be peace on Earth and NO global warming.

If I were in charge of the world
You wouldn't hear people yelling or older kids teasing younger kids.
You also wouldn't see wild fires destroying forests
There would be no guns, and there would be lots of happiness on Earth.

If I were in charge of the world
There'd be better technology,
More rechargeable batteries,
More ice cream to enjoy,
And even more cures for people who need help fighting diseases.

If I were in charge of the world
There would be more double layered Chocolate cake
And delicious chocolate chip cookies for dessert every day.
Also, a person who loves animals,
And even a person who DOES NOT like to go on roller coasters,
Would still be allowed to be in charge of our wonderful world.
Abby Hackert, Grade 6
Wrightstown Elementary School
*Patterned after "If I Were in Charge of the World" by Judith Viiorst

Senses of September
Watching rust-colored leaves fall from a giant oak,
Chimneys just beginning to issue white pillows of smoke.
Marveling at the ferris wheel as I wander through the bustling fair,
Staring as the season's first soccer ball goes whizzing through the air.

Listening to geese honking as they seek warmer ground,
Crackling bonfires and the band's drum-bangin' sound.
Old friends chattering as they reunite,
Chomping crunchy apples, juice spilling out with every bite.

Grimacing as a steaming mug of cocoa burns my lips,
My hand clenching as the ball misses the receiver's fingertips.
Palm throbbing as I finish my lengthy homework,
Pulling slimy guts out of a pumpkin always makes me smirk.

Sniffing scrumptious pumpkin pie, grinning from its sweet scent,
Taking in the musty smell of morning as I wake up in my damp tent.
Instinctively walking towards the sweet aroma of a farmer's market,
Plugging my nose from the harsh black smoke of a raging fire pit.

Savoring the last morsels of salty, Boardwalk fries at summer's end,
Sharing a bite of a sizzling hot dog at a baseball game with a friend.
Eating buttery, hot popcorn and watching movies late at night,
The thoughts and feelings of September overtake me — I go without a fight.
Taylor Mahlandt, Grade 6
Ephrata Intermediate School

Horses
The exquisite unique animals,
Can never be tamed,
They run so wild,
With the wind in their mane.

They gallop through the fields,
Feeling as free as they can be,
With their flowing tails up high,
And their hefty hooves hitting the ground.

The graceful powerful animals,
Obedient to God and man,
Running as fast as they can,
Anxious to see what's ahead of them.

They love everything about life,
And never want to let go of it,
They are proud to be who they are,
A majestic horse.
Merideth Lantz, Grade 6
Linville Hill Mennonite School

My Puppy
Coco is brown, black, white and gray,
Very small and very cute.
She playfully bites and chews.
Soft, silly puppy playing cheerfully outside.

Fluffy, frisky puppy
Cuddling on your lap.
When she goes to sleep,
She lays on her mat.

Lovable little puppy
Playing in the sun,
Feeling free
And having fun.

Little puppy
Growing, growing, growing.
As she swims in the water,
She goes putter, putter, putter.
Tiffany King, Grade 6
Linville Hill Mennonite School

Phillies
P ractice to do good
H it home runs
I can't stop watching them
L ose one game, win the other
L ove their jobs
I love going to the stadium
E very night my brother yells
S orry that the season is over
Olivia DuBree, Grade 4
McKinley Elementary School

Halloween Night
Ghosts, goblins, witches and bats
Hover over you and peer into your masks.

Running around knocking on doors,
Saying trick or treat and begging for more.

Halloween night is the time
So get ready to shout for you'll be mine.

If you make it home alive
Then you are lucky to have survived

Because Vampires come out on October 31st
To suck your blood and quench their thirst.
Megan Oberholtzer, Grade 4
Shady Grove Elementary School

Come Back Summer
Come back summer
Don't go away!
You don't have to go,
You're welcome to stay!

Please summer stay,
You're so much fun!
The reason is,
You shine the sun!

Come back summer,
You're welcome to play!
Come back summer,
Let's have a nice day!
Sebastian Ojeda, Grade 6
Immaculate Conception School

Chris Is My Dad
Chris is my dad,
He doesn't make me mad,
Always and always I'll be glad,
That he's my dad,

Chris is my dad,
He makes me feel glad,
He fought off a gator,
But that's a story for later,

Chris is my dad,
I'm so glad his name's not Chad,
He's so funny but he doesn't seem to mind,
That he's goofy all the time.
Alli DeCarlo, Grade 5
McKinley Elementary School

My Little Sister
It's time to go to bed.
I try to give her a hug.
She punches me in the head.
I fall to the rug.
She seems so nice and sweet,
In her pretty little dress.
Everyone wants to give her a treat,
She makes such a mess.
Jake Davis, Grade 5
Foster Elementary School

Little Chipmunks
Little chipmunks so fast and so free!
Little chipmunks so filled with glee!
Racing around like little rockets
Filling their mouths like little pockets,
Through the woods collecting nuts,
To hide at home in their homey huts.
On their own little collecting spree,
Taking all they want because it's free!
Christopher White, Grade 6
Home School

The Argument of My Book
I sing of ducks, and pink, and kittens,
the months June, September, and July,
Christmas, my birthday, Halloween,
snow, rain, and sunshine,
flowers, blossoms, trees,
tennis, soccer,
art, and music.
And THAT is the argument of my book!
Kate Powers, Grade 5
Copper Beech Elementary School

The Stormy Night
I'm in bed
I hear pit pat of the rain on my roof
Then it gets harder and faster
I hear the cracking of thunder
I look out my window
I see the flash of lightning
I lie back down and go to sleep
Kevin Borne, Grade 5
Saint Theresa School

Mouse/Cat
Mouse
Petite, fast
Running catching, biting
Whiskers, cheese, meow, kittens
Licking, purring, trapping
Sneaky, clever
Cat
Lisa Cunningham, Grade 6
St Maria Goretti School

High Merit Poems – Grades 4, 5 and 6

Costumes
Costumes can be anything,
A bat or a rat or a bird with wings.
They can be funny or scary,
Or pretty like a fairy,
Or big or small,
Or round like a ball.

You can be a laughing pumpkin,
Or a super hero named Dunkin.
You can be a sad dragon,
Or Red Riding Hood with a wagon.
Costumes are so much fun,
You'll be sad when Halloween's done.
Leah Barbacane, Grade 5
McKinley Elementary School

Nature in the Winter
It's about the cracking of leaves
the swaying of trees
the absence of life

It's about the bare bark
the rippling creek
the frost covered everything

It's about pricker bushes
the mud holes
the disappeared sun

It's about the forest in winter.
Katy Frey, Grade 5
Pocopson Elementary School

Holiday
Thanksgiving
When we all
Come to dinner
When we all have
To help clean up
And help
With cooking
When it is time to eat,
We all pray.
Thanksgiving
Is as awesome as
Watching a Super Bowl
For football.
Jordin Priddy, Grade 6
State Street Elementary School

Soft Warm Blanket
A soft, warm blanket
While I'm sitting by the fire
On a chilly night.
Forrest Seybold, Grade 4
Watsontown Elementary School

The Magic of the Guitar…
My fingertips practically on fire
Racing up and down the
Many bronze bumps
Forming grooves
Right under my nails

My other hand bouncing the
Teardrop-shaped pick along
The strings
Me thinking the letters it plucks

E A D G B E

Working together
Either
Ripping my ears off
With
375 watts of
EAR SPLITTING METAL!
Or
Producing a symphony
Subtle enough
To calm any beast.
Drake Jacobs, Grade 6
Ephrata Intermediate School

Family
When you're hurt
aches, bruises, or pains
they'll be there

When you need help
homework, advice, or just life
they'll be there

When you're in a bad mood
sad, grumpy, or angry
they'll be there

When you need encouragement
plays, tryouts, or tests
they'll be there

When you're sick
stomachache, flu, or sore throat
they'll be there

No matter what
even in your heart
your family will be there
Alayna Bonicky, Grade 6
Ross Elementary School

The Castle in the Mist
The castle in the mist
On top of that hill,
All surrounded with drowsiness.
Ominous,
And creepy.

The castle in the mist,
On top of that hill.
Inside is a grand ballroom
With a ceiling that held crystal chandeliers.
A huge dining room,
With a table for twenty.
Where they served chocolates,
And shrimp.

The castle in the mist,
On top of that hill.
Now
   Just
      Gray
         Stubble,
Like the beard of a grandpa.
Alison Pirl, Grade 5
Falk Laboratory School

In My Dreams
In my dreams there is another land
Another land where there is only peace
And there is only love
No more war, no more fights

In my dreams
There are pretty butterflies
With delicate wings
With beautiful colors

In my dreams
There are no weapons
There are no leaders
Everyone's in charge of themselves

You only make good decisions
Although there will be no free will
The Earth will stay beautiful
That is how it is in my dreams

Just the way God made it
Christina Strati, Grade 4
Jefferson Elementary School

Leaves
Wonderful yellow
The beautiful leaves falling
To the ground in piles
Lauren Stahl, Grade 4
Watsontown Elementary School

The Color Green
Green looks like trees blowing in the wind.
Green sounds like leaves falling from trees.
Green feels like grass touching me.
Green tastes like green eggs and ham.
Green smells like green mint candles.
Kira Mclendon, Grade 5
Clearview Elementary School

Football
Footballs feel like leather.
Footballs are as brown as dirt.
Footballs sound like a bullet.
The laces are as white as my teeth.
Footballs feel like rocks.
Sebastian Lewis, Grade 4
Wickersham Elementary School

Touching Life
When I touch the petals of a flower
It makes me count the days of my life.
Life is nothing like money.
The time is almost up.
I can feel it.
Cecilia Monaghan, Grade 5
Nether Providence Elementary School

My Favorite Fall Sport
Football
Active, collisions
Sprinting, hitting, tackling
Be your own blocker
Football
Matt Firuta, Grade 6
Pennridge North Middle School

Blue Whales
Whales
Enormous marine
Breaching, spouting, lobtailing,
Peaceful — throughout the sea
Blue.
Eva Gnegy, Grade 6
Trinity Middle School

The Weeping Willow
Willow
Breathing, waving
Giving us protection
Blowing in the whistling wind
Weeping.
Cameron White, Grade 5
Trinity East Elementary School

Excitement
Excitement is getting pumped up for the big game with my teammates.
Excitement is the Philadelphia Phillies bringing home a World Series victory.
Excitement is racing around the bases to beat the play.
Excitement is waiting impatiently on Christmas Day to open my presents.
Excitement is a bright neon green keeping me alert.
Excitement tastes like pop rocks leaping around in my mouth.
Excitement smells like spicy chili peppers fresh from the garden.
Excitement sounds like my precautious parents preparing popping popcorn in the kitchen.
Excitement feels like stroking my hand across a spiky cactus in the Sahara Desert.
Excitement looks like fireworks exploding with color on the 4th of July.
Excitement makes me scream and shout for joy.
Reilly Mercurio, Grade 6
West Allegheny Middle School

Excitement
Excitement is like the bright yellow sun in the early morning
Excitement is energy ready to explode like a volcano
Excitement is butterflies in my stomach ready to fly away
Excitement is the color yellow that is bright
Excitement tastes like a fresh orange that has just been peeled
Excitement smells like a hot day after it has just rained
Excitement sounds like a bird in the early morning chirping away
Excitement feels like the rough dirt on the softball field
Excitement looks like a softball team winning the championship game
Excitement makes me happy and full of energy showing all over
Excitement is the way flowers bloom in spring time
Sophia McNavish, Grade 6
West Allegheny Middle School

Love
Love is butter melting on your warm heart
Love is a soft pillow on a cold winter's day
Love is all the beautiful stars in the sky
Love is purple, like a flower at full bloom
Love tastes like a warm chocolate chip cookie combination in your mouth
Love smells like a flower, just right for picking
Love sounds like the thump of your heart when you go near them
Love feels like soft wool on a sheep's warm belly
Love looks like your puppy in the window, waiting for you to come home from school
Love makes me want to jump and shout to the world
Love is a light in your heart, shining through you
Brenna Marie Laughery, Grade 6
West Allegheny Middle School

Happiness
Happiness is the glowing crackling sun that lights the world
Happiness is cheerful birds singing their delightful song early in the morning
Happiness is the medicine needed to cure sadness, depression, and rage
Happiness is the color of bright yellow sunshine
Happiness tastes like delicious pink cotton candy looking like puffy clouds
Happiness smells like a batch of fresh chocolate chip cookies straight from the oven
Happiness sounds like an angel singing a saintly, holy song
Happiness feels like supple, smooth soft skin
Happiness looks like a cute adorable, warm newborn puppy waiting for a hug
Danielle Wicklund, Grade 6
West Allegheny Middle School

High Merit Poems – Grades 4, 5 and 6

Thanksgiving
T hankful
H arvest
A ngry turkeys
N o school
K indness
S pice
G iving thanks
I nteresting food
V ariety of foods
I like turkey
N o good manners
G ravy on potatoes
Nathaly Lora, Grade 5
Clearview Elementary School

Rain Forest
Rain
Nature
Temperature
Insects crawling
Life
Grace
Color
Beautiful
Environment
Sound
Green leaves
Calm feeding
Chloe Cusano, Grade 6
Nazareth Area Intermediate School

Autumn
Leaves falling in the air
Carving pumpkins in your yard
Costumes in the street
Scarecrows at the pumpkin patch
Sweet treats everywhere
Fast blowing wind in my hair
Chilly nights here and there
Bats flying into the sky
Crows cooing in air
Ghosts booing behind the walls
Corn mazes creating chaos
Leaves turning red all over heads
Justin Karolski, Grade 6
Carson Middle School

Fall
Fall is a beautiful time of year.
I hear the birds chirping.
The leaves are changing colors.
The smell of the nice, crisp air,
The relaxing crunch of leaves.
I love fall.
Emily Ewing, Grade 6
Chichester Middle School

Sun
What does the sun remind you of?
The sun is as bright as a baby's smile
It is very yellow
It is round and shiny
Why does it shine so much?
The sun gives us light
It is always so bright
It lightens up our day
How does the sun make you feel?
I feel happy when I see the sun
The sun makes me feel warm
Sun brings peace to my day
Sabrina McBride, Grade 6
St Jerome Elementary School

Chase
My dog, Chase, is chocolate brown
His puppy face never wears a frown
His eyes like gold and black nose wet
A long tail wags; he's always set
To play, to sleep, to run, to jump
My dog goes down with a great big thump
He sleeps a lot, and loves his treat
Like a bull in the house, he'll have you beat
Most of all, he's my best friend
he makes me happy and in the end
My dog, Chase is quite a guy
he is the apple of my eye!
Dylan Lock, Grade 6
St Jerome Elementary School

Winter
The snow is falling, a blizzard is near.
My mom yelled out, "You're off my dear!"
I sit down and watch the snow fall,
I see trees standing big and tall.
I see hot cocoa screaming with steam,
Ice skaters skating on the stream.
I hear children laughing, Ha! Ha! Ha!
Carolers singing, La! La! La!
The cars are covered in snow,
Big lights shine and glow.
Now you see my reason,
Why this is my favorite season!
Valerie Suder, Grade 6
St Jerome Elementary School

Grandparents Are
Loving you no matter what.
Being there whenever you need them.
Telling you stories from long ago.
Making new, cheerful memories.
Reading books together.
Going shopping together.
Kylee Jacoby, Grade 6
Moravian Academy Middle School

Louisiana Black Bear
L oving
O rnery
U nlucky
I nsect eating
S cary
I ntelligent
A ctive
N atural
A nimal

B lack
L arge
A nxious
C reative
K odak

B ig
E ndangered
A ggressive
R are
Emily Wahlgren, Grade 6
Nazareth Area Intermediate School

Why
Why must I be treated this way?
'Tis you who is like river,
'Tis I who is like sea
We are so much alike, yet
Why are we so different?
Why must I be treated this way?
I know 'tis unlike me to
Complain like so,
But I just want my paradise
That I call home.
Why must I be treated this way?
I am trapped in a
Hateful new world.
Dark, gray woods surround me
And I just
Can't
Find
My
Way
Out.
Mackenzie Damon, Grade 5
Boyce Middle School

Summer
S unny
U mbrellas on the beach
M ovie time
M agic of Disney World
E xciting
R ock and roll time
Allison Polovoy, Grade 6
Chichester Middle School

Gymnastics

Flipping, twisting, through the air —
It gives the spectators quite a scare!

Flexibility and strength attitude and desire —
Are all spectacular gifts to admire.

Frustration, commitment, determination and grace —
Are a few feelings a gymnast must embrace.

Hard work and discipline is all it takes,
Just always be positive and you'll be great!!!!

Hannah Gabrielle Baddick, Grade 4
Lincoln Elementary School

Me

Jaelyn
Nice, fast, funny
Sister of Dontae
Who loves mom, nan, and my family
Who feels silly about everything
Who needs my PSP, food, and to bother Shavon
Who gives toys, games, and a remote
Who'd like to see *Field of Screams*
Who dreams of having a little skateboard
A student of Miss Tadlock
JJ

Jaelyn Moore, Grade 4
Wickersham Elementary School

Happiness

Happiness is winning the championship game
Happiness is finding something you lost
Happiness is a smile on someone's face
Happiness is lime green shining in the light
Happiness tastes like crispy coated chocolate bars
Happiness smells like fresh baked cookies straight out of the oven
Happiness sounds like your favorite song repeating in your head
Happiness feels like sitting on clouds
Happiness looks like a colorful collage
Happiness makes me explode with laughter
Happiness is the greatest feeling

Laurel Zaborowski, Grade 6
West Allegheny Middle School

Pizarro

Francisco
Brave, nobleman, strong, war
Related to daughter of the colonial treasure
Cares deeply about money
Who feels he needs to find seven cities of gold.
Who gives more weapons
Who fears Indians.
Who would like to see the seven cities of gold.
Resident of Cibola.

Andrew Gallo, Grade 5
Indian Lane Elementary School

Ten

Ten, my first double digits,
Sad, I feel.
Mad, I feel.
Is my life moving too fast?
From being Superman for Halloween,
To sitting on Santa's lap,
Turning ten is like moving the first ten yards of a football field,
Only you can't go back.
I used to be afraid of monsters,
But now, I think of them as boxes,
They cannot move, breath, or live.

Then I look back at those yearbook pictures,
And those early childhood videos,
And I realize, I've changed.
In some ways I feel happy.
In some ways, I realize that it's not that bad to get older.
More privileges,
More opportunities,
But more responsibilities.

Max Hinkle, Grade 5
Copper Beech Elementary School

The Holiday Season

The holidays are an exciting and busy time.
Starting in November it's Thanksgiving time.
Gobble up turkey and yummy foods.
I like pumpkin pie, do you?

Next comes Christmas, in a very busy month.
Everybody is decorating to make their house just right.
After a busy day of putting up the tree,
You will go to sleep all night.

On Christmas day you open up your gifts.
It's fun to look and see what you get.
Have a nice Christmas Day.
Sit back, relax, do it your way.

After Christmas comes time to ring in the New Year.
Everybody loves to celebrate and cheer.
Then comes the countdown to the New Year.
Have all the fun you want, don't delay!

Emily Wright, Grade 6
Hopewell Memorial Jr High School

Apples! Apples! Apples!

Oh! How I love apples!
How would I ever live in a world without apples?
Never, ever would I live in a world without apples!
I can't imagine a world without that wonderful apple flavor!
Why, I would run fifteen miles every day for them!
Apples are best with caramel you know!
Don't you like apples?

Jessica Edwards, Grade 5
Oswayo Valley Elementary School

High Merit Poems – Grades 4, 5 and 6

Night
The beautiful night,
It is a powerful sight.
It has stars and a moon,
Now it's over, I'll see you soon.
Kaelin Brennan, Grade 4
St Joseph School

Summer
I love ice cream in the summer heat.
The nice warm road settles beneath my feet.
In the summer I go to the park.
Then I go home when it gets dark.
Mallory Taramelli-Dickinson, Grade 4
St Joseph School

The Pond
Dragonflies buzz near the pond
It is silent and peaceful
A frog jumps and the water gets on her face
A smile grows
Olivia Serafini, Grade 5
Nether Providence Elementary School

Love
L ooking back on the past
O range flowers, red trees
V ery loud laughter
E veryone dancing their lives away
Alexis Pickering, Grade 4
McKinley Elementary School

Thanksgiving Is
Turkey and mashed potatoes.
Seeing friends and family.
Pumpkin pie for everyone.
Eating food all night.
Katie Persin, Grade 6
Moravian Academy Middle School

Red Is…
As painful as the bleeding days
As beautiful as a new rose
As gentle as the great sunset
As red as fresh, new strawberries
Ana Jukic, Grade 4
Jefferson Elementary School

Dancing
Dancing is fun,
It's number one,
When I leap in the air,
All the people stare.
Julianne Jenkins, Grade 4
Jefferson Elementary School

Bravery
Bravery is a soldier fighting in Iraq for our country.
Bravery is someone proudly singing our beautiful national anthem.
Bravery is a cannon screaming victory at the enemy.
Bravery is a purple heart on a courageous soldier's uniform.
Bravery tastes like someone eating Brussels sprouts for the first time.
Bravery smells like fresh gun smoke clouding the battlefield.
Bravery sounds like a lion roaring to protect its pack from predators.
Bravery feels like an army truck driving up the rough Rocky Mountains.
Bravery looks like an American flag waving in the cool spring air.
Bravery makes me feel like I can go to sleep at night and not have to worry about getting hurt.
Bravery makes me feel like I can trust my country's decisions.
Bravery is like bombs booming in the blazing hot air.
Lexi Hill, Grade 6
West Allegheny Middle School

Excitement
Excitement is the tearing of paper opening a special gift
Excitement is the crack of the bat sending the ball way out in left field
Excitement is a new trampoline waiting for your company
Excitement is a bundle of colors jumping up and down
Excitement tastes like fresh juicy watermelon on a sizzling sunny summer day
Excitement smells like warm sugar cookies begging to be eaten
Excitement sounds like screams and laughter sent from a rickety roller coaster
Excitement feels like a basketball rolling off the tips of your fingers going in for a winning shot
Excitement looks like an acrobat flying high in the air during a circus
Excitement makes me feel as wonderful as winning a gold medal
Excitement is watching balloons of all colors take off in the blue sky
Excitement is a monkey swinging from vine to vine racing to get a ripe banana
Carolyn Stout, Grade 6
West Allegheny Middle School

Joy
Joy is a beautiful flower blooming in the spring.
Joy is a newborn puppy entering the big world.
Joy is a tasty chocolate covered Oreo cookie before bedtime.
Joy is a beautiful shade of blue in the clear sky.
Joy tastes like fresh baked bread from the oven.
Joy smells like home grown peaches from my backyard.
Joy sounds like the chirping of a bird on a summer morning.
Joy feels like fluffy, fuzzy fur on a frisky feline.
Joy looks like children happily playing on the playground at school.
Joy makes me feel like flying high in the sky.
Joy is taking long walks in the deep adventurous woods behind my house.
Savannah Webster, Grade 6
West Allegheny Middle School

Thanksgiving Dinner
I see my family members: aunts, uncles, and grandparents coming to the house.
I can hear my cousins chomping down the delicious mouth watering dinner.
I can taste the swirling Swiss mashed potatoes in my drooling mouth.
I can see my happy and friendly family sitting around the festive decorated table.
I can touch the soft melting cookies from the hot oven.
Amanda Choi, Grade 4
Colonial Elementary School

It's a Smoothie Day
It's a smoothie day
These days are great days
Strawberry-banana blending, crushing ice
Red and pink
Makes your mouth water
Brain freezes
While watching movies you then feel frigid
My frigid drink is gone
Until my smoothie day ends
Live life while you have it
Just love smoothies!
Briana Paige Gery, Grade 6
Pennridge North Middle School

Autumn
Autumn is a transition,
A time of change and color

Betwixt the muggy green of summer,
And the sharp whiteness of winter

Leaves like little fiery torches,
Flickering in the breeze

A beautiful time,
But, the quickest season.
Laurel McLaughlin, Grade 6
Pennridge North Middle School

The Great Game of Hockey
Hockey is the world's greatest game
No other game is the same
Players skate down the ice very fast
Among them the puck being passed
The goalies are fast as lightning
The speed of the puck is frightening
Players get hit
The coach makes them sit
The star player scores
The home crowd roars
Hockey is the world's greatest game.
Mason Schroeder, Grade 5
East Union Intermediate Center

Why?
why do the leaves fall?
why are the trees so tall?
why do we learn?
why can we turn?
why does it snow?
why does the wind blow?
why do dogs bark?
why does a fire give off a spark?
why?
Olivia Leng, Grade 6
St Joan of Arc School

Christmas Holiday
I wake up and look out my window
It's a huge breeze of white flakes
Everybody's houses are looking so pretty
For the holiday that's great
Red and green are hung from houses
Sleighs and Santas are out there too
Everyone is asleep and quiet like mouses
Now I know what to do
I run downstairs to see what I got
But first I have to wake everyone up
I go to my brother's bedroom first
My little brother is full of thirst
I get him some milk and cereal too
Then I go to my dad's room
I wake him and my stepmom up
Then we go look at Santa's cup
The milk's all gone and the cookies too
Uh oh my sisters are still in their room
We get them and go to the tree
Everyone is happy as can be.
Jocelyn Krotec, Grade 6
Hopewell Memorial Jr High School

The Ultimate Day
If I had the best day ever, I would wish for:
puppies
donuts
iPod touch
iPod Apple
my pet ferret Freddie
grilled chicken wrap
grilled chicken and shrimp Caesar salad
Thanksgiving dinner
banana split
flowers
cookies
cake
turkey legs
mashed potatoes with gravy
earrings
DSI
my trampoline
pumpkin pie with whipped cream
fried Twinkies
Victoria Rombach, Grade 6
St Sebastian Elementary School

McKinley School
Overlook school
Learning, teaching
Enjoying, working, sharing
Small, old, large, new
Helping, creating, drawing
McKinley School
Skylar Hunsiker, Grade 5
McKinley Elementary School

Vampire/Human
Vampire
Immortal, cold-blooded
Sucking, healing, living
Fangs, blood, teeth, food
Eating, bleeding, dying
Mortal, warm-blooded
Human
Allison Alejo, Grade 6
St Maria Goretti School

Teacher/Student
Teacher
books, papers
teaching, telling, grading
chair, grades, desk, tests
learning, listening, asking
assignments, projects
Student
Abby Caruso, Grade 6
St Maria Goretti School

Fire/Water
Fire
Hot, painful
Flaming, blistering, searing
Burns, blisters, bubbles, animals
Refreshing, soothing, cleansing
Clean, lively
Water
Elijah S. Trotter, Grade 6
St Maria Goretti School

Friends/Bullies
Friends
Courageous, intelligent
Loving, hard working, respecting
Beautiful, kind, careless, mean
Fighting, annoying, beating
Angry, rough
Bullies
Melina Owens, Grade 5
St Sebastian Elementary School

Friends
Friends
Cool, powerful
Loving, caring, respected
Heart, dream, argument, nightmare
Hating, hurting, unloved
Rude, disgusting
Bullies
Lydia Wirth, Grade 5
St Sebastian Elementary School

High Merit Poems – Grades 4, 5 and 6

Show Time!
Dog shows are fun
With some dogs you run
And other dogs just walk
But you shall not talk!
All groomed up and ready to go
It's time now for the show!

You are called into the ring
Now it's time to do your thing
You better listen to the judge
And hope your dog doesn't budge
If you want to place
You better put a smile on your face!
Anna Shoop, Grade 5
Saint Theresa School

Nature — Rain
I feel sorrow as the rain comes down
It feels so cold and wet
Plop! Plop! Plop!
The rain speaks to me
I let my head drop down low
As I wait for the bus to come
The driver cannot see
As we swerve down the road
I see lightning through the window
Hear thunder through the pane
The rain feels unappreciated
It streams down even harder
Voicing its madness at the world
Sara Korzuch, Grade 6
St Jerome Elementary School

At the Pond
I'm at the pond,
The water's cool.
I can't believe
I'm away from school.

I can float.
I can boat.
I can build a moat.

They day is ending.
I don't want to go.
I'm very sad.
I move quite slow.
Jacob Hines, Grade 5
East Union Intermediate Center

Thanksgiving Dinner
Delicious dinner
Roasted turkey, apple pie
It's goodness to me
Haley Miller, Grade 4
Watsontown Elementary School

Friends/Bullies
Friends,
Allies, companions
Loving, caring, sharing
Pal, mate, gangster, thug
Disliked, uncaring, unloved
Evil, mean
Bullies
Alexander Riccardi, Grade 5
St Sebastian Elementary School

Sweet/Sour
Sweet
delightful, pleasant
eating, licking, smiling
candy, mangos, warheads, lemon
eating, slurping, puckering
bitter, tart
Sour
Rebecca Sellinger, Grade 6
St Maria Goretti School

Baseball/Football
Baseball
Watchful, unpredictable
Running, batting, stealing
Pitcher, umpire, quarterback, referee
Catching, throwing, tackling
Quick, aggressive
Football
Andrew Blosky, Grade 6
St Maria Goretti School

Brother Dwain
Dwain
Wild, playing
Shouting, running, jumping
Screaming around the house
Yelling, eating, sleeping
Happy, funny
Brother
Marcus Allen, Grade 6
McKinley Elementary School

Family/Friends
Family
Fun, kind
Hugging, kissing, eating
Memorable moments in life
Shopping, working, playing
Cool, happy
Friends
Allison Hoy, Grade 6
McKinley Elementary School

The Ultimate Day
If I had the best day ever, I would wish for:
dogs
the beach
mashed potatoes
Christmas
my bed
basketball
TV
family
playing outside
action
fresh air
when it rains
softball
horses
playing with my dogs
making bracelets
my friends
steak
noodles
jumping on my trampoline
Julia Galbraith, Grade 5
St Sebastian Elementary School

Who You Are
You could spend your
whole life looking
for who you are who,
you could have been,
who you expected to
be. You can never be you because
you're always trying to
be he or she.
Striving to be unique
but your colors aren't
even on the rainbow.
But you won't see for
deep inside who you
could be… you could
spend your whole life
looking for who you
are who you could
have been who you
expected to be when
you were standing
there the whole time.
Ava Henderson, Grade 6
Colwyn Elementary School

Fall
As the leaves blow beneath my feet
And form a pattern that looks so neat,
I'm glad that I am here at all
To see this lovely scene of fall.
Laura Weiss, Grade 4
St Joseph School

A Winter Day
On a winter day, I grab my coat and gloves to go outside.
We build forts and have snowball fights.
But my favorite thing of all is the
Winter snow that falls on my tongue.
The great feeling you get when you get what you've always wanted
On Christmas Eve
I love the snowflakes
As they love me too
We're like two friends that will stay together till the world ends
So as the time goes we bounce and we play
Hoping the day will never end
We run off into the valley from mountain to top
Knowing each other is still there.
But as the day ends
The snow goes away
But it will be back another day to play

Austin Walker, Grade 6
State Street Elementary School

The Beautiful Things in Nature
If I were blue,
I would be the clear sky.
If I were blue,
I would be a kite flying in the air.
If I were blue,
I would be rain falling from the sky.
If I were blue,
I would be a puddle waiting to be jumped in.
If I were blue,
I would be a flower blooming.
If I were blue,
I would be a bluebird soaring in the sky.
If I were blue,
I would be the rivers all over the world.
If I were blue,
I would be the Atlantic Ocean crashing on the shore.

Jessica Atoo, Grade 5
Holy Child Academy

Baseball
Baseball is fun,
You have to run,
Most teams do have outs,
With the Phillies, there are no doubts.

The baseball sails out of the park,
Phillies fans are as happy as a lark,
Bases are loaded; players come home,
All celebrate victory with an ice cream cone.

It's not like a confirmation,
Foul balls make no affirmation,
The hitter catches an unlucky break,
The manager shakes his head at the mistake.

Michael Rudzinski, Grade 6
St Jerome Elementary School

Just the Beginning
It opens its eyes for the very first time,
Wondering, wondering, what will come to its mind?
It struggles to stand, but wobbles and falls,
Wishing to answer the wonderful calls.
Crawling and falling, such a devastating process,
Wanting to prance along the wonderful mosses.
It finally gets up wondering what to do next,
It jumps out its nest and simply guessed.
"Should I soar should I fly should I rise above the sky?
Should I stop should I drop, I don't want to die."
It turns to its mom asking what to do next,
she nods and calls to go back to the nest.
It flaps and flaps getting above the trees
but there's only one problem that's all it sees.
It goes back down and locates the nest,
and lays down to sleep for an ever long rest.

Gregory Nero, Grade 6
Hopewell Memorial Jr High School

Books
I love books
Books are like a personal television with words
They are really fun to read
You can make the characters come alive
Some of them even interact with me
Books come with a hard cover or in paperback
I can buy them at any store
They are really easy to search for
Books come in many varieties
Some are about love, friendship, school, and many more!
Some are long, and some are short
Some are for children, and some are for adults
You see, books can be for everyone
Why are books so fun to read?
They expand my vocabulary, and stir my imagination
Get a book; Read!

Basia Sobczuk, Grade 6
St Jerome Elementary School

About Me
I lay in silence in my room every day
I always see a bright sun ray.
I see my cat on my big bed
And I imagine his fur dyed red.

My mom kisses me on the head
And I go to school without making my bed.
My dad works every day
But on the weekends my dad and I go out and play.

My mom and I go shopping for food a lot
But we make sure the food doesn't rot.
In the summer I like to swim
And visit my Aunt Nancy and Uncle Jim!

Emily Susan Figliolia, Grade 5
St. Joan of Arc School

Freedom
Freedom is an animal
It is not not afraid against smaller animals.
But the bullies make the animal run away.
But every day it's gets stronger,
and stronger,
and stronger.
And the bullies get littler
and littler,
and littler.
And now the bully runs away
just like the little animal did.
Austin Adler, Grade 5
Copper Beech Elementary School

Colors
Colors, colors, 1, 2, 3
There are so many colors
Look and see
Orange, red, black and brown
All those colors make me frown
Blue, green, yellow, white
All those colors bring delight
there are so many colors
Don't you see
Colors, colors
Which would you be?
Alexander Zemaitis, Grade 5
Saint Theresa School

Ode to Alyssa Novak
Oh Alyssa is so fine and kind she is so funny
And is as sweet as honey.

Alyssa's favorite thing to do is ride horses
After she studies her school courses.

Alyssa can sometimes be a little shy,
But she is so confident, I ask myself why?

I am so glad Alyssa is my friend
And I hope our friendship never ends!
Alyssa Martinazzi, Grade 4
All Saints Catholic School

Fall Is Ending
Fall is here, I have no doubt,
That the leaves will fall about.
Leaves are falling to the ground,
Fall colors are all around.

Soon the winter winds will blow,
Then the leaves will be under snow.
That time has not come just yet,
But it will be soon, I bet!
Hunter Mravintz, Grade 5
East Union Intermediate Center

Thanksgiving
I talk with my family
I watch football
It's time to eat
I'll eat it all
Mashed potatoes
Fluffy stuffing
Here comes turkey
The oven is puffing
It's time to go
I'm very sad
But come to think of it
I'm very glad.
Andrew Krachie, Grade 4
Middle Smithfield Elementary School

Christmas
Christmas colors are red and green
A tree with candy canes I've seen
Under the tree next to cookies and milk
Sits my stocking made out of silk
Aunts, uncles, grandparents too
All together to see Y-O-U
A wreath sits upon the door
Nobody wants to go home anymore
Christmas stories here and there
People singing everywhere
People drinking eggnog here
The air is filled with jolly good cheer
Megan Sellers, Grade 4
McDonald Elementary School

Snow
Snow is bright
It is also very white
I adore snow
It has a little glow
Snow is very pure
I wish it would snow more
I love to see the glisten of the snow
It makes me happy; I love it so
It feels like a blanket when you lay
I hope the snow angels I made stay
When the snow dances into my eye
I will not make a sigh.
Jaime Pirrone, Grade 6
St Jerome Elementary School

Fire
Fire is the warmth
Of your heart.
It is the flame that enlightens us,
With love, affection, and hope.
And we all soon gather round,
To show that we care.
Alberto Girod, Grade 6
Chichester Middle School

Danny the Dog
Danny the Dog
Was sniffing around.
He is digging, Oh, no!
There are holes in the ground!
Danny the Dog
Thought he would get a smack.
He was in big trouble,
But we called him for a snack.

Danny the Dog.
Quickly came back.
He was thinking
He'd get a tasty snack,
But instead
He was put in his cage
And placed in a corner.
He went into a rage.
Deanna Arnone, Grade 4
St Andrew's School

Ricky the Rabbit
Ricky the Rabbit
Was running around
Going faster and faster;
He fell to the ground.
He felt a sting,
And he cried, "Ouch!"
He saw some bees
And started to crouch.

Ricky the Rabbit
Heard the bees yelling.
He said, "Settle down,
Or I'll be telling."
He turned around
And hopped to his house.
He told his mom
And they saw a mouse.
Gabriel Coleman, Grade 4
St Andrew's School

Opposites
Day
Light, sun
Opposite of night
Night
Dark, stars out
Opposite of day
Summer
Hot, sun out
Good time to go to
The beach/winter
Cold, snow, good for
Something hot to drink.
Danielle I. Matos, Grade 5
Hamilton Elementary School

The Meaning of Music
Music doesn't come from CDs
Nor the radio, or MP3s
It comes from your heart
And comes out of your mouth
It reaches our souls and never gets out.

Emotions of many kinds
Are sung with words
People will listen
To rhythm and beat
Music gives meaning to life

People of many colors
And many races
Can be tied together
By one simple thing…
Music

The music of people
The music of places
The music of cultures
The music of races
Makes the world go 'round
Megan Gmys, Grade 6
Ross Elementary School

Phillies
Phillies
Fast, strong
Amazing, fighting, competing
Winning the World Series
Performing, working, reaching
Muscle, determination
Champions
Aaron Zvyagelsky, Grade 6
McKinley Elementary School

Animals
Animals come in all sizes and shapes
There are dogs, cats, bears and apes.
Some grow large, some stay small
Some get very, very tall.
Some growl, some moo
Some like to chew on shoes.
Some eat hay, some eat plants
Some even eat ants.
Some like to run and play
Some like to sleep all day.
Some are wild, some are pets
When they get sick they go to vets.
Some are black, some are white
Some are dark, some are light.
Some are spotted, some are plain
But we love them just the same.
Zoe Ricketts, Grade 5
East Union Intermediate Center

Superstar vs Benchwarmer
Superstar
Sensational, sweaty
Running, hitting, slapping
Home run, all star, bench, cramp
Sitting, boring, watching
Uninterested, patient
Benchwarmer
Grace McNeill, Grade 5
Pocopson Elementary School

Fall
Leaves
Orange, red
Floating, crunching, flying
Trees, branches, sticks, twigs
Playing, raking, throwing
Colorful, falling
Fall
Joseph Santana, Grade 5
Hamilton Elementary School

Stadium
Homeplate
White, dirty
Running, winning, scoring
Homerun, player, pitcher, batter
Breaking, swinging, missing
Wooden, smooth
Baseball bat
Hannah Bailey, Grade 5
Pocopson Elementary School

Baseball Diamond
Hot dog
Tasty, mouthwatering
Chewing, gobbling, relishing
Ketchup, mustard, bubble gum, dugout
Sitting, yawning, watching
Unimportant, unpopular
Benchwarmer
Jessica Liu, Grade 5
Pocopson Elementary School

Winter
Winter is wonderful
I love the snow
Nobody is going swimming outside
There's lots of snow on the ground
Ears are going to be freezing
Reindeer are shooting across the sky

Norah McDonnell, Grade 4
McKinley Elementary School

Fall
Autumn leaves are falling,
There are people calling.
Hear woodpeckers, "Peck! Peck!"
From a distance, a speck.

Autumn trees are swaying,
Little children playing.
Fall! Fall! It is here!
Listen as we cheer!
Tatiana Taylor, Grade 5
East Union Intermediate Center

Ice Cream
It is nice and cold,
For the young and old.
It's a summer treat,
To bring home to eat.

Bring a jumbo cone,
I'll eat it alone!
It makes a great day,
Hip, hip, hip, hooray!
Joella Miller, Grade 5
East Union Intermediate Center

My Great Dog
My dog is very loyal,
I treat him like he's royal.
He smells when his coat is wet,
But he is still just my pet.

We run along the main street,
Man, my dog has some fast feet!
My dog, he loves to come eat,
But he is really so sweet!
Jarrett Crowe, Grade 5
East Union Intermediate Center

Pittsburgh Champions
The glorious Pittsburgh champions
Stealing the spotlight
On the most magnificent night of all
In the Lions' den — Detroit
All for one thing — the Cup!
Dillon Clark, Grade 5
Ross Elementary School

Thanksgiving
Thanksgiving is…
Playing with cousins.
Watching football.
Eating too much turkey.
Making mashed potatoes.
Getting together.
Julia Costacurta, Grade 6
Moravian Academy Middle School

Video Games

How lovely are video games?
The things you can do in them are quite insane
The actions you perform are really crazy
When you're playing them you could be lazy
Some games are really tricky
So many games to play no need to be picky
Video games are as fun as playing sports
Except you don't' have to wear gym shorts
Bam!! Slam!! Video games are exciting
Try them for yourself; you'll find then delighting
There are many games that you can play
You can't play them all in one day

Bobby Lawless, Grade 6
St Jerome Elementary School

Football

Football is a really great sport
It's played on a field, not on a court
Sometimes football gets kind of rough
To play football, you must be tough
Running backs are as fast as lightning
The linemen's size is often frightening
The players are soldiers; the coaches are kings
Fighting for their crowns and rings
Playing in the cold is really the worst
Even when you're crushing the boys from Rhawnhurst
Now you know why football is fun
The whistle just blew; my poem is done

Tom Robinson, Grade 6
St Jerome Elementary School

NASCAR Race

I'm in a race not an ordinary race.
Fast down the track just seeing black.
I can't look back now I'm in the lead.
Here comes Jimmie I need to keep going before he catches me.
I'm just a rookie he's a pro.
We're approaching one lap to go.
I'm on turn four he's right behind me.
This one's going down to the wire.
What's that he blew a tire.
Whoopee now we can celebrate.
He lost I won.
What a great day for a NASCAR Race.

Griffin Curry, Grade 6
Hopewell Memorial Jr High School

Love

Love is sweet as sugar, honey and molasses
love is as sugary as a lollipop
it's the warm feeling you get in your heart
when you think about the one you love
butterflies, hearts and kisses fill your stomach
love is all around and everywhere

Tamaiya Hawkins, Grade 6
John G Whittier School

Joy

Joy is a bright sun lighting up your day
Joy is a warm blanket when there is a frigid snow outside
Joy is flowers blooming on a spring morning
Joy is a shining gold coin you receive
Joy tastes like fresh brownies dancing in your mouth
Joy smells like chewy, crunchy cookies on Christmas Eve
Joy sounds like laughter on a playground
Joy feels like a plush stuffed animal hugging you
Joy looks like your best friend making you smile on your worst day
Joy makes me want to smile all the time
Joy makes the sun shine every day
Joy is enjoying the time you have with your friends

Reilly Zimmerman, Grade 6
West Allegheny Middle School

Sadness

Sadness is being sucked into a dusky hole that you did not see
Sadness is a frown on a smiley face
Sadness is a storm cloud that follows you around
Sadness is indigo like the color of an ocean after a storm
Sadness tastes like rotten eggs that have sat outside for a week
Sadness smells like expired milk hidden so no one can find it
Sadness sounds like thunder in a storm, BOOM! BOOM!
Sadness feels like the slimy yoke of a newly cracked egg
Sadness looks like a little cloud all alone in the sky
Sadness makes me wish I was on a beach
Sadness has one leg and is unstable
Sadness is like losing someone you love very much

Jenna Josey, Grade 6
West Allegheny Middle School

Snow

Pure, white snow fell to the ground,
Glistening like diamonds.
Winter is here.
Fluffy snow covers the bare trees
Like a warm, white blanket
As I watch it fall, it swirls and drifts
The snowflakes dance
During a peaceful walk
On a cold winter's day
The snow crunches under my feet
How happy and content I feel
Enjoying the sparkling, spectacular, splendid snow.

Timothy Wolfe, Grade 6
St Jerome Elementary School

Halloween

Scary, freaky
popping out, scaring people, freaking out
werewolves, zombies, Superman, mummies
surprising people, trying to scare people, terrifying
crazy, shocking
fright night

Miguel Vasquez, Grade 5
Hamilton Elementary School

Summer Fun
School ends, summer starts
Swimming practice at the club
Sizzling grilled hot dogs
Blazing heat, tan lines hurting
Frolicking fun at the beach
Lily D'Angelo, Grade 5
Holy Martyrs Elementary School

The Beauty of Maine
Damp, rocky beaches
Clams crunching under sandals
Sweet and tender lobster tails
Salty, cold ocean water
Crashing waves thunder to shore.
Sean Patrick Farrell, Grade 5
Holy Martyrs Elementary School

Sunshine
Sunrise
The sun rises
Yellow, bright in the sky
Orange ball moving down slowly
Sunset
Emil Bajgoric, Grade 4
Jefferson Elementary School

Christmas Time
Christmas bells chiming
Bringing happiness and joy
Santa's on his way
Children playing in the snow
Smells of pine and gingerbread
Ricky Bradley, Grade 5
Holy Martyrs Elementary School

Chilling at the Beach
Jumping on hot sand
Seagulls flying up above
Hear the waves crashing
Sand castles dotting the beach
Collecting large, bright conch shells!
Julia Dellaporta, Grade 5
Holy Martyrs Elementary School

Birthdays
Floating red balloons
Smooth and creamy chocolate cake
Excite and delight
Wrapped, multicolored presents
Noisy chatter of guests
Juliana Burns, Grade 5
Holy Martyrs Elementary School

Aggression
Aggression is like a spiraling tornado of hatred bottled up inside of you.
Aggression is the downpour of rain that comes out of nowhere on a sunny day.
Aggression is like a volcano erupting inside you.
Aggression is the color of blood seeping from a wound.
Aggression tastes like a freshly grilled hot dog with flaming hot jalapeños.
Aggression smells like a gigantic stack of salty sauerkraut.
Aggression sounds like the explosion of a huge bomb on a calm night.
Aggression feels like rough sand paper rubbing against your back.
Aggression looks like the center of a battle field in the middle of the war.
Aggression makes me want to overcome my fears and battle my enemies.
Aggression creeps up on you like a thief in the night.
Aggression is the feeling of anger boiling inside of your mind.
Ryan Rohm, Grade 6
West Allegheny Middle School

Love
Love is a mother's comforting hug, after a long day at school.
Love is a newborn baby child resting in a mother's gentle arms.
Love is a girl elegantly waltzing around her bedroom
Love is the color of a velvety rose waiting to be smelled.
Love tastes like a warm, delicious, heart-shaped sugar cookie.
Love smells like a fancy, fresh, fragrance a princess would wear to a dance.
Love sounds like a soft coo from a baby, after a long nap.
Love feels like a fluffy, warm, blanket always there to comfort you.
Love looks like a beautiful wedding after the prince saves the damsel in distress.
Love makes me want to listen to cheerful music.
Love is a lavender violet saying, "I love you" from a bashful, loving person.
Love is a faint, soft whisper, "Goodnight."
Haley Grogan, Grade 6
West Allegheny Middle School

Bird
Bird, Bird, how do you fly?
No one taught you.
Should you go high or low?
How do you sing such a beautiful song?
Eagle why do you shriek but the bluebird sings?
Bird why can you do so many things?
Cats lay around and chase yarn balls.
Dogs bark and chase their tails.
You're one of the only creatures that take flight.
Wonderful bird
Beautiful bird.
Bird.
Erin Markham, Grade 5
Copper Beech Elementary School

Furious
Furious is flaming red
It sounds like the screaming on a dark, scary night
It smells like the burning coal on a fire, oh so bright
It tastes like burnt chicken left in the oven all night
It looks like an angry bull charging at the matador in his sight
Furious feels like a tornado coming at your house with unstoppable might
Joseph Lozito, Grade 4
Anne Frank School

High Merit Poems – Grades 4, 5 and 6

Leaves
Leaves
are falling
as colorful as
can be leaves are
falling as you
can see
leaves!
Jeryka S. Diaz, Grade 5
Hamilton Elementary School

Changes
Summer has left us.
Autumn has replaced Summer.
It's getting chilly.

Fall has come to us.
There are dead leaves on the ground.
See you soon Winter.
Hiram Santiago, Grade 5
Clearview Elementary School

It Is Fall
Fall is here now
Leaves are falling
They are all different colors
Like red, yellow, and brown
They look so pretty
There's a pile of leaves
I'm going to jump in them.
Gia Lisco, Grade 4
Middle Smithfield Elementary School

Summer
We play all day in the summer.
Going to school is a bummer.
Riding along in my hummer.

In the summer I can swim.
It is better than the gym.
The water is at the brim.
Sydney Lerda, Grade 5
Our Lady of Grace Elementary School

Summer and Winter
Summer
Fun, sunny
Playing, swimming, laughing
Pool, beach, ice, snow
Snowing, flurring, skating
White snowflakes, frozen
Winter
Allie Dych, Grade 6
St Maria Goretti School

The Ultimate Day
If I had the best day ever, I would wish for:
the smell of the dogs
the smell of chocolate cookies
my grandparents' two dogs
their dogs barking
patting their soft fur
my grandpa
my grandma
my aunt Katie
my fave black shorts
my fave palm tree shirt
my fave black flats
the coolness of the pool
the beautiful night sky
so many stars
the pretty day sky
the smell of citrus fruits
the nice neighbors
the hot water
the nice days every day
Haley Mondragon, Grade 6
St Sebastian Elementary School

The Ultimate Day
If I had the best day ever, I would wish for:
Brownies
Flat screen TV
Fuzzy blankets
Movies
iPod
Laptop
Cell phone
Crafts
Saturdays
Roses
Pools
Winter
Cake
Bagels
Friends
Christmas
Rome
Family
Summer
Adelyne Bejjani, Grade 6
St Sebastian Elementary School

Apples
Apple orchard's buckets full.
Green, shiny, stick, leaf,
Core, seeds, small tree
White, red, yellow
Comes from
An apple tree's branches.
Aubrey Gall, Grade 5
Maxwell Elementary School

Snowmobiles
S ometimes dangerous
N oisy engines
O utstanding races
W orth watching
M agnificent machines
O nly can be driven in snow
B e aware of things on the track
I ncredible crowds
L ittle snowmobiles are made
E ncourage yourself before racing
S afety gear is needed
Kayla Seitz, Grade 5
East Union Intermediate Center

My Birthday
March is the month that I like the most,
A birthday party for me that I host.

Friends and family are everywhere,
The birthday cake, there's none to spare.

I look around the room and what do I see,
A ton of presents standing in front of me.

After a long day it's time to go to sleep,
I doze off and count presents, not sheep.
Noelle Manchini, Grade 5
East Union Intermediate Center

Skateboarding
Faster, faster, faster I go,
Kick flip in the air and land.
Then go, preparing to perform,
A difficult move…3, 2, 1, "go!"
As I do my trick, I put a twist on it,
I go for a grind.
I'm falling behind,
Crashing to the ground.
I fail to do my trick
I wonder if I can do
A twisted side-flip?
Jason Johnson, Grade 6
Chichester Middle School

Christmas
C old and snowy
H ot chocolate and presents
R udolph and reindeer
I gloos and snow balls
S kiing and snow boarding
T ons of fun
M aking cookies
A fraid of blizzards
S nowmen and snow children
Peter Hamel, Grade 5
Foster Elementary School

Space

Filled with no gravity
Stars scattered here and there
Planets surrounding the sun
Black holes to the unknown

Dark as night
Moons for the planets
Human space travel
Aliens may be on the planet Mars

Built to be explored
Many places to see
Constellations fill the spaces that can't be filled
Space is a beautiful place

Aidan McGuckin, Grade 6
St Jerome Elementary School

The Red Devils

Our soccer team is doing very, very bad,
It's making all my teammates sad.

This makes Coach Sean kind of mad,
And he frequently talks about this with my Dad.

We used to win with all the talent we had,
Now most of our opponents are our old comrades.

Maybe our team's lucky streak was just a fad,
But all that winning was really rad.

With our down spirits and stinky pads,
When this terrible season is over I'll be glad.

Spencer Heastings, Grade 6
Carson Middle School

My Mysterious Winter Friend

Cold snow crisp and clear
My friend is coming,
He'll soon be here.
I get things ready to start our fun.
Maybe a snack. Yes a nutritious one.
A long stick of orange speckled with green.
Also bits of nuts would be very keen.
A set of hats and scarves I get for us two.
A hat for him with the colors of green and blue.
Now some sticks and some rocks he may want indeed.
But why would he want that.
You may question me.
Cold snow crisp and clear,
My snowman friend is finally here.

Jill Goodman, Grade 6
William Penn Middle School

The Thankful and Lovable Horse

I'm thankful so very much,
For all the things I love to do,
Including the things that include you,

I'm thankful for shelter,
I'm thankful for speed,
But, I also am thankful for how you take care of my every need,

My beautiful mane blows in the wind when I run,
I love to speed, speed, speed,
I mostly love to run with sun,

Well, those are the things I love and more.
These are also the things I'm thankful for!!!

Gabrielle Alley, Grade 6
Interboro GATE Program

Friendship

It was a beautiful day at Foster School
Everyone was outside and the playground was full.
The birds were flying up high in the air,
The kids were playing, at each other they would stare.

Suddenly a scream shook the ground,
It was a student who had fallen down.
The nurse rushed out to the playground to check,
The student was bleeding from a cut in his neck.

I went to his house to see him the next day
I asked him what happened and he said he was OK.
I asked if he wanted to be my friend
And from that day on, time together we did spend.

Herminio Ramirez, Grade 5
Foster Elementary School

Outdoors

I like when I go outdoors,
But not when I have to do my chores.

As the sun shines down upon my face,
It gives me energy and I run all over the place.

I love to smell beautiful flowers,
Especially after a morning rain shower.

As the breeze blows the trees begin to move,
The rain comes again and I soon disapprove.

I run for cover and go and hide,
When the weather clears up I'm back outside.

Emma Govachini, Grade 5
Ss Simon and Jude Elementary School

Basketball

When you play basketball
Everyone wants to play ball,
But only one team
Can go and win it all.
With 30 teams in the league
Everyone wants a star,
But can they make a three
Away from the basket by far?
You play 82 games in a season
Some people think it's a lot,
If you think it is
Try to make every shot.
When you are close to the basket
You want to slam dunk,
But when it goes off the rim
You hear a big clunk.
With every game you play
The championship is near,
But when you make that winning shot
Your name being chanted is all you hear.
Adam Barkman, Grade 6
Hopewell Memorial Jr High School

The Ultimate Day

If I had the best day ever, I would wish for:
potato chips
pretzels
bananas
apples
winter
Thanksgiving
my friends
popcorn
chocolate covered almonds
corn
cupcakes
chocolate cake with white icing
ice cream sandwiches
my family
soccer
basketball
cross country
pizza
everything to do with Harry Potter
Gillian Kasper, Grade 6
St Sebastian Elementary School

Happiness

Happiness is yellow
It sounds like a toddler's laughter
It smells like sunflower's blooming
It tastes like lemon pie
It looks like Lilly of the Valley
It feels like a warm day at the beach
Ahyanna Brooks, Grade 4
Anne Frank School

The Ultimate Day

If I had the best day ever I would wish for:
Cedar Point
Lemonade
Halo 3: ODST
BZ Power
Lego
Bionicle the Legend Reborn
Pomegranate
Bionicle shirt
Licorice (dog)
Diary of a Wimpy Kid (book)
Rice crispy treat
Ocean City
Halo: Combat Evolved
Sweetarts
Star Wars: Republic Commando
Windows Vista computer
Family
Marshmallow
Bionicle comics
Ryan Marks, Grade 5
St Sebastian Elementary School

The Ultimate Day

If I had the best day ever, I would wish for:
Hamburger with ketchup and pickles
American Pie
Turkey on wheat bread with pickles
TV
Ketchup on corn
Blankets
Family
Friends
Gym
Pets
Vacation
My bed
Pizza
Christmas
Spring
Fall
Time with family and friends
Halloween
Chocolate covered pretzels
Alexander Boone, Grade 6
St Sebastian Elementary School

Autumn in the Forest

F alling
O range leaves in fall
R otting
E xcellent sight to see
S oaking wet in the morning
T owering trees.
Zachary Ecker, Grade 4
Trinity East Elementary School

Pets

Pets are part of my family.
They make me smile.
They make me laugh.
Sometimes they make my parents mad.
Sometimes one is noisy.
The other one is quiet.
One is very furry.
The other one has a shell.
One is a mammal.
The other is a reptile.
My dog is a girl.
My turtle we are not sure.
Pets add joy to my family.
Joey Belmont, Grade 5
St Joan of Arc School

Shooting Star

S ailing in the skies above
H alting never for any reason
O pen to everyone to see
O nlookers watch your ongoing shine
T hey wish upon your radiance
I njuring no living creature
N ormally in the night
G ift to all humans

S o pretty in so many ways
T iny thou are not
A lways near
R emember to wish
Erin Iams, Grade 5
Foster Elementary School

If Fall Could Be…

If fall could be a color,
It would be orange.
As bright as the leaves.
If fall had a taste,
It would taste just like apple pie.
If fall could be a smell,
It would be freshly baked pumpkin pie.
If fall could be a sound,
It would be the crunch of leaves as you step.
If fall could be a feeling,
It would be crisp and crunchy.
If fall could be an animal,
It would be a tasty little turkey!
Elizabeth Escott, Grade 5
Clearview Elementary School

The Cold Day

The warm fireplace
I drink my hot chocolate
On a snowy day
Samuel Reed Pawling, Grade 4
Watsontown Elementary School

Apple Pie
A wesome
P erfect
P eaceful
L uxurious
E xcellent

P henomenal
I ntriguing
E nchanting
Nino Itri, Grade 5
East Union Intermediate Center

Candy
Candy can be soft like gumdrops,
It can be hard like lollipops.
Candy can be sweet and sour,
I can eat it for an hour.

Make sure you do not eat too much,
Or you might get a sugar rush.
Although candy is good and sweet,
Be careful 'bout how much you eat!
Katelyn Slagel, Grade 5
East Union Intermediate Center

Corvette
Cherry red
Heated seats
I can feel when its heart beats
Black on brown
When you hear that sound,
You'll know…we're going to go
Caution yellow
Be my good fellow,
Roll Roll Roll!
Brandon Zhitnitsky, Grade 6
Hillcrest Elementary School

Chocolate
Hershey's,
Sweet, candy,
Chocolate is sweet,
Yummy, crunchy,
Hershey's chocolate.
Kayleigh Izzo, Grade 5
Russell Elementary School

Family
F un to be with
A mazing people
M y favorite people
I love them
L ucky I have them
Y ou would love them too.
Anthony Oliphant, Grade 4
McKinley Elementary School

Silver
Silver is cold frozen
cool as ice
Silver, cloudy as snow
ice crystals glow in clouds
Silver is steam evaporation
it fills the Earth with joy
Silver, the magnet on the teacher's whiteboard
Silver, the sky when it's about to rain
silver, color of my morning
Silver!!
  Silver
    Silver
      Silver
        Silver
J'Lynn Matthews, Grade 4
Wissahickon Charter School

Earth
The wind whispers in my ears
The leaves fall off the redwood trees
The big city was near
I could feel the breeze
In the city of Pittsburgh
Stood houses and skyscrapers
Just like Harrisburg
I saw some newspapers
In the rural towns
Stood silos and farms
The windmill spun around
I saw a big red barn
Earth has many qualities
That we can't deny
It has a large quantity
Of people who rely
On everything the earth gives to us
Barbara Matthews, Grade 5
East Union Intermediate Center

My Birthday
My special birthday
Surprises and loads of gifts
Games, movies, and party treats
Isabel Parsons, Grade 4
McKinley Elementary School

No Freedom
In 1946 Russia took over Berlin and blocked people from getting out.
Lots of people risked their lives to be free
By climbing over the wall built by the Russians all around Berlin.
"Down with Russian soldiers," the Germans said.
And one day they were free.
Avery Skiviat, Grade 5
Foster Elementary School

Hockey Exhilaration
When I step onto the ice
It feels so nice.

The room is so cold
But it never grows old.

With my stick in my hands
I look at the stands.

I shoot the puck
I don't always have luck.

It makes me feel strong
And the game seems to last so long.

My team spirit will never die,
As long as my team's flag flies high.
Matthew Giampa, Grade 6
St Jerome Elementary School

My Brother and Myself
My brother
Loud, crying
Never sleeps
Always cries
Not phenomenal
Bugs me
Always pooped
Cutie pie
A baby
Me, myself
Cute funny
Nice helpful
Good friend
Smart student
Good daughter
Loud active
Big sister
Lianis Ojeda, Grade 4
Wickersham Elementary School

Night Pond
Nightmoon glistening,
Reflecting in my window,
The pond in my yard.
Kay I. Casturo, Grade 4
Jefferson Elementary School

High Merit Poems – Grades 4, 5 and 6

Cherry the Chipmunk
Cherry the Chipmunk
Was reading a good book,
But when the sun comes out,
She goes out of her nook.
She finds a flower,
And gives it to a friend.
She wishes this day
Would never end!

Cherry the Chipmunk
Crawled into bed,
Said, "Goodnight,"
Then lays down her head.
Cherry the Chipmunk
Wakes up on the floor,
Makes some oatmeal,
Then is hungry no more.
Callie Burgan, Grade 4
St Andrew's School

David the Dragon
David the Dragon
Was flying up high.
He was so tired
He fell from the sky.
He was close to Minnesota.
He hurried up to the sky.
He fell down,
And he took a sigh.

David the Dragon
Started to fly.
He went up and up
Into the sky.
He looked around
And saw a plane.
The pilot asked him
To give him his name.
Jeffrey McKissick, Grade 4
St Andrew's School

Summer
When June arrives summer's here
It only comes once a year
It's as hot as walking on the sun
I'm half asleep when the day is done
The ice cream truck rides down my street
The ground is hot beneath my feet
No school or teachers to please
It's as if I hear the singing of the bees
Waiting in line for the Ferris wheel
The roller coasters make me squeal
Summer's a blast, but by the end
I can't wait for school to start again
Hannah Savage, Grade 6
St Jerome Elementary School

Shawn Hoy
S ports are my favorite thing to do.
H ave four family members.
A pples are my favorite snack.
W ater is the best sports drink.
N ever know what's going to happen!

H annah is my dog.
O n my birthday I have pumpkin pie.
Y ankees are my least favorite team.
Shawn Hoy, Grade 4
McKinley Elementary School

Our Beautiful World
Crystal clear water
Gorgeous dolphins
Hawaiian trees
And coconuts falling.

Summer sun
Bright blue sky
Sparkling sand
Summer, oh my!
Sumir Czopek, Grade 4
Fairview Elementary School

I Forgot My Poem
I forgot the poem I'm supposed to write,
The bulb above my head just won't light,
So now I'm writing random letter,
And getting scolded by my betters,
Now I'm afraid I must bid you good-bye,
And to remember my poem,
I soon again will try,
I guess until then this is it,
I just realized my bulb was lit!
Lauren Daukaus, Grade 5
McKinley Elementary School

Maple Tree
Maple
Towering, huge
Climbing into thin air
Playfully blowing in the wind
Giant.
Abigail Faust, Grade 5
Trinity East Elementary School

Soccer
S ave the ball
O h joy! We won!
C hampions
C oaches
E xcellent kick
R eally good team
Grant Gow, Grade 4
McKinley Elementary School

All About Fall
Leaves
Crunch leaves
Jump into leaves
Brrr it's cold out
Fall

Fall
Cold, wet
The wind blowing
Time to go inside
Autumn
Alexis Fenstermacher, Grade 5
Clearview Elementary School

Halloween
Halloween is a favorite time for me
There are lots of things to do and see.

In all the houses on my street
You get some tricks and treats to eat.

It is one of my favorite times of year
It can give some kids a terrible fear.

I can't wait till Halloween night
But make sure for safety carry a flashlight.
Justin Greegus, Grade 5
Ss Simon and Jude Elementary School

Winter
Winter is my favorite time of year
it's the time for holiday cheer.

I like the cold white snow
I jump on a sled and off I go.

Snowball fights are very fun
but only after my homework is done.

Christmas is in the air
the most wonderful time of the year.
Justin Skirda, Grade 5
East Union Intermediate Center

The Great Sport of Softball
Oh how I love to play softball,
I play it every spring and fall!
First base is where I like to be.
The ball is always thrown to me.

My team's the best, there is no doubt.
We cheer for each other, scream and shout.
Deer Lakes is great, we scored a run!
No better way to have such fun!
Brooke Zawalnicki, Grade 5
East Union Intermediate Center

Christmas

Christmas is coming, it is almost here
Movies are on and my family is near
Walking in the snow
Caroling as we go

Baking cookies is fun
We are always on the run
Putting up decorations is such a tease
When it is all over, you are at ease

Christmas in December,
Is so much better than September
"Jingle Bell Rock" is my favorite song
It's a shame the season is not long

Maria Murray, Grade 6
St Jerome Elementary School

Winter

Snow, snow, snow
I love it so
Snow, snow, snow
It gets so cold
Snow, snow, snow
Equals a lot of fun
Skiing, snowboarding
All so fun
Coats, hats, gloves,
And scarves keep me warm
I wait and wait
Until the jolly guy comes
Then I hurry under my covers
Because I felt a little numb

Sean Hiteshew, Grade 6
Immaculate Conception School

The Thankful Snake

I'm thankful for my home, a rock
I can eat big things when
my jaws are unlocked.

I'll move more slowly towards my prey
My scales act as camouflage
So I'm hidden that way.

I'm thankful for my venom
that shines in the light
even when I'm hunting late at night.

These are the things I'm thankful for
I like these things and many more.

Andrew Bucher, Grade 6
Interboro GATE Program

Knowing

Almost everyone I know
Knows someone who has fought
To let us live a good life
And live in peace

These brave soldiers fought
Tyrants
Dictators
And all affiliated armies

They risked life and death
And saw close friends die
Right before their eyes
At the speed of light

To them I can only say
Thank you
Thanks for risking your life
Thanks for everything

Sarah Kathryn Witherow, Grade 6
Pennridge North Middle School

Nature

Nature
Fun, exciting, beautiful, magnificent
Child of Earth
Lover of ecofriendly items,
The environment,
Nature study
Who feels…
Pain when deforestation happens,
Anger at pollution,
Full of vengeance
Who fears…
Deforestation,
Over-polluting
Global warming
Who would like to see…
Forestation,
Everything ecofriendly,
Earth purified
Nature.

Ethan Dolata, Grade 5
Pocopson Elementary School

What Is a Friend?

What is a friend?
Someone you can trust
Someone you want to be with
Is always kind
Likes to be with you
Cares about you
Loves to play with you
That is a friend.

Alyssa Spagnoletti, Grade 5
Saint Theresa School

Bubba

Bubba likes to play ball
He brings it back when I call
Bubba likes to run
He's as fast as a bullet from a gun

Even though he is only one
Like an elephant, he weighs a ton
Bubba is strong as an ox
His fur is the color of a fox

Bubba is lucky to be alive
Into any water he will dive
He has an amazing thirst
His favorite food is liverwurst

Bubba cuddles with me in bed
Where I put my arm, he lays his head
My mother tried to give him away
For him to stay I always pray

Julianne Blank, Grade 6
St Jerome Elementary School

Matt at the Bat

Here I am
In the on-deck circle.
I'm almost up,
About to hurl!

My teammates cheer,
I can hear.
It's in my ear,
Batter struck out — it's very clear.

One out and down by one,
Being up next is such a stun.
What's he doing, he's gonna bunt,
Throw him out; go get the ump!

Now, I'm up,
With two outs gone.
1, 2, 3, strike him out,
At the old ball game!

Matt Ready, Grade 6
Chichester Middle School

Shopping

S uper savings
H alf off
O utlet malls
P ay day!
P ayments spent and gone
I n the fitting room
N othing too expensive
G ifts for friends

Kelsey Young, Grade 5
Saint Theresa School

High Merit Poems – Grades 4, 5 and 6

Copies

We make copies, more and more
I don't like copies
Yes, I'm sure!
Copies take up so much time
It should even be a crime
You push the button over again
So much, it adds up to ten
And when the copiers get all jammed
It makes your schedule much more crammed
We make copies, more and more
I don't like copies
Yes, I'm sure!

Donovan Oakes, Grade 5
Saint Theresa School

Autumn

Orange leaves frame black-birch bark,
Sun rises into pink horizon.
Icy snow dusting soft green grass,
Wind ripping at the flags and tousling your hair.
Earthworms smile out of apples.
Cold nights get colder.
Darkness falls earlier,
And light waits longer to return.
Sun melts into purple waters,
Lapping at a sandy beach.
Days are shortening,
Autumn has come.

Carrie Mannino, Grade 5
The Ellis School

Excitement

Excitement is catching an interception to set up the offense
Excitement is hearing you have club seats for the Steeler's game
Excitement is getting the MVP in a championship game
Excitement is orange like some of the leaves in autumn
Excitement tastes like your favorite calzone at Pepperoncini's
Excitement smells like your Grandma's house on Thanksgiving Day
Excitement sounds like your favorite song on a hot summer day
Excitement feels like lying on a cloud talking to the world
Excitement looks like crispy chocolate chip cookies
Excitement makes me smile like a smiley sticker
Excitement is as beautiful as the springtime
Excitement is the BANG you hear in a cannon

Jordan Cecil, Grade 6
West Allegheny Middle School

I Sing Of…

I sing of animals, bunnies, and swans that swim in streams
I sing of flowers, blue birds, and lilacs in the spring
I believe in love, youth, and time saying wow
I write of legends, stories, and poems like right now
I sing of tulips, and clouds, and morning dew
I sing of friends like me and you!

Grace Campbell, Grade 5
Copper Beech Elementary School

Envy

Envy is the water that boils up inside you
Envy is the pain that seeps down all around you
Envy is the jealousy that's undeniable
Envy is the red that fills your body with hatred
Envy tastes like a lemon with a super sour flavor
Envy smells like sour milk five days past its due date
Envy sounds like the bang that comes out of a gun
Envy feels like sharp rocks piercing through your feet
Envy looks like the beast that comes to you when you are sleeping
Envy makes me angry whenever I feel it inside me
Envy sneaks up on you whenever you are not ready for it
Envy is the water that boils up inside you

Brennon Grubb, Grade 6
West Allegheny Middle School

Holiday Cheer

Snowflakes falling to the ground
Not even making a bit of sound.
Now we know that Christmas is near
That special day with holiday cheer.
Run down the stairs and open the presents.
It's the day you can say will be very pleasant.
It is a beautiful day with carols galore
Feasts, family, cheer, and more.
The holiday's over it is time to go to bed.
But don't be sad, the New Year is ahead.
Merry Christmas, Happy New Year.
The wonderful days with holiday cheer.

Benjamin Goodwald, Grade 6
Hopewell Memorial Jr High School

Bravery

Bravery is a bold, brown, bull
Bravery is a first place medal at my volleyball tournament
Bravery is a slithering snake stalking for its prey
Bravery is red showing strength and encouragement
Bravery tastes like devouring a scorching hot wing
Bravery smells like smoke from a large fire
Bravery sounds like a thump of a drum
Bravery feels like rubbing an enormous, slimy snake
Bravery looks like two exhausted climbers
Bravery makes me feel strong and self assured
Bravery is a backhand spring mocking me
Bravery is the sound of bullets in a war

Lauryn Long, Grade 6
West Allegheny Middle School

My Mom

My mom is as pretty as a flower.
My mom is as nice as a bunny.
My mom is as sweet as a flower.
My mom is as small as a leprechaun.
My mom is funnier than a joke book.
My mom is as pretty as a flower.

Kayana Torres, Grade 4
Wickersham Elementary School

Yummy Goodness
Food, oh delicious food!
Yummy, scrumptious
Warm and sweet
Bitter cold, tart and neat.

Food, oh food
Creamy, silky
Zesty, milky
Thick and musty.

Food, it melts in your mouth.
Moreish, munchy, crunchy
Soft and gooey
Sloppy, plain.

That baked goodness;
I love it!
That scrumptious,
Delicious food!
Victoria Smoker, Grade 6
Linville Hill Mennonite School

Bailey
Bailey is my adorable cat
He's as cute as can be
I love him so much
Just as much as he loves me

He's tailless and thin
Always wants to eat
He's colored like a pumpkin
Always under my feet

He likes to sit and watch
The many birds outside
He scares easily at noises
Always runs and hides

Bailey is my cat
But also my friend
For the many ways he comforts me
There is a list that has no end
Kaitlyn McGlinn, Grade 6
St Jerome Elementary School

Werewolf
I wish I were a werewolf.
I would be like a dog.
I wish I were a werewolf
because vampires aren't for me.
That would make me happy.
I would be out at night.
I would fight for what's right.
Yes, that would make me happy.
Marina Woodson, Grade 5
East Union Intermediate Center

My Thumb, My Gum
My thumb, short and stubby,
My thumb also rhymes with gum.
Also when I think of some gum,
I find that I want some.

I use my thumb to read and write,
Gum I love to chew and bite.
Thumbs are handy to suck on,
When all of my gum is gone.
Yrsa Owings, Grade 6
Chichester Middle School

Batter
Hey, Batter, standing like a brick wall,
Thinking of the home run ball,
Flying in like "Air Force One,"
The first strike, "Call 911!"

In the crowd, they cheer and woo,
Too bad, it was called strike number two!
You wish you could touch home with glee,
But too bad, it's called, "Strike Three!"
Michael Franzini, Grade 6
Chichester Middle School

Shane Victorino
V ictorious on the field and off
I ntimidating to other players
C enter fielder for the Phillies
T hrowing the guy out at home
O pposite field hitter
R ounding third base
I nside the park home run
N ever gives up
O utstanding player
Bobby Jones, Grade 6
Chichester Middle School

Birds
Birds
Miniature, vivid
Flying, constructing, sleeping
I think they are charming.
Beautiful
Timothy Johnston, Grade 5
St Anselm School

Grandparents
Staying at their house on the weekend.
Spoiling you till you're rotten.
Always good to see.
Happy when I'm around them.
Comforting friends.
Good advisors.
Lauren Smith, Grade 6
Moravian Academy Middle School

Fall Numbers
Fall
Two colossal pumpkins
Three bags of leaves
Four plump squash
Five apple pies
Six Halloween baskets
Seven jack-o-lanterns
Eight students in costumes
Nine pumpkin pies
Ten trees dead with no leaves
Nyrell Arias, Grade 5
Clearview Elementary School

I Wish
I wish I had 15 pumpkins.
I wish I could fly in the leaves.
I wish it snowed a lot.
I wish it stopped raining.
I wish there was no school.
I wish more leaves would fall.
I wish I had apple pie.
I wish I could eat turkey.
I wish I could play football in the fall.
I wish I could be a basketball player.
Tahjae Becker, Grade 5
Clearview Elementary School

The Bouncing Basketball
Basketball, dribble, pass, shoot
score, run, hussle, fake
rebound, lay-up, competition
win, lose, good sportsmanship
never giving up, jump shot
pump fake win!
Dribble down the court
shoot the ball.
Go up for the rebound
watch it go in the net.
Tiffany Spisak, Grade 5
Maxwell Elementary School

Rain Forest
Wind
Water
Butterflies
Environment
Mud
Frogs
Spiders
Animals
Crawling insects
Leaves
Elio Diaz, Grade 6
Nazareth Area Intermediate School

Fall
leaves
yellow, brown
changing, rustling, crunching
The leaves are fun to jump in
Autumn
Serena Derosa, Grade 5
Hamilton Elementary School

Following My Dreams
A cartwheel on the beam
Is harder than it seems.
While on the bars
I reach for the stars.
Gymnastics fills my dreams.
Megan Zaremski, Grade 5
East Union Intermediate Center

Joyful
Joyful is blue
It sounds like it is peaceful
It smells like fresh air
It tastes like blueberry muffins
It looks like a delicious cookie
Dymeere Ancrum-Lowery, Grade 4
Anne Frank School

The Kingdom's Marriage
There once was a king named Jim,
Who loved his queen named Kim,
But when they got married,
They found out they varied,
On ruling the kingdom of Sim.
Cassandra White, Grade 6
St Joseph School

Family
My dad is a lad,
My mom is the bomb,
My brother likes book covers,
And
I am a hockey player.
Nikolai Portner, Grade 4
McKinley Elementary School

Christmas
Christmas
fun, cheery
gathering, sharing, caring
time to bake cookies
Holiday
Samantha Coleman, Grade 6
St Joseph School

My Cat Henry
My cat Henry is quite friendly,
Though he can be a troublemaker.
We used to have another cat, I don't think he liked that.
He chased it 'round like a rat. You could hear them running tat, tat, tat.
He'll usually sleep all day. But when my sister comes he walks (or runs) away.
So he has a knack for trouble.
But we still love him double.
Alex Hessler, Grade 4
Lincoln Elementary School

Humor
Humor is bright yellow like a rising sun at the crack of dawn
   from an admirable view from my freshly scrubbed windows.
It looks like a smile chuckling in two gleaming scarlet lips.
Humor tastes like rich caramel chocolate cradled in a candy wrapper.
It smells like the mint of a tasty Tic Tac being chewed slowly.
It sounds like a hyena in the audience of the Howard Stern show.
Humor feels like a throbbing heart bungee jumping in my chest.
Rick Wattenmaker, Grade 6
Our Lady of Ransom School

Jealousy
Jealousy is a green gruesome grudge on a cloudy day in late April.
It looks like fire burning in the devil's eyes because of his desire.
Jealousy tastes like a sour lemon-lime lasting forever in my mind.
It smells like rotten cheese on a humid day stuck outside in the sun.
It sounds like fingernails going down a chalkboard in the middle of class.
Jealousy feels like someone clawing my heart out on Valentine's Day
   smothering all my hopes and dreams.
Samantha McCarry, Grade 6
Our Lady of Ransom School

Seasonal Trees
Leaves say above our heads in the spring
May's flowers bring showers that shatter on the damp ground
giving water to the trees as a gift of forgiveness for the strong storms
Fall winds throw the leaves to the ground cleaning up for winter's arrival
Cold gusts of winter air blow through every corner inside of the forest
When summer arrives the birds fly back to perch on the branches of the seasonal trees
Emma A. Graham, Grade 5
Lincoln Elementary School

Fall Night
The warmth of the campfire and the sound of the crickets singing through the night
And the stars shining so bright, you don't even need a flashlight
The ashes chasing each other around
I love these fall sounds
The vibes that the sounds send
I don't want this night to end.
Claire Carpenter, Grade 4
Fawn Elementary School

The Nice Bee

Once there was a bee
The bee loved to drink the pollen out of the tree

Everybody needs bees
And trees
To keep us alive

Then the bee goes back to the beehive.

Aimee Keenan, Grade 4
Fairview Elementary School

The Scary Night

Look at the vampires down the hall.
And you can hear the witches call.

Look at the scary house.
What about that very spooky mouse?

Look up at the dark night sky.
You can hear the children shout "Why?"

Molly Dougher, Grade 4
Cathedral School of St Catharine of Siena

Halloween, Halloween, Halloween

In your dream it's a fright
So don't wake up on Halloween night
Roaming goblins on Halloween
Just listen to all the kids scream
Skeletons, Werewolves, and Witches too
They're all coming out to say Boo!
Scary costumes left to right
Halloween is gonna be a fright

Jennifer Tran, Grade 4
Cathedral School of St Catharine of Siena

Fall

Fall is for people, short and tall,
as long as you like to have a ball.
Jumping in leaves is a lot of fun,
until your parents say you're done.
The leaves are beautiful everywhere,
even though they might have a tear.
Fall is a season for love and thanksgiving,
even though the temperatures might have you freezing.

Jessica Mattiace, Grade 5
St John Neumann Regional Academy - Intermediate School

Colors

Red is the love that we all share
Orange is the stars that shine bright at night
Yellow is the color that represents the soft, sinking sand of the beach
Green is the smell of fresh cut grass
Blue is the water that replenishes our thirst
Black is the night when we rest

Victoria Kotwica, Grade 6
Ross Elementary School

For You and I

For my sisters and brothers who are trying to hold their hate,
For my fathers and mothers trying not to hesitate,
For the cats and dogs roaming to find their way home,
For the babies in the bathtub playing with the foam,
For the bats that are in flight all night,
And the squirrels that play all day.
For you and I, and the friendship we have,
I wish we can spread wings and fly.

Alexis Griess, Grade 4
St John Neumann Regional Academy - Intermediate School

Gold, the Brightest Color of Them All!

Gold is a golden retriever barking for its ball.
Gold is a duck quacking with its bill.
Gold is the lion shaking its mane.
Gold is the American Goldfinch singing on a branch.
Gold is my goldfish shimmering in her bowl.
Gold is a beautiful canary's gold fallen feather.
Gold is the fallen leaves right outside my bedroom window.
Gold is the summer sun that used to shine on my face.

Maya Brown-Hunt, Grade 5
Holy Child Academy

Black Things in Nature

Black is the night filled with stars.
Black is the color of an eclipse.
Black is the stripes on a bee's back
Black is the color of the pupils in my eyes.
Black is the center of a sunflower seed.
Black is the crow soaring over the forest.
Black is the color of a cat's fur on Halloween night.
Black is the soul of the devil.

Griffin Anderson, Grade 5
Holy Child Academy

My Favorite Baby Blue

Baby blue is the calm ocean on sunny days.
Baby blue is a dolphin doing flips in the air.
Baby blue is a sky during a sunny day.
Baby blue is the box with my pencils in it.
Baby blue is my pen when I have to write a paragraph.
Baby blue is the walls of my classroom.
Baby blue is the dictionary that I look up my words.
Baby blue is the lollipops I get when I win the review game.

Kiera Devers, Grade 5
Holy Child Academy

Shy

Shy is aquamarine
It sounds like a low-pitched voice that no one can hear
It smells like a flower that just doesn't want to sprout
It tastes like a boiled egg that doesn't want to come out of its shell
It looks like a child who just doesn't want to say, "Hello"
Shy feels like a butterfly that needs back his cocoon.

Paige Mininall, Grade 4
Anne Frank School

Thanksgiving
T urkeys
H ome for the holiday
A big feast
N ovember
K eep on eating
S o many helpings
G ravy, please
I 'm stuffed
V acation time
I ndians
N ow we're all together
G iving thanks for one another.
David Kozlowski, Grade 5
East Union Intermediate Center

The Thankful Armadillo
I am thankful for my shell.
It helps my living oh, so well.
My tail is neat and divine,
It has been passed down over time.
The food I eat is just so sweet
I love the tasty, tender treat.
I was not born with a fin,
But my camouflage does help me win.
I always burrow during the day,
I make a tunnel the right way.
I thank you God, you are so helpful,
For my existence, more than a handful.
Valerie Perry, Grade 6
Interboro GATE Program

Cheerleading
C heerful
H appy
E nergetic
E ncouraging
R eliable
L oud
E nthusiastic
A thletic
D ynamic
I magination
N oisy
G leeful
Marlie Bergman, Grade 5
Central Elementary School

Thanksgiving Is
Time to eat the turkey.
Hanging out with friends and family.
Being thankful.
Having the best meal of the year.
Drooling over the turkey.
Making a memory.
Greg Caubel, Grade 6
Moravian Academy Middle School

Christmas Eve
15 grandchildren,
6 families
Loved ones coming together
Rip! Presents are opening
Wrapping paper everywhere
Singing Christmas carols
Cousins are playing outback
Everyone having fun
We are as loud as a train
pulling into the station
People enjoying themselves
My family and I
On Christmas Eve
Shannon Boyle, Grade 6
St Jerome Elementary School

A Waterfall
A narrow waterfall
Brings me joy
Calming and cooling
Sounds of music
Gets me through the difficult day
Sitting by it for relaxation
As blue as the night sky
Peaceful noises
Crystal clear water
Shining in the sunlight
A home for many fish
Trickling sounds
Watching water fall into the river below
Caroline Simmer, Grade 6
St Jerome Elementary School

Squirrels
Squirrels are
　Jumping, leaping
　　Running, eating
　　　Playing, chasing
　　　　Climbing, hiding
　　　　　Bouncing, sprinting
　　　　　　Chewing, gnawing
　　　　　Pouncing, hopping
　　　　Hanging, hovering
　　　Plunging, plummeting
　　Falling,
　Plop.
And doing it all over again!
Wesley Holdcraft, Grade 4
Lincoln Elementary School

Dolphins
Splashing, having fun,
Swimming freely in the sea,
Dive to capture fish.
Kaylor Dodds, Grade 5
East Union Intermediate Center

The Magic Bottle
Although the journey hard,
　the reward,
　the toil...
First you must climb down the mountain,
　to your quest you must be loyal.
Through the shadowed valley,
　where rattle snakes do coil,
If you wish to pass the test,
　still, you must be loyal.
Now walk across the rock,
　BEWARE!
Beneath you doth hot lava boil.
Now climb down another mountain.
You are reaching the end.
Now if you've found the treasure,
　you have proven yourself loyal!
Erin Wayman, Grade 4
Commonwealth Connections Academy

Every Day
Every day before I get to my
classroom, I eat breakfast. Every day
before I eat breakfast I get dressed.
Every day before I get dressed I brush
my teeth. Every day before I brush my
teeth, I brush and comb my hair.
Every day before I brush and comb my
hair I wake up. Every day before I
wake up I am asleep. Every day before
I am asleep I am eating dinner.
Every day before I eat dinner I
get in the shower. Every day before
I get in the shower I am outside.
Every day before I am outside I
am at tutoring. Every day before I
am at tutoring I am in school learning.
Kalina Brown, Grade 6
Colwyn Elementary School

Winter
Winter is as cold
as the ice that I hold
on a cold winter day.
The snow falls like hay,
like a bitty, bitty mouse
on top of my house.
An hour later I wake up in bed
my stomach waiting to be fed
and on my way downstairs
my eyes stop and stare
outside the window.
Snow! Snow! White, white snow!
Here comes fun and relaxation
on a cold, cold winter day!
Michael Wlodarczyk, Grade 4
Middle Smithfield Elementary School

The Shark Attacks!
The cold-blooded, unmerciful shark
Emerges from the darkness
Dawn and dusk
In the ocean bay
The shark tries to catch the prey.
Calvin Chmura, Grade 6
Ross Elementary School

The Tide
The glistening sand
Rolls patiently
Into the night
On the beaches
Waiting for the tide.
Eric (Yu) Cao, Grade 6
Ross Elementary School

Wolf
Barking, howling, eating
hunting, sleeping, playing,
running, sprinting, growling
scratching, biting, traveling,
stalking, sneaky.
Krys Lewis, Grade 5
Maxwell Elementary School

Rain Forest
Rain
Hot weather
Birds calling
Insects crawling
Wet
Ally Sandt, Grade 6
Nazareth Area Intermediate School

Rain Forest
Wet
Flowers
Bugs climbing
Lizards crawling
Rain
Owen Backer, Grade 6
Nazareth Area Intermediate School

Wet
Wet
Forest
Leaves dripping
Birds flying high
Trees
Devon Adelbock, Grade 6
Nazareth Area Intermediate School

Corvus Leucognaphalus
C row
O utside habitat
R eddish iris
V ery glossy with a heavy black bill
U nlikely to eat plants
S tocky bird

L arge black crow that can be in the range of 42-46 cm big
E ats a large amount of fruit
U nlike any other bird
C orvidae family
O utstanding crow
G enus is the corvus genus
N ever live in cool places
A nd they are known to live in the Dominican Republic, Haiti, and Jamaica
P opulation size is around 2,550 up to 9,000
H ard and strong bird
A nd the population trend is decreasing
L ive in warm tropical places
U sually flies in groups
S mart and intelligent bird
Daniel McGee, Grade 6
Nazareth Area Intermediate School

Anger
Anger is like being trapped in a cage with nobody there.
Anger is like coal burning in a campfire.
Anger is like everyone disappears and you are left all alone.
Anger is red like a blazing fire.
Anger tastes like a rotten egg that has been in the refrigerator for months.
Anger smells like a skunk after it has been scared.
Anger sounds like a car crashing into a pole.
Anger feels like quills on a porcupine.
Anger looks like a tornado ripping through the sky.
Anger makes me feel like I am going to explode.
Anger is rough, raw, rage.
John Matesic, Grade 6
West Allegheny Middle School

The Magic of Books
You pick up a book and zap!
Your eyes are glued.
The book has trapped you in the pages so you can't escape 'til the very end.
Your head conjures up vivid details of the events occurring.

Suddenly *you* are the main character.
One day you are a gorgeous princess, and the next you are an evil witch.
Books take you on thrilling, wild adventures.
These adventures can never bore you.

Books are the never ending possibility of imagination!
The magic of books is in the story and how you make it seem.
Finally you reach the end and return from being trapped in the pages.
It's time to start a new adventure!!!!
Nicole Welsh, Grade 6
Ross Elementary School

The King of the Forest
O bstacle to humans
A nimals' homes
K ing of all trees

T aken down for building tables
R oots as big as the tree
E xtraordinary
E ntire forests.
Jeffrey Ecker, Grade 4
Trinity East Elementary School

Soccer
Soccer balls,
Soccer goals,
My teammates,
Coaches, cleats,
Shin guards, whistles, yelling,
Stinky pinnies and sports drinks.
My water.
Tired, sweaty.
Alison Smith, Grade 4
St Anne School

Baseball
B aseball
A ll-star
S tealing
E xtra innings
B atting practice
A thlete
L ead off batter
L eft field
Ryan Stipe, Grade 6
Chichester Middle School

Football
F ans
O ffense
O ut of bounds
T ime out
B all
A ll players play
L ead block
L ove the game!
Steven Brown, Grade 5
Central Elementary School

The Sea
The sea
As peaceful as it can be
I seem to wonder
What's out there way out yonder
One day I will sail out there
And smell the fresh air
Katie Hogg, Grade 5
Saint Theresa School

What a Great Thanksgiving
Too much food
I can't believe my eyes
You couldn't count it all
From turkey to pies

Food all over my face
My belly hurts
Why so cruel

My eyelids droop
And I want to sleep
But I'd rather stay up
And watch the fire flickering

"What a great Thanksgiving,"
I say to myself
And I fall asleep.
Emily Evans, Grade 5
Falk Laboratory School

Winter Walk
Giant trees tower overhead
The air is crisp and cool
You can hear leaves
Crunch underneath your feet
Winter's coming 'round the bend.

The leaves are turning brown and orange
Their branches white with snow
They'll soon break off
And fall to the frosty ground
While you walk through the woods.

You have to wear a jacket
At this time of the year
Or suffer from the freezing cold
You can see your breath
In the frosty morning air.
Courtney Labritz, Grade 6
Ross Elementary School

Gray
Gray is broken down
Gray sounds like a beating drum
booming and rushing you
Gray shows the wrinkles within you
like gray hair right in front of you
like listening to the rain
as it rides around your ears
Gray darkens you
Gray keeps you away from what's inside
Gray draws tears in a smooth way
Gary hardens you up
That's how gray makes me feel
Alexus Tomlinson, Grade 4
Wissahickon Charter School

Natural Feelings of Fall
The sun is rising
Bursting at the pinkish sky
Fall is arriving

Feel the crisp breeze blow
Softly at your red cheeks.
Fall is arriving.

You see the dim light
Of the sun behind the clouds.
Fall is arriving.

Shadows of trees dance.
Walking down through the black light.
Fall is coming.
Allyah Harrar, Grade 6
Pennridge North Middle School

Penguins
Penguins, penguins, penguins.
You are cute and fluffy!
Penguins, penguins, penguins.
You waddle around all day
and slide on your bellies.
Penguins, penguins, penguins.
Oh how I love penguins.
As you jump into the sea
to get some grub!
You grab fish for you
and your young!
A beautiful sight of the
little one's waddle,
soon to know…it will be
just like its parents.
Chelsea Komorowski, Grade 4
Middle Smithfield Elementary School

Independence Hall
I really love Independence Hall
Even though, it is so small.
The building breathes history
It is more fun than reading a mystery.
It all began at this historical place,
Where many famous people paced.
The Declaration of Independence
was signed here.
Even though some delegates had
doubts and fear.
It was the starting point for our
government's formation.
The corner stone of our great nation.
It's like an anchor for a U.S. ship.
It would make a great field trip.
Colin Kendra, Grade 6
St Jerome Elementary School

Peace

Peace is light blue like a crystal, cool river with swans swimming sprightly down the shore to a refreshing waterfall.
Peace looks like a calm waterfall running down a long stream full of fish on a fateful February Friday.
Peace tastes like a tasty Thanksgiving turkey made on that special November evening.
Peace smells like a warm batch of brownies made for family and friends in a beach house
    near the shore during a sunset in August.
Peace sounds like chirping crying crows looking for their mother on a long, lonely day during a rainstorm in March.
Peace feels like warm wet water from a hot tub with bursting bubbles washing away your troubles.

Aeneus Evans, Grade 6
Our Lady of Ransom School

Laughter

Laughter is sapphire blue like the serene ocean in the Caribbean islands in July.
It looks like a gorgeous radiant raging rainbow roaming in the sky on the first day of summer.
It tastes like freshly baked chocolate chip cookies on your kitchen counter on a cold crisp winter's night.
It smells like brownies that just came out of your oven on a frosty white Christmas morning.
Laughter sounds like a marvelous mystical waterfall flowing on a bright sunny day in June.
It feels like smiley faces jumping up and down in your heart on Thanksgiving Day with your family.

Samantha DiBiase, Grade 6
Our Lady of Ransom School

Thanksgiving

I can see my friendly, kind family setting the beautiful table, and my brothers and cousins playing my addicting Wii.
I can smell the buttery rolls that I know will taste like bits of heaven when they hit my drooling mouth.
I can taste the fabulous desserts that are as colorful as the magnificent fall day and hot turkey like the chestnut, brown trees.
I can feel the ceramic bowls as they are passed around the majestic, decorative, wooden table.
I can hear the laughing and talking of my marvelous mom and all our wonderful guests.

Kaitlyn Duff, Grade 4
Colonial Elementary School

Thanksgiving

I can see my loving, joyful family sitting around the cheerful table decorated in lace tablecloth.
I can smell the mouthwatering food and the aroma of the fresh, homemade pumpkin pie.
I can taste the appetizing corn delightfully bouncing on my taste buds.
I can hear my mom putting a Thanksgiving movie in the shiny DVD player as I snuggle up on the cozy couch.
I can feel the warmth of my wonderful mom, as I slip into her arms and watch the fantastic film.

Aish Ramesh, Grade 4
Colonial Elementary School

Thanksgiving at the Heffelfingers' House

I see all of my friendly family members walking all around the glamorous looking house.
I smell the chestnut brown turkey sizzling inside my mouth.
I hear all of my wonderful family members declaring how enjoyable all of the delicious food is.
I feel the slimy, greasy wishbone peeling off of the spectacular looking turkey.
I taste the snow white mashed potatoes dancing on my tongue while my mouth is drooling.

Jessica Heffelfinger, Grade 4
Colonial Elementary School

Great Thanksgiving Night

I can see my amazing family gobbling on different appetizing foods watching addicting football.
I can hear my pop sharing wonderful stories and singing "God Bless America" like he loves to do every year.
I can smell the aroma of the steaming hot mashed potatoes as they are placed on the decorative table.
I can feel the sensation of joy through the house on this dazzling day.
I can taste delicious turkey as I shove it inside my drooling mouth on this great Thanksgiving day.

Brian Paul, Grade 4
Colonial Elementary School

Nature's Beauty
All day I learn more
Hearing beautiful birdsongs
Watching flowers bloom
Ashley Rogliano, Grade 6
St Joseph School

Scarecrows
Scarecrows stand out there
Guarding the rows of cornstalks
Crows come anyway!
Isaiah Derr, Grade 4
Watsontown Elementary School

Hunting
Walking through the woods
Through my scope I see a deer
Playing in the snow
Chad Snyder, Grade 4
Watsontown Elementary School

Halloween
Halloween is fun
Trick-or-treaters getting scared
Because of a ghost
Gage Anzulavich, Grade 4
Watsontown Elementary School

Snowmen
Dancing at late dusk
Melting at the sight of sun
Slush litters the lawn
Jack Vukelich, Grade 6
St Joseph School

Halloween
Get your costumes out
Ready for trick-or-treating
Halloween is near
Emma Burrows, Grade 4
Watsontown Elementary School

Christmas
Bright lights all around —
Much excitement in the air,
Many gifts to give.
Keira Mull, Grade 6
St Joseph School

My House
Welcoming always.
Cozy like a puppy's fur.
Home base forever.
Jack Walsh, Grade 6
St Joseph School

Anger
Anger is an oak tree giving you the evil eye ready to burst at any time.
Anger is a slithering cobra running through my head giving me poisonous thoughts.
Anger is as cold as an icicle stabbing you right in the heart after you lose
   the championship game.
Anger is an afternoon detention and a call home for not listening to your teacher.
Anger is beating red tomato sauce boiling over your hot stove.
Anger is gray like a storm cloud as big as a yellow school bus.
Anger tastes like jalapeño peppers burning intensely in my fiery mouth.
Anger smells like a skunk spraying their defense all around the neighborhood.
Anger sounds like your heartbeat thumping rapidly after your terrible grade.
Anger is a pointy porcupine persistently rubbing against my skin.
Anger looks like a furrowed forehead, piercing eyes, and a frown on your face.
Anger makes me want to scream, shout, and pout until I let my anger out.
Lexi Cogis, Grade 6
West Allegheny Middle School

The Artist
The artist sets her pen on paper, sets the first word down beautifully
For she is not an artist of color, she is an artist of words
She writes the first word, imagination is taking flight
Soaring across the now golden room, climbing on imagination's feathery wings
The journey begins. Jumping from cloud to cloud
Guided by imagination's wings. Looking down at the ground she smiles
For there are some childhood friends, fairies, elves, maybe a gnome or two
Glancing up surprised, she rushes through the legs of a giant
Flying backwards in the past, forward to the future
Reaching up and touching the stars. She glides safely home on imagination's wings
Through an open window. She sets her pen on paper
Sets the last word down beautifully, for she is not an artist of color
She is an artist of words, writing her words eloquently
Emily Weller, Grade 6
Commonwealth Connections Academy

Happiness
Happiness is someone simply smiling.
Happiness is an oozing chocolate fountain.
Happiness is a laugh when hearing a joke.
Happiness is a rainbow of bright colors.
Happiness tastes like a freshly picked peach from the garden.
Happiness smells like a freshly baked batch of chocolate chip cookies.
Happiness sounds like the boom of an exploding firework.
Happiness feels like a soft and squishy cotton ball.
Happiness looks like a splash of sparkling colors.
Happiness makes me feel grateful for life.
Happiness is as bright as the gleaming sun.
Josh Castelluci, Grade 6
West Allegheny Middle School

The Touchdown
Before the quarterback called the play the crowed cheered "Hooray!!"
They're down on the line ready to ready to run while someone's out with an injured thumb.
The quarterback calls hut and the crowd starts to cheer while the other team stands in fear.
He pitches the ball to number one wile the crowd yells "Run, run."
So he runs and runs and runs some more until the crowd yelled "He scored, he scored."
Robert Mcelhaney, Grade 6
Hopewell Memorial Jr High School

Under the Streetlight
Every so often
If the stars are lined up right
The moon is full and blue
It casts a low hanging gloom
The shadows are waking up

Jumping out of trash cans
Pushing aside heavy grates
Climbing out windows
Crashing through double doors
They become one in the street

They've come together
A blob of absolute black
Misunderstood dark
All they want is to have fun
Dancing under the streetlight
Robert Colville, Grade 6
Ross Elementary School

Randall the Rabbit
Randall the Rabbit
Was hopping around,
Flopping and flopping
Stomping on the ground.
Randall the Rabbit
Was trapped in a cage.
He wanted to watch
The movie "Ice Age."

Randall the Rabbit
A friendly mouse found.
He set the rabbit free.
His owner fell on the ground.
Randall the Rabbit
Went on a hunting trip
With his happy friends.
He went skip, skip, and skip.
Nilay Parekh, Grade 4
St. Andrew School

The Past and the Present
I used to be in 1st grade
but now I'm 5th grade
I used to have short hair
but now I have long hair
I used to drink out of bottles
but now I drink out of cups
I use to be short
but now I'm tall
I use to have black hair
but now I have brown hair
I use to wear regular clothes
but now I wear uniforms
Asia Phillips, Grade 5
Hamilton Elementary School

My Life
I used to be a little girl
But now I am a bigger girl
I used to jump on my bed
But now I know better
I used to be lazy
But now I do ballet
I used to play game boy
But now I play D.S.
I used to go to Puerto Rico
But now I go to Florida
I used to sleep in
But now I wake up early
Mayra Rivera, Grade 5
Hamilton Elementary School

Billy the Dog
Billy loves to play
I could play with him all day
Billy is so furry
He loves to scurry
Billy always barks
When he is out in the dark
Billy takes a nap
When we visit our Pap
Billy always has fun
When he is playing in the sun
Billy is so silly
That is why we named him Billy
Abby Fredley, Grade 5
East Union Intermediate Center

Soldiers
Soldiers will always be your friend
They will fight until the end
They go from our country to another land
Where they try to kill another man
The grenades say Click! Whooo! Boom!
The bullets flying by saying Zoom! Zoom!
Bullets running like track stars
Bullets hitting and blowing up cars
They call in support
They never want to abort
They always get the job done
Even if their parents lose a daughter or son
Jimmy Kowalski, Grade 6
St Jerome Elementary School

The Trees of the Forest
F rom hickories to
O sage orange, to
R edbuds, to
E lms and
S pruces —
T rees
Michelle Biksey, Grade 5
Trinity East Elementary School

Willis the Whale
Willis the Whale
Wanted to possess a Wii.
He asked his mommy,
But he should have asked me.
Willis the Whale
received something in the mail
He tore it open fast,
And told his neighbor, Dale.

Willis the Whale
Found a Wii in the box.
He turned it on,
And found out it talked.
He started to play
His favorite game, Wii Sports.
He played some tennis.
He appeared on the court.
John Yoder, Grade 4
St Andrew's School

Buddy the Butterfly
Buddy the Butterfly
Was flying around.
His wings were so tired
He fell on the ground.
Buddy the Butterfly
Was making a pie.
Then he said,
"Let's go look at the sky."

Buddy the Butterfly
Was flying a kite.
After that
He went on a hike.
Buddy the Butterfly
Had a piece of cake.
Then he didn't feel well
Because he had a stomach ache.
Alexa Stephens, Grade 4
St Andrew's School

Ode to Crab Legs
Oh crab legs
You are so juicy and sweet
Hot crab dipped in butter
I can't wait to eat
Oh crab legs
So fun to crack your shell
Juice squirts in my eye
It makes me want to yell
Oh crab legs
You are my favorite food of all
I love all kinds of crabs
Even ones that are small
Cameron Dunmyer, Grade 4
All Saints Catholic School

Fall

Rain, wind
dripping, pouring, blowing
leaves, colors, Thanksgiving, November
harvest, covering, flowing
fog, haze
Autumn

Felton Dro, Grade 5
Hamilton Elementary School

Servant of the Queen

The waves of jewels and gold
Like water at the ocean's edge
I can tell I am almost to the queen's throne
For riches of thankfulness
I arrived to the throne of the queen
And she made me the general of her army.

Tanner Navarro, Grade 5
Nether Providence Elementary School

Jesus

Jesus is our Savior,
Jesus is God's only son,
Jesus forgives us when we ask,
Jesus makes us happy,
Jesus is our Father,
Jesus is the light of the way.

Alexandra Parisi, Grade 6
St Joseph School

Basketball

Basketball is my favorite sport,
Especially when I am on the court.
Running, shooting, working hard,
Even if you are a guard.
I wish I will never quit,
No, not a bit.

Anna Conover, Grade 5
Foster Elementary School

Joys of Heaven

H appy place to be
E verybody that I miss
A ngels to see
V ery quiet
E njoy the place forever
N o sickness there

Emily Costlow, Grade 4
All Saints Catholic School

Basketball

I know I'm tall
I shall not be small
Sometime I fall
But I score the winning ball

Madison Banaszak, Grade 4
Burgettstown Elementary Center

Planted Life

I sit, on my porch and watch,
Watch the wind whip across the prairie and see,
The withered plants try to wiggle back into the ground,
And hear their cries for rain.
As the wind calms a fine mist of dust and sets in the prairie slowly seeps into it.
I'm like the withered plants just trying to stay rooted and not picked up by the dust
And blown away.
As I look at the prairie it looks like my heart, cracked, and smooth with dust,
I wipe the grime from my eyes, and stare at the dust,
That swallowed up lives, homes, and happiness taking everything.
When I look one more time at the prairie
And know now I see faintly, a blade of grass and think,
Life never gives up and will find a way to keep being planted.

Tess Weaver, Grade 6
Haine Middle School

World Series

The World Series, wild and crazy and a battle to the end.
Hoping your favorite team makes it.
Never knowing who will win and who will lose.
Watching all five games
And maybe even going to a game yourself
Having big parties
And celebrating the win of each game
And when all five games are over and you know who won
You have the biggest party of all
You stay up all night to party because of all the excitement and sugar
And you can't wait until next season comes
And you hope your team is in the World Series again.

Ryan Gartenmayer, Grade 6
Hillcrest Elementary School

The Vision

The vision is peaceful,
Very peaceful.
I can see the beach with full of brightness, laughter
The cool tide waves.
I can see the mountains standing tall and still
The clouds beginning to depart.
I can see the rain, full of clear water falling from the sky.
I can see the stars aligning, so bright in the pitch dark nighttime sky.
I can see snow falling, Little kids being very creative
Making snowmen, snow angels, making snowballs and snowforts.
I see everything in my mind.
Do you have a vision?

Trae Morgan-White, Grade 6
William F Harrity School

Love

Love is a fuzzy feeling you get with compassion for another
butterflies in your stomach, tingles in your fingers
love can be tricky
it can be synthetic or true
you'll know when you find the right person to quench your heart's thirst

Dominique Holland, Grade 6
John G Whittier School

Happiness

Happiness is all of the brightest colors in the world put together
Happiness is a pathway that leads to success
Happiness is a smiling kid at an amusement park
Happiness is rosy pink cheeks on a cold winter morning
Happiness tastes like bubble gum when it makes the popping noise
Happiness smells like fresh, clean clothes right out of the dryer
Happiness sounds like ducks in a pond going, splash, splash, splash
Happiness feels like sticky, soft, silky cotton candy on a hot summer day
Happiness looks like beautiful, lavender flowers blooming in the spring
Happiness makes me jump up and down like waiting in line for a brand new roller coaster ride
Happiness is living in a world of paradise
Happiness is growing younger every minute

Angeline Peng, Grade 6
West Allegheny Middle School

Frustration

Frustration is a hot oven that you are stuck in
Frustration is a person trapped in horrible thoughts
Frustration is a football player fumbling the football and missing the fabulous field goal
Frustration is checkered brass and rust on the walls of every room you walk into
Frustration tastes like bitter grapefruit making its way down your sore throat
Frustration smells like rotten milk when all you wanted to eat was a bowl of cereal
Frustration sounds like a knock on your door when you're trying to do your homework
Frustration feels like a lumpy bed before an early event
Frustration looks like a single mom, with five kids, that just lost her job
Frustration makes me want to shred a pillowcase into hundreds of pieces and throw it at someone
Frustration greeted me at the door today and just will not leave me
Frustration is working very hard on something for a long time and not achieving it

Jessica Crider, Grade 6
West Allegheny Middle School

Excitement

Excitement is a winning game of soccer
Excitement is a game splashing in puddles on a rainy day
Excitement is the winning goal that drives past the goalie's hands
Excitement is racing red
Excitement tastes like freshly made crumbly, chocolate chip cookies right out of the oven
Excitement smells like freshly delivered pizza
Excitement sounds like the booming of bright fireworks bursting in the air on the Fourth of July
Excitement feels like the perfectly cut grass tickling my feet
Excitement looks like an A on a test
Excitement makes me smile from ear to ear
Excitement is a little kid inside of me jumping up and down
Excitement is the best feeling you could ever have

Emily Nolan, Grade 6
West Allegheny Middle School

Why We Love

Do you ever wonder why we live or die.
It's cause of love why we live and when we die we will know why we lived a life of love.
It makes you feel great, Triumphant, and cared for even more than before.
Just the sound of it makes you want to jump up and down.
It's when you're feeling down that just one hug or kiss will bring you through the day and when it's over you will say I loved my life.

Zachary Hovanec, Grade 6
Hopewell Memorial Jr High School

The Life Cycle of a Tree
seed
miniature, covered
flowering, living, building
homes, food, oxygen, flowers
leaning, rotting, toppling
rich, soft
dirt
Kelsey Reese, Grade 5
Trinity North Elementary School

Halloween
My! A ghost is here,
I am scared of ghosts a lot,
Go get some candy.

Wind is howling hard,
Boo, ah someone just scared me,
It was my brother.
Yaridis Rosado, Grade 5
Clearview Elementary School

The Mighty Oak
oak
mighty, tall
growing, towering, aging
leaves, acorns, habitat, shade
staying, sheltering, reproducing
peaceful, beautiful
tree
Sierra Hermann, Grade 4
Trinity East Elementary School

Halloween
Halloween is fun,
Do not eat too much candy,
Wear a warm costume.

Ghosts are coming now,
I am very scared of ghosts,
Hairy ghosts are coming.
Jessica Hernandez, Grade 5
Clearview Elementary School

Fall
Fall
is beautiful
Fall is nice
if you jump into
my pile of
leaves you'll
pay the price.
Christopher Lazo, Grade 5
Hamilton Elementary School

The Beach
Wish, wash goes the wave,
Roaring back and forth,
Calmly flowing in and out,
It will never go off course.

Sailboat very far away,
Sailing the deep blue,
Going with the flow of water,
Wish I was in the boat too.

Hot sand beneath my feet,
Burning like the sun,
Making me want to run really fast.
I am having so much fun.

The water going in and out,
Feels like ice,
Oh, how much I love the beach,
It is my paradise.
Katherine Peters, Grade 5
Foster Elementary School

Hawaii
Look at those dancing dolphins!
You don't see them often.
The water was so pretty
Almost like it was glittery.

Food as sweet as candy,
Yet as sour as lemons.
Thick juicy tender meat
What a grand feast!

There are so many animals
Like the fine flippy fish,
And the largest golden finches
Along with the rest.

The sky was like sparkling water.
The clouds were like ice cream.
The sunset was like a rainbow.
When you get there, you don't want to go.
Lenéa Riehl, Grade 6
Linville Hill Mennonite School

Thanksgiving
Thanksgiving is a wonderful time
For friends and family, especially mine.
To get together and have a feast
To laugh, drink, and eat, like a beast
Friends and family gather to have some fun
But you can't go out and play in the sun
It's almost time to put up the tree.
Thanksgiving is very special to me!
Justin Kirstein, Grade 6
State Street Elementary School

Hawk
Hawk
glides swiftly, like an owl, with no sound,
smooth as fabric, flowing white,
looking down, plummeting down, down,
landing on two feet.
Hawk
glowing circles yellowish red,
peeking through the darkened shadows,
lands on a branch, shakes a tree,
I have to squint to just barely be able to see,
Hawk
claws like knives, ready to attack,
rushing water, running back,
gliding, searching for its prey,
back to staying where it needs to stay.
Hawk
prey can't go in and come out,
makes it want to scream and shout,
dark and deep, with unpenetrable walls,
never-ending black.
Hawk
Campbell Kurlander, Grade 5
Falk Laboratory School

What Is Green?
Green is beautiful grass tickling our feet
Gentle, calm a color so sweet
This color is seen all around
A lucky clover found on the ground
Juicy pickle sour lime
The color of green on summer leaves
The feeling of green is a winter breeze
A color so safe is what you need
It's a color of envy and a color of greed
Green plant, green peas
Green eyes, green teas
A long lasting evergreen tree
Green is in everything I see
Makes you strife
The color of life
Can be on something that you wear
The feeling of Christmas in the air
Across the world
Across the land
A color so alive, a color so grand
Where would we be without green!
Victoria Chhor, Grade 6
St Hilary of Poitiers School

Night and Day
When day turns to night,
There are spiders to fright.
When night turns to day,
The sun will light the way.
Madeline Jones, Grade 4
St Joseph School

My Mom and My Dad

My mom is as nice as an angel.
My mom feels as soft as a pillow.
My mom smells as good as perfume.
My mom is as small as a leprechaun.

My dad is as hard as a rock.
My dad is as spooky as a ghost.
My dad is as sticky as gum and glue.
My dad is as tall as a giant.

Carmen Rodriguez, Grade 4
Wickersham Elementary School

Inspiration of Life

The owls hoot happily, loudly,
For now their time had come,
To hunt with the wind
and move with the trees.
As I sit here alone, tired,
I hear the sound of a hundred bats,
who fly with the grace of a star
and I want to fly with them.
My energy back, my bad thoughts gone.

Erin Sebastian, Grade 6
Sewickley Academy

Halloween

H ollowed out jack-o'-lanterns.
A utumn colorful leaves.
L aughter of young children.
L oudly heard rain.
O ctober brings crispness.
W indy mornings.
E arly nights of darkness.
E erie sights and sounds.
N aked trees without leaves.

Janessa Delgado, Grade 5
Clearview Elementary School

Costume

Costume
Beautiful, amazing
Horrifying, disguising, shocking
Wow! that costume was frightening
Scream

Matthew Tucci, Grade 5
St Anselm School

Curious

Curious is rose red
It sounds like a dog barking
It smells like a taco
It tastes like dry bread
It looks like a monkey
Curious feels like a book

Hiren Patel, Grade 4
Anne Frank School

Lucky Glove

Baseball season is coming around.
My dad bought the tickets and we went downtown.
We saw the game it was filled with action.
I turned around to see the score and all I heard was the crowds roar.
I looked up so high in the sky and saw the ball coming.
I patted my mitt, lowered my cap, and all I heard was smack.
I looked in my glove and there the ball was.
I took the ball out and raised it up high, so proud of myself for catching the fly.
There I was on the big screen as happy as could be.
I had the time of my life and my dad shared it with me.

Nic Anastasi, Grade 6
Holy Rosary School

Shrieking!

Boom! Boom! The storm speaks in a loud, thundering voice.
Splat! Splat! The storm's ferocious rain splatters on umbrellas.
Squishy! Squashy! Bright yellow rain boots splash through the squishy mud.
Boom! Boom! The storm is speaking even louder, almost shrieking!
Wisp! Crash! The harsh wind slaps umbrellas out of children's' hands.
Cry! Shriek! The storm is speaking a little softer.
Pitter, Patter! The storm has been drumming on my roof.
Suddenly, softer, softer. Finally the storm is over.
Lots of laughter! Kids squish through the happy mud.
A good ending.

Hanna Hummert, Grade 4
The Ellis School

We Need Each Other

What is a cone, without a huge scoop of ice cream
sitting upon it, waiting to be licked away?
What is a wrapper, without a piece of delicious candy inside it?
What is salt, when there is no pepper to balance it out?
What is a sock when you have no shoe to protect it?
What is love when you have no heart?
What is a laugh, when you have no one to share it with?
What is a smile, when no one is there to see it?
What is a person, without a friend to help them overcome tough times?
What is the world, without a big bowl of happiness?

Sara Rowlands, Grade 6
Hillcrest Elementary School

Courage

Courage is a glittery gold like getting a badge
on a shimmery, sunny Sunday morning when winning a righteous race.
It looks like a brilliant reward on a Monday afternoon after winning a competition.
It tastes like a chocolate creamy candy bar on Tuesday night on Valentine's Day.
It smells like the clean, clear chemosphere on a bright morning at the park.
Courage sounds like a bright glossy, glistening, glowing bell ringing when Mass starts.
Courage feels like doing something marvelous on the 4th of July.

Gabriela Flores, Grade 6
Our Lady of Ransom School

High Merit Poems – Grades 4, 5 and 6

Hockey
The blistery winds of winter are drawing close,
It's time for my favorite time of year.

With thrills and chills hockey season begins,
I prepare to do my part.

A championship goalie I have been,
My grand entrance will make heads turn.

My teammates play the game with great hearts,
Our job is to keep the other team from getting a goal.

The crowd roars with exciting noises,
I know again we will win this year.

My coach is as proud as my mom is,
We played the game, to fulfill our dreams.

Justin Burroughs, Grade 6
St Jerome Elementary School

Polar Bears
Cuddly bears who are soft, fuzzy, and white
Be careful because they might bite
They're able to go in the frozen waters
To find a frenzy of fish to feed their son or daughter
Not because of any bad behavior,
The Polar Bears are now in danger,
People are destructive in so many ways,
Especially by polluting our beautiful ice age
I love the warmth I see in their heart
The sorrow I feel for them tears me apart
The Earth would be upset if they tragically left forever
Let's all team up as we go hand in hand to make it better
They need our help so they can live on
And not to fear the creak of dawn
Don't you want your kids to see the majestic creatures?
As they live on 'til the end of Earth's features.

Brooke O'Hare, Grade 6
St Jerome Elementary School

Colorful Pens
C an I borrow some of your pens?
O f course you may but don't blunt the ends.
L aughing with joy, my friend takes them from me.
O h! What wonderful implements they be!
R ainbow colors are sure to please.
F ancy colors are like a disease.
U ntold mysteries yet to be told.
L ittle bundles of joy to unfold.

P ens so plentiful, collection in demand.
E nough for friends, at my command.
N ever complete homework in black and white.
S o pens not returned — that's still my plight.

Samantha Ludlum, Grade 6
The American Academy

We Are Thankful
I am thankful for…
A ll the colorful leaves on the trees that are falling off.
B rings me a lot of wet grass in front of my house.
C olorful trees bring me a lot of colorful leaves.
D elicious, wonderful tasting leaves from the rain.
E ach colorful pumpkin shining so bright at night.
F alling leaves come off every tree.
G reat big blowing, howling wind, blows towards you.
H igh winds blowing leaves everywhere onto the sidewalk.
I n the fall you go trick-or-treating.
J oin in with the kids that trick-or-treat.
K isses from the sweet howling wind.
L ie on the pile of leaves.

Taniyah Preux, Grade 5
Clearview Elementary School

I Am Thankful for Fall
I am thankful for…
A ll the trees that bring me
B eautiful leaves.
C olorful plants that are beautiful too.
D elightful rain that waters the plants.
E ach jack-o'-lantern shining bright at night.
F all's wonderful colors are beautiful all the time, and my mom's
G reat hot cocoa too!
H alloween is so much fun!
I n the fall we pick up pumpkins and carve them.
J oining in with everyone to trick or treat, it's really so much fun!
K ittens that wander the streets and
L aughter from my family.

Jordan Holzheimer, Grade 5
Clearview Elementary School

Bunnies
There are bunnies all around,
But they never make a sound.
They come in colors: black, brown, and white,
And they are usually up at night.

Whenever I see bunnies hop,
Their ears always flop.
Sometimes when we're away,
They come out to play.

Alina Snopkowski, Grade 4
Sacred Heart School

Christmas
Christmas mornings, so much fun
Down the stairs the children run,
They run down like a herd of cattle
The they'll spread their Christmas joys.
Though Christmas is just one of the seasons,
There are still many reasons,
Why we celebrate, Christmas!

Nicole Santry, Grade 6
State Street Elementary School

My Dream
I dreamed
I was a tree
Near a lake
Listening to the wind
Silently.
Jessica Ashmore, Grade 4
Trinity North Elementary School

The Yew in Peru
I once saw a tree in Peru.
Our guide said it was a yew.
It started to sway,
We all ran away.
The trunk fell down in the dew.
Ben Artuso, Grade 5
Trinity East Elementary School

Bats
Bats
Spooky, creepy
Flying, scaring, feeding
Frightening people down low
Ahhhhhhh! Bat!
Michela Rehfuss, Grade 5
St Anselm School

Brave
B e brave like a soldier
R ely on your friends
A s tough as titanium
V ery bold and strong
E veryone fights
Josh Main, Grade 4
Fairview Elementary School

Brave
B orn to tussel
R eady to fight
A ble to give us freedom
V aluable soldiers stay
E ach soldier daring
Jeddy Young, Grade 4
Fairview Elementary School

Bats
Bats
Eerie, mysterious
Eating, sleeping, flying
Creatures of the night
Frightening.
Olivia Molinari, Grade 5
St Anselm School

Honor
Honor is the valuable possession a soldier has
Honor is the only thing he has left
When he leaves the battlefield he walks off with pride
He will still walk the earth another day

Whenever a man falls he is called a hero
He is just one more reason we should fight harder
We should fight harder every time a man falls
It gives us one more reason not to give up

When he gets off the plane he gets on his knees and he prays
When a man comes home he carries a new part to his life
He comes home with a story to tell his family and friends
When he comes home people cheer for his loyalty

Someone gets a letter from the army saying a man died
Their family will cry, we all cry when a man has fallen
It gives us one less man, but one more hero to remember
When a man comes home he has and will always have honor within him
Brody B. Giblin, Grade 6
Pennridge North Middle School

BreAnna
Peace, I'm BreAnna I listen to Gloriana.
They're a country band, and they've got tons of fans.

Music is my forte it really makes my day.
I especially like Taylor Swift she really has a gift.

In my free time I like to draw, in pencil, that is all.
Friends and family mean a lot, a bunch of them I've got.

I have two sisters too, a mom and dad, that's true.
Macaroni and cheese is my fave, it's something I normally crave.

Reading's a preferred pastime, though some people think that it's a crime.
I want to become a lawyer, with a very good employer.

I think I'm done with this couplet, about myself, I love it!
So here, forth I send, so here it goes, The End!
BreAnna Bechtold, Grade 5
St Anne School

I Wish for Fall
I wish the leaves would change to green, yellow, orange, or red.
I wish the moon would shine orange like a pumpkin overhead.
I wish that I could eat sweet pumpkin pie.
I wish I had time to watch the wind blow the leaves by and by.
I wish I could watch the crows fly so high in the sky.
I wish that I could too fly ever so high.
I wish I had lots of candy corn and other sweets to eat.
I wish that it would soon be time to shout trick or treat.
I wish that I could hear big blackbird's call.
I wish that I would not have to wait any longer for the wonderful season of fall.
Erica Anewalt, Grade 5
Clearview Elementary School

High Merit Poems – Grades 4, 5 and 6

Glory
Down the court we're racing.
On the sidelines, coach is pacing.
We go for the score.
The ball bounces off the rim and hits the floor.
The ball smacks my palm and I grasp it.
Triple threat and dribble to the basket,
This could be the winning shot.
Swoosh! My team yells and cheers a lot!
We win the game in overtime
And all the glory is mine!

Greer Jeffrey, Grade 6
St Joseph School

Deliciousness
Deliciousness is the taste of biting into a warm cookie
Deliciousness is ice cream melting on my tongue
Deliciousness is the smell of a fresh baked pie
Deliciousness is like the color of a red rose
Deliciousness is a melted s'more made over a campfire
Deliciousness is waking up to the smell of breakfast waiting for me
Deliciousness sounds like popcorn popping
Deliciousness feels like Jell-O as it slides down my throat
Deliciousness makes me feel good inside
Deliciousness is everywhere and everything that is happy

Isabelle Lesko, Grade 6
West Allegheny Middle School

We Give Thanks
Turkey Day is the best day of all,
It's during November, in the fall.
There is turkey (of course!) who wouldn't deny,
Stuffing, cranberry sauce, and pumpkin pie!
But this day isn't just about a great feast,
It's the thing we think about this day the least.
This is the day we thank the Heavenly King, the Father,
For all the things He has provided us, like food, shelter, and water.
So on Thanksgiving, thank God for all He has done,
And you will have a Thanksgiving that will be so much fun!

Julia Strohl, Grade 6
St. Joseph School

Joy
Joy is like hitting three clay pigeons with one shot
Joy is opening a piñata filled with candy and money
Joy is winning the lottery three times in a row
Joy is the color green for the world going green
Joy tastes like the world's biggest pizza
Joy smells like the beginning of spring and fall
Joy feels like landing in a big soft pile of feathers
Joy looks like a new baby deer being born
Joy makes me the happiest person in the world
Joy is the first day of summer

Quintin Lemashane, Grade 6
West Allegheny Middle School

Juan
Juan Ponce de Leon
Adventurous, brilliant, smart, soldier
Related to Dona Inez
Cares deeply about being a soldier
Who feels excited about exploring
Who needs to find the Fountain of Youth
Who gave his life
Who fears the Moors
Who would like to see the Fountain of Youth
Resident of Cadiz, Italy

Ross Colon, Grade 5
Indian Lane Elementary School

The Championship
The ninth inning in the ball game
All eyes on me…
I threw the first pitch.
The batter took a wiff.
I knew the ball was hit far.
I didn't know if the outfielder would catch the ball.
He jumps like a cougar and hits the wall.
What a catch!
He caught the ball
And we won it all!

Jarret Cunnard, Grade 6
State Street Elementary School

Happiness
Happiness is a summer day
Happiness is a new bike
Happiness is winning a football game
Happiness is like an indigo sky
Happiness is like the crack of a bat hitting a ball
Happiness is the smell of chocolate chip cookies
Happiness is the taste of pepperoni pizza
Happiness is the texture of a Nike football
Happiness is playing baseball in the spring
Happiness is biking all day

Max Clements, Grade 6
West Allegheny Middle School

Vespucci
Amerigo Vespucci
Explorer, leader, sailor, navigator
Related to Guido Vespucci
Cares deeply about tracing the routes of famous navigators
Who feels excited about going out on an exploration
Who needs love, care, food, and water
Who gives leadership and guidance
Who fears sea creatures and the boat sinking
Who would like to see today's United States
Resident of Cadiz, Italy

Erin Gilligan, Grade 5
Indian Lane Elementary School

The Ball Park
Chase Utley
Spectacular, awesome
Hitting, running, fielding
Second basemen, hitter, ketchup, mustard
Cooking, eating, enjoying
Tasty, long
Hot-dog
Ally Roberto, Grade 5
Pocopson Elementary School

Hunting
H unter safety
U nderstand surrounding
N ight spotting
T arget shooting
I nstincts
N avigate
G utting deer
Tyler Hotovec, Grade 5
East Union Intermediate Center

Player and Spectator
Player
Athletic, sporty
Running, catching, fielding
Glove, bat, popcorn, hot dog
Eating, yelling, booing
Lazy, nervous
Spectator
Nick McGlade, Grade 5
Pocopson Elementary School

Orange Is
As soft as a peach
As quiet as a kitten's purr
As beautiful as a Tiger Lilly
As graceful as a tiger running
As rough as a Chinese dragon's scales
As colorful as the busy day
 ends with a sparkling sunset.
Emma Luther, Grade 4
Jefferson Elementary School

Holidays
Halloween
Spooky, dark
Screaming, lurking, scaring
Pumpkins, candy, shamrock, gold
Tricking, spotting, catching
Leprechaun, clever
St. Patrick's Day
Brett Lomas, Grade 6
Hillcrest Elementary School

Friends
Friends are nice,
Friends care about you,
No matter what you do,
Your friends are there for you,
A true friend likes you for who you are,
If your feelings are hurt call your friends,
And they will tell you what to do.
Near or far,
Your friends are in your heart.
If you're sick,
Your friends will send you get well cards.
Your friends are the ones that will help you,
If you're in trouble,
Or don't understand,
That is what a friend is.
Tiffany Gwardzinski, Grade 5
St Joan of Arc School

What Is White
White is snow
Soft and crunchy
The clouds on a nice day
A dove flying high
In the air
White is on the top
Of a mountain
It is the color
On Santa's hat
White is winter
It is a soft boom, boom
Like a mushroom cloud
The smell of white is blooming flowers
The taste of white is vanilla ice cream
White is the color I dream
Sean Barry, Grade 6
St Hilary of Poitiers School

What Is Blue
Blue is the ocean
As blue as the sky
Blue is the color
Of childrens eyes
Blue is rain
Blue are the snowflakes
Blue is flying
While reading a good book.
Blue is cool
Swimming in the pool
Blue are the blueberries
Covered with powdered sugar
Blue is ice
Where people skate
Blue is the place where there is no hate.
Jake Barcza, Grade 6
St Hilary of Poitiers School

Pink
Pink is the sunset
hiding behind the trees

It makes me feel loving
about my mom giving me a kiss
on my cheek
before I go to bed.

It makes me feel happy
when I run through a meadow
on a sunny day
picking pink flowers

It makes me feel sweet
drinking cold pink lemonade
on a hot day

It makes me blush when
I am full of shyness
Jordyn Caldwell, Grade 4
Wissahickon Charter School

Calvin Isaac Wamser
C ool
A thletic
L ikes pie
V ictories
I lluminating
N ice

I ce hockey
S imple
A wesome
A sks a lot
C urious

W acky
A wesome
M aster
S illy
E xtra nice
R eally fun
Calvin Isaac Wamser, Grade 4
McKinley Elementary School

My Friend and I
My friend and I love to play.
We love to make things out of clay.
Sometimes we play in the rain.
We also like to eat candy canes.
We both like money,
And we are also funny.
We both love to go to the shore.
And eat to the apple core.
David Miazio Jr., Grade 4
McKinley Elementary School

High Merit Poems – Grades 4, 5 and 6

Love
Love is a dog wanting to come home to you.
Love is a hug from mom and dad.
Love is a new present on Christmas.
Love is pink like a Valentine card.
Love tastes like a chewy chocolate peanut cookie.
Love smells like a bunch of roses in a garden.
Love sounds like birds chirping on a sunny morning.
Love feels like a warm fireplace on a cold night.
Love looks like two hearts formed into one.
Love makes me feel happy inside.
Love is everlasting.

Reanna Turner, Grade 6
West Allegheny Middle School

Birds
Birds, birds how you talk to people in a certain way
ease their pain when they're feeling down

Birds, birds the way you glide across the sky
like a missile shooting from a rocket launcher

Birds, birds you're a singing airplane
the way you ride the wind like a sailboat

Birds, birds, you're a man working a full time job
you barely have time to rest for you work so hard every day

Tariq Boyer, Grade 6
John G Whittier School

Happiness
Happiness is a smile on a person's face
Happiness is laughing and having fun with friends
Happiness is a rainbow coming out after a rainy day
Happiness is yellow like the sun shining on a summer day
Happiness tastes like ice cream on a super hot day
Happiness smells like chocolate chip cookies baking in the oven
Happiness sounds like birds chirping on a sunny morning
Happiness feels like a kitten's soft fur
Happiness looks like kids having fun
Happiness makes me smile
Happiness is a lazy Saturday afternoon with nothing to do

Katie Quasey, Grade 6
West Allegheny Middle School

Fun Boxes
Big boxes are fun! To dream in, to draw in,
better than toys, a place to make noise,
become what you want, do what you want!
These will give you a thrill!
You don't need an electric drill or a grill!
You just need your imagination!!
You may think it sounds fun, so rush right out and buy one!
P.S. Call 555-728-4 in the next minute or you will lose
a chance to get a free small box. No batteries included.

Hannah Metcalf, Grade 5
Oswayo Valley Elementary School

Happiness
Happiness is a test that I have passed.
Happiness is new friends that are made every day.
Happiness is a pet that you get on your birthday.
Happiness is a gold shining star in the sky.
Happiness tastes like sweet apples and pears.
Happiness smells like lavender fragrance in your house.
Happiness sounds like loud laughter in my heart.
Happiness feels like smooth water against your skin.
Happiness looks like a big smile on your face.
Happiness makes me want to fly away like a bird.
Happiness is my heart beating like "thump."

Brandon Macasek, Grade 6
West Allegheny Middle School

The Best Time of the Year
I wake up to a nudging in my side
I wonder who it could be
I open my eyes
Not a thing in sight
"What is going on," I think
I walk to the window but all I see is…
Yes, yes it must be, it has to be, I can't believe I am seeing
Santa Claus!
Then I remember what today is
The best time of the year…
Christmas!

Jennifer Cranmer, Grade 6
Hopewell Memorial Jr High School

Little Bird
Little bird
Out on my feeder
Looking in.
Makes not a peep nor chirp
But instead stares in at the rosy glow of my house
With eyes that shine with longing
To get in at the warmth.
Even he realizes that he can't get in
And with that,
He flies away
Into the cold dark winter night.

Rachel Waddell, Grade 6
Ephrata Intermediate School

The World
What a magnificent world…

The humpbacks dance in water every single day
While the shark's skin glows in the underwater rays.

What a wonderful world…

The plain grass flows with joy in the wind
The sun's light is wonderfully bright it can sometimes sing.

Matthew Harrison, Grade 4
Fairview Elementary School

Siblings
Brother,
Handsome, rough
Playing, wrestling, smiling
Boy, funny, girl, kind
Laughing, styling, playing,
Pretty, gentle,
Sister
Eileen Burner, Grade 5
McKinley Elementary School

Friends/Bullying
friends
helpful, kind
loving, feeling, hoping
nice, happiness, anger, enemies
hating, hurting, fighting
mean, tough
bullying
Joshua Krull, Grade 5
St Sebastian Elementary School

Dogs
Barking, drooling,
playful, fun, soft,
loving, cute, fury,
big, small, different
types, chewing, puppy,
dog food, digging,
sleepy, happy
Thannushka Perez, Grade 5
Hamilton Elementary School

The Baseball Stadium
Stands
Crowded, noisy
Selling, sitting, cheering
Hot-dogs, fans, players, water
Coaching, catching, running
Diamond shaped, flat
Field
Irene Liu, Grade 5
Pocopson Elementary School

Fireflies
Their lights flash on warm
Summer nights
They send out green flashes
Throughout the night
After the night is over they
Give one more flash to say
Goodbye until tonight
Tyler Vivio, Grade 5
Central Elementary School

I Like School
I like school
The teachings of teachers.
The bubbling of beakers.
The tap of a pencil.
The shape of a stencil.
The bounce of a ball.
The story of Saul.
We sing and we sing,
until the bell rings.
In math there's a fraction,
and in gym we take action.
It's the end of the day,
sit down and now pray.
I like school.
Lauren McGonigle, Grade 6
Notre Dame School

Writer's Block
Writer's block is very bad;
It makes your English teacher mad.

What should this poem be about?
I do not know, without a doubt.

I'm getting writer's block, it's true;
I need a subject that's something new.

As I write this I get quite sad
Because I know this poem is bad.

If you are reading this, stop now
Because this is the end, anyhow.
Nathan Master, Grade 6
The American Academy

All About Me!
I used to like soccer,
but now I like softball.
I used to like cats,
but now I like dogs.
I used to like watching t.v.,
but now I like playing with my friends.
I used to like fish,
but now I like chicken.
I used to like DS's,
but now I like DSI's.
I used to like playing tennis,
but now I like basketball.
I used to like swimming,
but now I like going to the beach.
Kylie Myers, Grade 5
Hamilton Elementary School

The Meaning of Thanksgiving
T hanking friends and family
H aving another year together
A pples and cider filling the room
N ever letting each other down
K ind gestures and smiles
S melling turkey in the oven
G ourds and pumpkins decorated outside
I n the joy of having family
V isions of the feast of Thanksgiving
I n the love and friendship of each other
N eighbors and friends joining together
G iving thanks to everyone and everything!
Jaimie Bohatch, Grade 5
Central Elementary School

As the Sun Sets
As the sun sets,
It goes down
It gets dark
All around.

As the sun sets,
The moon comes up
It becomes night time.

As the sun sets,
Everything is calm
And the moon shines brightly.
Julia Reedy, Grade 4
Burgettstown Elementary Center

One Warm Autumn Day
In the warm autumn sun
Children were having so much fun
Trying to catch fluttering leaves as they fall
They want to be outside and not at the mall
Watching tractors go by
They look up at the sky
And see the blueness of it
Then they sit
As they start to pick apples from trees
They start to see some bees
But they did not care
They were just glad to be there
Sydney Carlin, Grade 4
Fairview Elementary School

Teachers
A teacher is loving,
A teacher is kind,
A teacher is a guardian,
A teacher is a role model,
A teacher is a friend,
And a teacher is a gift from God.
Kaleigh Strohl, Grade 6
St. Joseph School

High Merit Poems – Grades 4, 5 and 6

I Love When It Rains

It rains fastly, on a June summer's day
It's pure cloudy and gray
Where is the sun, is it hidden behind the clouds?
Good, I want it to stay there for awhile
I like the rain, so refreshing and pure
I love the rain, more, and more
So graceful it falls all over town
It taps away on the graveled ground
Then suddenly, it thunders very loud
Lightning strikes lighting up the sky
It looks like a flashlight shining right in your eye
Later on, the rain goes away
It turns out to be a beautiful rainbow day

Gabrielle Boronsky, Grade 6
Hopewell Memorial Jr High School

Mr. Moon

Mr. Moon, I have a question
On this extremely bright night
How do you glow ever so bright?

Did it hurt when a flag got stuck into you?
Do you watch the grass get its morning dew?

Mr. Moon, can you see global warming?
And if you can, why didn't you give us a warning?

Are you friends with other moons?
Is your enemy the sun?
Or do you all work together to make your job more fun?

Nicole Naticchia, Grade 6
Wrightstown Elementary School

Halloween!

H appy as a person on their birthday,
A ll around me people laugh,
L ooking for a costume as scary as a monster,
L ooking for someone to scare,
O vereating on candy,
W itches, ghosts, monsters and more,
E ating as much candy as you can,
E njoying every second of trick-or-treating,
N ever going to bed all night.

Sarah Palandro, Grade 5
McKinley Elementary School

Ode to Heaven

Oh heaven so wondrous.
Above the sky.
All of the exquisite saints, angels, and everybody there.
Special is heaven with the superb, excellent, and wonderful God.
Creator of all creation.
I am excited to go to heaven.
With the Virgin Mary.

Nick Moschgat, Grade 4
All Saints Catholic School

Different

Why must they trap me in this dark place?
Where the sun doesn't shine,
Where I'm a disgrace.
Back at home I was treated with care,
Why here must be like any old chair?
This place is so different to me,
The fish and the bird, both you see,
But on land or in water, where will I be?
I would tell you if I could see past any tree.
The gray of the water here is so bleak,
There's nowhere colder, except for the highest peak.
But the blue and warmth of Barbados' shore,
Falls from my mind at this unwelcoming door,
Where all to do is work and work more,
I feel so lonely as I scrub the floor.
All I have to look forward to,
Is the return of William Ashby who,
Is content with simply staring at you.
Alas I stare at the unwelcome door,
I can dream of Barbados as mine no more.

C.J. Stott, Grade 5
Boyce Middle School

Under the Butterfly Bush

It sleeps in sweet quiet rest,
a little stone marker upon its chest.
It feels no heat, it feels no cold, as the sun gently sets
under the butterfly bush.

I wonder what it would have been.
Would it have been fat or maybe thin?
Would it like to be tickled under its chin,
under the butterfly bush?

Does it chase its tail at all
or pounce with its four little paws?
Does it play or dream at all,
under the butterfly bush?

Seasons will come and seasons will go,
and as they pass I too will grow.
And, I will smile because I know
you are there,
under the butterfly bush.

Christina Donatelli, Grade 5
East Union Intermediate Center

The Turkey

When the turkey came to town, everyone started gathering around.
The turkey wondered why everyone was carrying knives and forks.
He guessed that they were probably going to eat some pork.
But he was wrong.
Because before he knew it, he was being eaten on a piece of rye.
Then he soon realized it was Thanksgiving not Fourth of July!

Kelsey Jachimowicz, Grade 6
Assumption School

Pretzel Rods
I love my mom's snacks
She makes chocolate pretzel rods
They are so yummy!
Kylan Kurtz, Grade 4
Watsontown Elementary School

New England
Rocky mountains cry
Snowing on hills of New England
Where snow is softly made
Bennett Palumbo, Grade 4
Jefferson Elementary School

Halloween
Pumpkins are orange,
Witches are green,
Happy happy Halloween!
Olivia O'Brien, Grade 5
McKinley Elementary School

My Cat
When the cat meows,
Likes to play with his catnip,
That's why I love him.
Alyssa Plotnick, Grade 5
Russell Elementary School

Snow
Big blanket of white,
It covers the ground and street,
Snow is everywhere.
Josh Dracup, Grade 5
Russell Elementary School

Thanksgiving Feast
Pie smells so yummy
Roasted turkey is tasty
Such delicious food
Pacey Howard, Grade 4
Watsontown Elementary School

My Little Dragon
My little dragon
His fire burnt my homework, ouch!
Funny little guy
Nia Lewis, Grade 5
McKinley Elementary School

It's Winter!
Winter's coming soon.
The frigid air stings my hands.
Still I'm having fun.
Luke Burrows, Grade 4
Watsontown Elementary School

Excitement
Excitement is riding the Aero 360 when you're upside-down
Excitement is the feeling when you win the championship game
Excitement is wandering the zoo trying to find the growling tigers
Excitement is lime green popsicles on a hot summer day
Excitement tastes like a fresh new pickle out of the jar
Excitement smells like freshly planted roses
Excitement sounds like a new song by Taylor Swift blasting in your iPod
Excitement feels like a soft new cuddly kitten
Excitement looks like all A's on your report card reaching out to you
Excitement makes me feel jumpy like a green bouncy ball
Excitement is spending a sunny summer day at the pool
Excitement is the best feeling in the world
Marissa D'Amore, Grade 6
West Allegheny Middle School

Courage
Courage is as proud as soldiers after a war
Courage is hardworking teammates in a championship game
Courage is sad clouds crying rain every day
Courage is proud purple pounding against the heart
Courage tastes like sizzling shrimp right off the grill
Courage smells like sweet cinnamon sprinkled on top of a cake
Courage sounds like clapping after giving a speech at a special occasion
Courage feels like a soft silky jacket rubbed against your face
Courage looks like a BOOM of fireworks going on for millions of miles
Courage makes me happy to have a great life
Courage is the feeling that makes me feel most grateful
Courage is one word with millions of meanings
Taylor Schmac, Grade 6
West Allegheny Middle School

Friendship
Friendship is being there for your friends when they need you
Friendship is caring for your friends
Friendship is being with your friends through good and bad
Friendship is true blue like the ocean water on a warm summer day
Friendship tastes like milk and cookies before bed
Friendship sounds like the beautiful blue birds chirping a song
Friendship smells like my grandma's yummy pumpkin pie fresh from the oven
Friendship feels like a big cozy bear hugging me to sleep
Friendship looks like two people watching fabulous fireworks boom in the sky
Friendship makes me happy seeing my hamsters after school
Friendship is like eating ice cold ice cream on a hot and humid summer day
Friendship is being there for your friends when they need you
Abigail Shipley, Grade 6
West Allegheny Middle School

Delighted
Delighted is sapphire blue
It sounds like people happily playing at the beach on a sunny day
It smells like flowers and candy
It tastes like the first cupcake a child has ever had
It looks like someone's new puppy, which they are so grateful to have
Delighted feels like I can't breathe because of so full of excitement
Alyssa Taylor Smink, Grade 4
Anne Frank School

High Merit Poems – Grades 4, 5 and 6

A Cow with a Towel

I once saw a cow
That was holding a towel.
The cow held the towel over his eye,
And said, "Now what kind of cow am I?"
He put the towel over his brow,
Now he is a pirate cow!

Lydia Walker, Grade 4
New Freedom Christian School

Winter

Winter is a very fun season
And here is the reason.
A sled riding race!
Wow! I'm in second place!
My friend throws a snowball
Ahhh! I'm hit and down I fall.

Ashley Dojcak, Grade 5
Foster Elementary School

Blooming Blue

Blue makes me
feel like the sky with
all the beautiful birds,
Water dripping like rain
Blue makes me feel shy
and sad like nobody's around.

Kne'aja Padgett, Grade 4
Wissahickon Charter School

Christmas

Christmas is a day of
celebration and a day
where you get together
with your friends and
relatives and get gifts
and presents.

Larice Mejia, Grade 5
Hamilton Elementary School

Leaves

L eaves dance in the wind.
E very leaf runs in the grass,
A nd skips on the ground.
V iewing leaves swim in the water.
E nough of them dive from trees.
S o many glide through the sky.

Justice Large, Grade 5
McKinley Elementary School

Halloween

Scary, fun
Screaming, frightening, terrifying
Trick-or-treating
October

Jeaninah Namukwana, Grade 5
Hamilton Elementary School

Happiness

Happiness is…the smell of a new daisy.
Happiness is…the warm cuddly feeling when you're chilly.
Happiness is…the colorful garden of flowers.
Happiness is…the color electric blue.
Happiness tastes like…the sweet delicious chocolate chip cookies fresh from the oven.
Happiness smells like…rich candles that smell delicious.
Happiness sounds like…the first chirp of a new baby bird.
Happiness feels like…the smoothness of a new kitten's fur.
Happiness looks like…a gigantic bed of beautiful flowers.
Happiness makes me…want to laugh out loud.
Happiness is…the feeling you get when you're with your family.

Makenzie Hays, Grade 6
West Allegheny Middle School

Fear

Fear is a monster coming out of your closet.
Fear is an ugly, reddish animal charging at you because it's starving and wants your blood.
Fear is something invisible ripping you to shreds.
Fear is crimson red and jet black.
Fear tastes like cold, bitter, tasteless sand.
Fear smells like a burning, rancid, horrible carcass.
Fear sounds like a harsh cry hissing at you.
Fear feels like a gooey, greasy piece of rotten meat.
Fear looks like a stormy, hazy, murky sky.
Fear makes me feel like it's eating me from the inside out.
Fear is a feeling you never want to have.

Brianna Bence, Grade 6
West Allegheny Middle School

Anger

Anger is a volcano that will burst into a billion pieces.
Anger is a kid that gets all F's on his report card.
Anger is the monster that scares you when you look under your bed.
Anger is red like the blood rushing through your veins.
Anger tastes like the most rotten apple from the most evil tree.
Anger smells like a smell that should never be smelled by a human.
Anger sounds like a screech of a chalkboard that goes eeeek.
Anger feels like the roughest piece of sandpaper.
Anger looks like the meanest cloud about to burst.
Anger makes me feel like all the happiness has been sucked out of me.
Anger is a deep dark dangerous ditch.

Michael Messner, Grade 6
West Allegheny Middle School

Tyson*

I love my dog Tyson. He would never let me down.
Tyson was so special you could never imagine how much he meant to me.
But then on June 18, 2008 was my worst nightmare.
I had to say farewell to my best friend. I really hated it.
But I knew he would feel better. I miss him so much.
I still have Capone my other dog,
I love him just as much but he will never take Tyson's place.
I will love them both forever.

Alexis Slavicek, Grade 5
East Union Intermediate Center
*Dedicated to Tyson 9/01/01 to 6/18/2008

Christmas Fun
Candy canes dance in my stocking.
The house is decorated with colorful lights.
Granny sits on the rocking chair knitting a Christmas sweater.
The ice is hanging from the house.
We are waiting for Santa to bring our Christmas presents.
Stocking are hung and waiting for Santa, too.
Christmas is fun!

Liam Malone, Grade 5
McKinley Elementary School

The Rocky Beach
Rocky hills and the gentle waters of the ocean
Pine trees that are very tall and seagulls that fly around the shore
Tons of white and pink shells
The seagulls squawking and the wind through the trees
The pine trees and the salty ocean
The water I brought and pretzels
The bumpy rocks and the sun against my back

Maria Howe, Grade 4
St Anne School

Thanksgiving Day
Sitting around the table,
Eating and laughing with your family and friends.
You could play games,
You might see all the leaves falling or already on the green grass.
But no matter what
You'll be around family and friends
On Thanksgiving Day!

Katie Gannon, Grade 4
Middle Smithfield Elementary School

Earth
Mostly water,
shaped like a sphere,
many living things live here.
Blue and green is the color,
cavemen, dinosaurs, humans and lots others.
It's where we live, help keep it clean,
it's got so much to give, protect, recycle, go green.

Andrew Pacheco, Grade 4
Middle Smithfield Elementary School

Beautiful Blue
Blue is the roaring salty sea,
Blue is the dark-blue bluebirds flying against the light blue sky,
Blue is how the lake glistens when the warm sun hits it,
The blue morning glories that awaken in the morning,
The sweet deep blue of blueberries when you eat them,
The clear, light blue raindrops quenching the plants,
The light blue robin's egg ready for life, speckled and fragile.

Samantha Dengel, Grade 5
Holy Child Academy

Mystery Box
I could see a big box that was waiting for me,
For my ninth birthday — what a mystery!
Italian wedding soup, Caesar salad, apple tart —
Lunch was done; opening presents would start.

I went to open this mystery box.
I thought it would just be some frocks or socks.
They made me open it with my eyes closed.
I didn't know what would be exposed.

After unwrapping it, I opened one eye.
What I saw made me want to cry.
"Smartfood Popcorn" was written on it.
I did not like this present, not one little bit.

My mom told me to keep on going,
But all I found was fabric for sewing.
Finally I picked up a piece of red linen.
Inside the fabric — a flute was hidden.

The flute I was playing had been rented.
It was fine, but just a bit dented.
This present has given me so very much joy.
I knew I was growing up when I didn't want a toy.

Sarah Null, Grade 5
The American Academy

Summertime
When summer starts it's fun,
because school is done.

I'll swim in my pool,
instead of being at school.

I can sleep in late,
and not go to the place I hate.

There are no more tests,
and I can leave my room a mess.

I can jog and run my dog,
or read about a hog.

I will get a tan,
then cool down by a fan.

I'll go on vacation,
and pet a big Dalmatian.

I can do so much in summer,
because there's no school, which is a bummer.

J.R. Rutkauskas, Grade 5
Our Lady of Grace Elementary School

Colors

Blue like the sky that looks down on you and me.
Orange like a goldfish swimming in the sea.
Pink like the flamingos at the zoo.
White like a ghost that yells "boo!"
Red like a wonderful blooming rose.
Green like that plant that always grows.
Purple like that monster hiding under kids' beds.
Yellow like the sun shining over my head.
Without colors our world would be dull,
So let's enjoy them now everyone let's all!

Caitlyn Reading, Grade 5
East Union Intermediate Center

Freedom

Freedom is the soldiers defending our country with their lives!
Freedom is our life that we live!
Freedom is everyone's friend!
Freedom's color is red, white, and blue!
Freedom tastes like ice cold water on a hot summer day!
Freedom sounds like your favorite song on the radio!
Freedom feels like a warm cotton blanket in the winter!
Freedom looks like our American flag!
Freedom makes me joyful and proud!
Freedom is our Country!

Alyssa Sundgaard, Grade 6
West Allegheny Middle School

Mr. Cheese

I'm Mr. Cheese
I'm the best thing on this table
I'm the most cheesy and the most gooey
And I have so many different kinds of cheese
Everybody is looking at me
I'm about to go into somebody's stomach
Am I the only one hot in here?
Stop drooling over me!
Move!
I think I'm about to get eaten...

Micah Saunders, Grade 4
Wissahickon Charter School

Christmas Day

Christmas day comes each year,
a day that brings both joy and cheer.
At midnight the tree becomes filled with toys,
all kinds of toys for both girls and boys.
The children wake to see,
all of their presents under the tree.
They grab a present big or small,
that can be a toy truck or even a doll.
Christmas day is not about toys,
it is about happiness and joy.

Casandra Mullen, Grade 6
Hopewell Memorial Jr High School

Explorer LaSalle

Robert de LaSalle.
Nobleman, explorer, Jesuit, French.
Related to his brother Jean.
Cares deeply about finding the Northwest Passage.
Who feels brave.
Who needs more boats.
Who gives claimed land to France.
Who fears Indians.
Who would like to see the Pacific Ocean.
Resident of France.

Austin Kreeger, Grade 5
Indian Lane Elementary School

The Master

You ever heard of the Master?
His name is James, oh yes sir!
He's really, really, really smart,
And he's especially good at art.
His hobby is computer programming,
Compared to him Bill Gates is a youngling!
His academic skills are so great,
Einstein hails him as a saint!
Do you know who the master is?
He's the one who wrote this poem, oh yes he is!

James Pickering, Grade 5
McKinley Elementary School

Witches' Stew

The witches are done cooking in their pot.
Their homemade recipe is done.
Their stew is what they've been waiting for.
They've been cooking all day.
The recipe they've made has horrid things in it...
Bat wings, spider legs, snake skin and bear claws.
Human nail, dog tails and snails.
What are the witches doing now?
Eating their stew...
And there are leftovers for *YOU!*

Elena Isabelle Montenegro, Grade 5
Lincoln Elementary School

Thanksgiving

Thanksgiving Day I watched the parade.
That was the day the turkey and stuffing were made.
We went to my Gram's,
As the brown sugar wiggled through the yams.
After we cleaned, it was time for pie.
Eventually, it was time to say good-bye.
My mom and I went to battle the crowds and long lines,
We saw thousands of people and a ton of discount signs.
When I got home, I crawled into bed, and that's where I stayed.
I slept until noon before I played.

Maya Niven, Grade 6
State Street Elementary School

If I Were in Charge of the World

If I were in charge of the world,
I'd cancel wars, problems,
Sadness and secrets.

If I were in charge of the world,
There would be World Peace,
Recycling bins,
Happiness and laughter
And lots of friendship.

If I were in charge of the world,
I wouldn't have yelling or fighting,
And absolutely no violence,
Annoyances or sarcasm.

If I were in charge of the world,
I'd like to see answers to all of our questions,
Knowledge of all we can know,
And cures to all of the diseases and sicknesses
Of the world, like Cancer.
And a person who thinks a little too hard,
Can still be in charge of the world.

Alexandra Kothe, Grade 6
Wrightstown Elementary School

Baseball Is Ready

White is the long straight line of a baseball field.
White is a fastball thrown.
White is the player's soft jersey.
White is the hard bat hitting the ball.
White is clouds shading the players from the hot sun.
White is the player's socks protecting the player's tired legs.
White is the player's eyes focusing on the ball.
White is the fan's rally towels swinging in the air.
White is the lights shining on the field helping people see.
White is the base ready to be clutched by the pointy cleats.

Theo Strahan, Grade 5
Holy Child Academy

Basketball

It looks just like any old ball
But it jumps to life after all
It is orange as a pumpkin with stripes that are black
If the other team scores it's time to get it back

You dribble, you pass, you shoot
Get five fouls you get the boot
Box in, box out, rebound, get feet set
The object of the game; put the ball in the net

Basketball is the best sport around
The crowd cheering is such a great sound
It is a great feeling to drive down the lane
I have a great passion for this game.

Conall Murphy, Grade 6
St Jerome Elementary School

October

Fall leaves are crashing down while a deer is hiding
In beautifully colored trees.
Cows are grazing peacefully, in a pasture
Of wild flowers.
These are things I see.

Up above,
A plane soars overhead.
There glides a crackling crow
Flying in the wind.
These are things I hear.

A smoky air fills the world with clouds
Of smoke.
The sweet aromas,
Of rainy days.
These are things I smell.

Zach Gawronski, Grade 6
Pennridge North Middle School

Penguins

Waddle, waddle all day.
Sun, rain, snow just all day!
Time for lunch!
Jump in the water,
Grab the fish!
Slide on your bellies all day.
Sun, rain, snow just all day!
Time to relax.
After a big feast.
Then it's time to play!
All the little penguins,
Waddle around,
Except one little penguin,
Who's all by himself.
"Come on let's play!" The little penguins urged.
He wasn't sad at all!
He just had a big feast today!

Jesenia Vizcaino, Grade 4
Middle Smithfield Elementary School

The Outside

Green and happy
Big blue sky
Dancing leaves
Cold and hot
I love it so much
Trees that fight the wind
Ants that crawl over me
Oops I stepped on a bee
It's home to all no matter how big or small
It gives food and shelter
If my arms were big enough I would give the earth a big hug
Thank you, nature.

Richard Abbott, Grade 6
St Jerome Elementary School

High Merit Poems – Grades 4, 5 and 6

The Ultimate Day
If I had the best day ever, I would wish for:
hot dogs
touchdown
swimming pools
dogs
winter
Jordan shoes
summer
Jordan clothes
pizza
cake
ice cream
facebook
Playstation 3
Wii
Xbox 360
Call of Duty World at War
candy
laser tag
lunch
Halo 3
Jayson Dean, Grade 6
St Sebastian Elementary School

Why
Why, oh why am I treated so?
why must they shut me up,
in this dark, dismal place,
in this land of muck and mud,
in this despairing place,
spit at and mock me,
shun and ignore me?
Though we are as different,
as land and water,
as black and white,
still, you must shun me?
Just because we are different,
gives you no right,
to treat me as you do.
I am still adjusting,
as I realize I must,
lest you shun me more,
I feel like a tropical bird,
landed on the wrong land,
I am used to a different world,
should you not welcome me?
Oceanne Fry, Grade 5
Boyce Middle School

Teeth
Brush your teeth
Make them shiny
Make them squeaky
Then they're pearly white
Trinity Duncker, Grade 4
Fishing Creek Elementary School

What Is Green
Green is the color of children's
Toys on Christmas day
The color of a tree that sways,
In the calm air
The color of an emerald stone
That every woman admires
Green's scent is like peppermint,
Eagles are green and chewing gum
Green sometimes makes me
Want to cry or fly
Green are birds chirping
In the morning brisk air
Green sounds like a big bear
That roars in the open space
It tastes like honey
And is the color of money
Green is my mother's favorite color
Green is humming while running
Green is Irish just like me.
Sean Jarrett, Grade 6
St Hilary of Poitiers School

How I Feel
It's amazing how much I liked you
the first day I spent time with you
I looked in your eyes
and it was like magic
but when we broke up all I could
do was think about you!
And how yet I still do,
when I told myself don't think
about the past I apologize but I
can't help the fact that I love
your personality just as well you.
Sometimes I don't know what to
do when my mind's all on you!
I don't know what you do but
you really got me loving you!
I would do anything for you!
I know I lied to you in the past
but if you gave me one more chance
we can make it last!
Jillian Rightmyer, Grade 6
Colwyn Elementary School

Our Beautiful World
Our beautiful world delights me.
With its frosty winter mornings,
Marvelous elegant ocean waters,
Pleasing Siberian tigers,
Glamorous bald eagles,
Scent of wild daisies,
Skies of blue,
And colorful green meadows.
Connor Shank, Grade 4
Fairview Elementary School

The Beach
I run, I wade —
Into the ocean
The waves splash
It feels good on my face.
I love the beach.

That dolphin look!
Watch me ride
Through the waves,
Into paradise
Oh! I love the beach.

The way it feels to have a watery friend,
The way the water feels
The sand.
It pulls on my feet
Wanting to go back in like me.

What! Oh no it's time to go
I tell my mom
"We just got here"
But even I know
We've been here four hours.
Alana Pugh, Grade 5
Carroll Elementary School

Christmas
It is Christmas time
Presents just for you and me
All under the tree

Santa comes tonight
Bringing presents and candy
From the North Pole

The angels watch us
As we sing for peace and joy
On this Christmas night

Jesus' birthday
Comes tonight under the stars
And the pretty sky

Fun festivities
On this happy holiday
Time for joy and cheer

Let us celebrate
On this cheerful day
Christmas! It is here.
Sophie Boyle, Grade 5
Southern Lehigh Intermediate School

Tennis
Tennis
Played with racquets
Use only tennis balls
Singles, doubles, soft court, indoors
Tennis

Stephen McGough, Grade 4
McKinley Elementary School

Space
S tars and suns
P lanets
A steroids
C omets
E arth

Emily Bigley, Grade 5
East Union Intermediate Center

Christmas
Christmas is a time for joy.
Christmas is fun for girls and boys.
Christmas is when we get new toys.
Christmas is fun for everyone.
Christmas has no sun.

Gabriel Greenway, Grade 5
East Union Intermediate Center

Basketball
Basketball
Dribble, hardwood
Passing, shooting, bouncing
Orange and black colors
Big

Trevor Coyle, Grade 4
McKinley Elementary School

A Man Was Once Ill
A man was once very ill.
He didn't want to take his pill.
He got a shot.
He sat on a cot.
Now he feels less ill.

William Palmiere, Grade 5
East Union Intermediate Center

Smiles
Smiles are so beautiful
warm rosy cheeks
pearly white teeth
glossy lipped grin
Smiles make me happy

Mallory Marzolf, Grade 5
East Union Intermediate Center

Fall
As I sit on top of the giant school, I observe the children
giddily running up the obstacles of hills, working as a team.
A single, blue, unappreciated flower, trampled upon by children,
if only to protect it with a DO NOT CROSS LINE.
Abundant trees, different colors, still life, a painter's dream.
The simultaneous cool breeze and disappearing sunshine. A single house caressed by trees.
One turn and a barren field appears, no bird lay upon its creviced floor.
The smokiness, ascending form a chimney, a cat near it falling asleep.
A sour smelling pollen, its aroma crinkling my nose,
not ever wanting a flower like that I land on, as I soar.
A squirrel, or tasty treat scurrying up the misshapen tree,
thinking I'm not watching it, not making a peep.
A lonely bare tree, cold and alone, the gorgeous leaves it once had was no more.
My ears do not deceive me, for Perkasie has awakened,
cars hustle and bustle startling me with a BEEP.
I peer over the school and startled by its beauty,
the horizon coated with mist, the color in the background becoming poor.
For the last time, I gaze at the frostbitten ground, the frozen air,
and children in coats, when I leave I hope these memories I can keep.
The children gaze up at me and I spread my wings,
I leap off the building, catch the wind and roar my falcon roar.

Douglas Kern, Grade 6
Pennridge North Middle School

I Am
I am an actress and a reader
I wonder what will happen next when I am reading
I hear the voice of what I think the character in my book sounds like
I see the people in the audience staring at me
I want to be an actress when I grow up
I am an actress and a reader

I pretend that I am the character that I am in my play
I feel like I am in the book I am reading
I touch the hard cover of my book
I worry that I will forget my lines during a play
I cry about the sadness or happiness in my book
I am an actress and a reader

I understand how the people in my book feel
I say the words on my script as I am trying to memorize it
I dream that one day I will be a professional actress
I try to read whenever I have spare time
I hope that some day I will find my favorite book
I am an actress and a reader

Judy Gallagher, Grade 5
Nether Providence Elementary School

Thanksgiving Is…
Dogs greeting people at the door by jumping on people
A fresh turkey waiting with gravy and raspberry sauce
A football on TV with uncles and grandparents waiting to be watched
Throwing a baseball or football with my uncle
The laughter of little cousins

Colin McQueen, Grade 6
Moravian Academy Middle School

The Nature of White

If I were white,
I would be a graceful penguin gliding across the ice.

If I were white,
I would be a protective mother polar bear guarding her young.

If I were white,
I would be a scurrying mouse running from a human.

If I were white,
I would be a bunny hopping away from a fiery fox.

If I were white,
I would be a beautiful flower blowing in the breeze.

If I were white,
I would be a crystal gleaming in the bottom of a volcano.

If I were white,
I would be a fluffy, beautiful floating cloud in the morning.

If I were white,
I would be a snowflake floating to the ground on a winter's day.
Courtney Ray Loomis, Grade 5
Holy Child Academy

Late

I woke up this morning and looked at the clock
It said that it was precisely 8 on the dot

"Oh no," I had thought, "This is really not cool"
"My alarm must be broken; I'll be late for school"

I scanned through my drawers for something to wear
I did it so quickly I forgot underwear

I hopped on my bike and I pedaled as quick
As it would take to break a small, flabby stick

I rode through the streets like a leopard on wheels
Then my bike hit a nail, my bad luck was unreal

I flew off my bike and onto the street
I dashed down the sidewalk, my speed couldn't be beat

Just then, a newspaper hit me smack on my knee
I read and it said something that startled me

"November 11" it showed in white and grey
"Have a happy Veteran's Day, no school today"
Cailin Umbaugh, Grade 5
Lincoln Elementary School

Yellow in Nature

If I were yellow,
I would be a butterfly fluttering from flower to flower.

If I were yellow,
I would be the sun on a hot summer day.

If I were yellow,
I would be a bee rushing to its hive.

If I were yellow,
I would be a yellow flower growing in the spring.

If I were yellow,
I would be a sunflower growing with all my friends.

If I were yellow,
I would be a star sparkling in the sky.

If I were yellow,
I would be a leaf during autumn, floating in the wind.

If I were yellow,
I would be the full moon with the stars up in the sky.
Sophia Scarpone, Grade 5
Holy Child Academy

Tasty Orange Food

If I were orange,
I would be a tasty orange.

If I were orange,
I would be a juicy grapefruit.

If I were orange,
I would be a lollipop waiting at Citizen's Bank.

If I were orange,
I would be smushed squash lying on the ground.

If I were orange,
I would be a delicious tangerine.

If I were orange,
I would be a cantaloupe waiting to get put into the refrigerator.

If I were orange,
I would be a mango waiting to fall off a tree.

If I were orange,
I would be a papaya waiting to be eaten by a happy child.
Domenique Aguirre, Grade 5
Holy Child Academy

Friends
Friends are the chocolate chips to your cookie.
They are like the peanut butter to your jelly.
They are like laces to your shoes.
They are the pages to your book.
They are the leaves to your tree…
The snow to your winter…
The sun to your summer…
Friends are something you simply can't live without.
Sienna Brock, Grade 6
State Street Elementary School

Soaring
The wind ruffled my feathers as I flew over Puerto Rico.
The insects on the trees seem to wave at me.
I flew down to catch a big black juicy one.
As I soared up my yellow shoulder gleamed in the sunlight.
I looked down at my treetop nest.
Then the wind pushed me up beckoning me higher
And I felt that I could fly 5,000 miles.
I am the Yellow-Shouldered Blackbird.
Angela Baranowski, Grade 6
Nazareth Area Intermediate School

Max
There was a dog named Max
Max stroked at his prey like a T-Rex
Max ran as fast as a cheetah
He was also very kind.
Max let all the little boys and girls play with him
He would lick their faces nonstop.
Max would never hurt a human.
And best of all he's my dog!
Josea Rubenstein, Grade 6
State Street Elementary School

Me and My Scooter
I like to ride my scooter.
I love to go down hills.
My friends and I love to do tricks.
We always play razor.
It is when one kid does a trick and your job is to do the trick.
If you bail you get the letter R.
You don't want to get razor or you can't play anymore.
That is one of my best talents.
Dylan Defuria, Grade 4
McKinley Elementary School

Fall Is…
Fall is the sound of the leaves crunching under my feet
Fall is the beauty of leaves changing color
Fall is the smell of smoke running through the air
Fall is the feeling of the wind pushing the leaves off the trees
To fall softly to the ground to greet you
Fall is the beauty of one season.
Madison Rebuck, Grade 6
Pennridge North Middle School

Tangy Taco
I hate being eaten
It doesn't make sense
I don't like to be gone
I'm just so great
It's hard not to be tempted
But I'm just a little bit of meat, cheese, lettuce and sauce
Maybe not all maybe more
But please don't eat me
I'll hide in my shell
Please don't eat me if…
I'm less at Taco Bell
What am I? A taco of course
But please don't eat me or there will be no more.
Meredith Roteman, Grade 4
Jefferson Elementary School

What Is Green
Green is the color of money in my pocket.
Green is the color of fireworks my dad sets off on Christmas.
Green tastes like a fresh crunchy pickle.
Green sounds like trees waving in the morning.
Green is the color of Christmas and the lights on my tree.
Green is the color of salads I eat.
Green is the color of my dad's car.
Green is as soft as the grass in front of my house.
Green is joyful like the tree that talks to me.
Green is a color of a football field.
Green is as bright as the sun.
Green is the color of the frogs that live in the flower bed.
Green is fine and it's mine.
Joseph Wasekanes, Grade 6
St Hilary of Poitiers School

Hawaiian Crow
H awaii is my home
A lala is my Hawaiian name
W ear feathers of dark brown
A black bill, feet, and legs I have
I depend on the Koa Tree
I lived in Kai Malino Ranch and Kona Coast of the Big Island
A nuisance I was to them
N ourished on berries and flowers

C ontinued to decrease in numbers
R escued from extinction
O nly kept in a zoo now
W ild no more
Aubrey Baranowski, Grade 6
Nazareth Area Intermediate School

Morning
I woke up in the morning.
I was sleeping on my fingers.
My breath right now is the opposite of my soul.
Kevin Cecchine, Grade 5
Nether Providence Elementary School

Kite

Kite
diamond, air,
wind, fly, paper, triangular
long string
tail

Ashley Turchan, Grade 5
Maxwell Elementary School

Kittens

Kittens
Playful and cute
Are good pals, friends, and fun
Are super, sleepy, and funny
Loving

Danielle Andrews, Grade 4
McKinley Elementary School

LeBron James: The Chosen One

Blaring directions
Fans cheering The Chosen One
A game winning shot
Powder exploding in air
Tension rising when he dunks

Cole Storm, Grade 5
Holy Martyrs Elementary School

Santa

Santa is a wise old man
Even though he does not have a van
Santa has a sleigh
That he pulls presents for children
"Hooray!"

Kayla Fox, Grade 5
Fishing Creek Elementary School

Arizona's Beauty

Carved rock everywhere
The Colorado River
Hiking down long paths
River rushing in your ears
The beautiful Grand Canyon!

Catherine Reedy, Grade 5
Holy Martyrs Elementary School

Nature

The birds fly high in
the sky as the
trees blow slowly
in the
wind.

Alexandra Millan, Grade 6
Notre Dame School

Happiness

Happiness is the feeling you get when you accomplish something new
Happiness is soaring high in the sky
Happiness is hitting a home run in the ninth to win the championship game
Happiness is the blue, calm waters of the vast Atlantic Ocean
Happiness tastes like a hot fudge sundae on a sizzling summer day
Happiness smells like snicker doodle cookies fresh out of the oven
Happiness sounds like wind chimes chiming softly on a spring day ding, ding
Happiness feels like my puppy's fur
Happiness looks like a rainbow in the brilliant blue sky
Happiness makes me feel gigantic like the Empire State Building
Happiness is taking leisurely evening walks with my dog, Rudy

Jimmy Martin, Grade 6
West Allegheny Middle School

Imagination

Imagination is like a movie or daydream dancing.
Imagination is like a cartoon where everything can be possible.
Imagination is like something hiding in the closet but nothing was there.
Imagination is like shiny white stars in the twilight.
Imagination tastes like candy and chocolate chip cookies.
Imagination smells like blueberry flowers.
Imagination sounds like a bell ringing inside my head: ding dong.
Imagination feels like I'm touching something soft.
Imagination looks like I'm acting in real life.
Imagination makes me feel special and happy.
Imagination is thinking about what is in your mind.

Kevin Hernandez Rivera, Grade 6
West Allegheny Middle School

Bravery

Bravery is diving on a grenade to save a man's life
Bravery is three-hundred men facing off against one million for their love of Greece.
Bravery is standing up for a kid when he's being bullied
Bravery is red rolling thunder
Bravery tastes like a hot dog sizzling on the grill
Bravery sounds like the screams of thousands of men coming at you
Bravery smells like the battle it was born on
Bravery feels like rocks, fire, and gravel mixed together
Bravery looks like an army of men
Bravery makes me feel amazing
Bravery is very good to have

Joshua Loyer, Grade 6
West Allegheny Middle School

Everything Orange

If I were an orange, I would be a big juicy orange waiting to be picked,
If I were an orange basketball I'd be getting ready to be shot in a net,
If I were an orange orangutan, I would swing all around,
If I were an orange pumpkin I'd be getting ready to be carved into a jack-o'-lantern
If I were an orange flower, I would be waiting for the sun to help me grow,
If I were an orange book, I would be waiting to be read,
If I were orange, curly hair, I would be waiting to be brushed,
If I were the sun, I would stay shining bright.

Monqualine Subah, Grade 5
Holy Child Academy

Art and Music
Art
Colorful, fun
Cutting, drawing, painting
Brushes, paint, notes, bars
Playing, making, listening
Peaceful, creative
Music
Alexis Staley, Grade 6
St Maria Goretti School

Orange
Orange is the color of my favorite dress
Walking down New York City
Waving to people
Some people might think I am crazy
I saw a hot dog stand
"Give me two please."
Amirah Rose, Grade 4
Wissahickon Charter School

Autumn
A mazing colors
U nder the beautiful sky
T iny brown acorns
U gly jack-o'-lanterns
M ummy costumes
N ights good for trick-or-treat
Becky Lee, Grade 4
All Saints Catholic School

Monsters
Creepy, scary
Hiding, stalking, lurking
Zombies, bats, vampires, mummies
Eating, scaring, chasing
Seeking, noisy
Creatures
Eniya Brooks, Grade 5
Hamilton Elementary School

Love
Love is fragile like a heart
a very strong four-letter word
it's a key
someone in this world has one for you
if the key doesn't fit, it's not meant to be
you'll find out what love really is
Quaintesha McKinney, Grade 6
John G Whittier School

Deer
Deer in the corn field
I'm ready to shoot at it
Meat in the freezer
Brodie Hollenbach, Grade 4
Watsontown Elementary School

Happiness
Happiness is a perfect view of a sunset over an ocean.
Happiness is another spectacular victory over an enemy.
Happiness is a great party with the sounds "clap, snap, bang."
Happiness is the bright, beam of a brindled blue.
Happiness tastes like delicious homemade cookies.
Happiness smells like spring, when all the flowers bloom.
Happiness sounds like the beat of your favorite song.
Happiness feels like a soft cloud in a calm afternoon sky.
Happiness looks like the smile on your baby sister.
Happiness makes me feel calm, but also wanting to dance at the same time.
Happiness is a spectacular feeling you should always have.
Tommy Burke, Grade 6
West Allegheny Middle School

Honor
Honor is showing respect for the fallen heroes
Honor is admiring the people that died on 9/11/01
Honor is clapping for someone that got hurt during a football game
Honor is the color of the American flag still standing after a well fought battle
Honor tastes like juicy steak coming off the grill
Honor smells like the blooming flowers in the spring
Honor sounds like all the people roaring for a war hero coming back from Iraq
Honor looks like a hero getting a gold medal for a long fifty years at war
Honor makes me feel like I tried my best on something
Honor is the stars and stripes posing proudly on the American flag
Honor is not being a sulking sore loser after losing the championship
Jared Colbert, Grade 6
West Allegheny Middle School

Humor
Humor is loud laughter when I hear a funny joke
Humor is Will Farell dancing in a music video in *Step Brothers*
Humor is the yellow banana cream pie thrown at a clown
Humor is the morning riddles trying to be funny
Humor feels like the BUZZ from the hand buzzer when you shake a joker's hand
Humor tastes like chocolate chip mint ice cream sliding down my throat
Humor smells like a clown's red face paint
Humor sounds like the noise made by a Whoopee cushion
Humor looks like seven silly smiling clowns
Humor is practical jokes on April Fool's Day
Humor makes me happy when I hear a funny joke
Tory Elghatit, Grade 6
West Allegheny Middle School

Veteran's Day Heroes
Thank you for risking your lives for our country.
Because of you, I am here today, because of you I am free.
You are my hero, you are an unknown hero that fights for what you believe in,
Thank you so much,
Some people know you as soldiers,
Some people know you as brave heroes,
Heroes that fight for our safety and our freedom,
You are brave people, through the fear and dangers of war.
Thank you again for going through all that trouble to support our country.
Joshua Randall Glover, Grade 6
Pennridge North Middle School

High Merit Poems – Grades 4, 5 and 6

Touchdown!
Quarterback drops back
Receiver goes deep
D-line gets through
Quarterback gets away
Throws the pass
Defender tips it
Crowd gets quiet
Wide receiver catches it
Crowd goes wild
Home team wins!
Noah Richason, Grade 5
Maxwell Elementary School

Sister
A sister is someone
that is there for you.
Someone that cares for you.
There is no one like a sister.
You can have a best friend
but no one can compare to a sister.
There is no one like a sister.
Even though we fight and fuss
we still love each other so so much!
There is no one like a sister.
Tynetta Tull, Grade 6
Colwyn Elementary School

Rain
Rain, rain, rainy days
Oh, how I hate rainy days
Rain can drizzle
Rain can pour
No matter what
We get more and more
Rain makes puddles
Lots of them
But to me
Rain is a treasured gem!
Catherine Gregoire, Grade 5
Saint Theresa School

Cookies
Cookies and cream
Oh, what a dream
Oh, so good
For you and me
One giant cookie
What a big treat
Krazy Kookie Killer Kookies
I love cookies!
Everyone have a taste
So crunchy!
Maura Cudahy, Grade 5
Saint Theresa School

Birds
Forest
Tropical
Insects crawling
Green
Rain
Noises
Exotic
Innocent
Fresh
Angelica Timar, Grade 6
Nazareth Area Intermediate School

Babe Ruth
B oston Red Sox
A great baseball player
B ambino
E veryone knows him

R BI master
U nder Hank Aaron for most homers
T he sultan of swat
H e died of throat cancer
Timmy Gallagher, Grade 4
McKinley Elementary School

A Change That We Need to See
We all need to make a change
Use your imagination for different things
Use your pride and quickness
Trust me you will have a good Christmas
listen to me and not a bee
Finally you would get to see
the help I gave to you from me
Let's make a change for everyone
to see.
Ahmier Torrence, Grade 6
Colwyn Elementary School

My Backpack
My backpack is as light as a penny.
My backpack is as colorful as a rainbow.
My backpack smells like a flower.
My backpack is as big as a giant.
My backpack is as nice as a clock.
Nhi Phan, Grade 4
Wickersham Elementary School

Skateboarding
It is so cool.
I love the wind in my face.
It is so rad, man.
I like the new tricks.
Bumps and bruises.
Hard falls.
Jimmy McGinn, Grade 4
McKinley Elementary School

Phillies
P hils are always winning
H ow far will they go to win?
I banez hits a single
L idge always throws a strike
L ow scores are always sad
I n the field they do not fail
E ven when it is raining
S ee how good this team is!
Peirce Robinson, Grade 4
McKinley Elementary School

Green
Green makes me nervous
like the first day of school
and when my mom takes me to parties
with people I never met before.

Green reminds me of being
at the doctor's office to get my shots
Sometimes I want to disappear.
Ayanna Graham, Grade 4
Wissahickon Charter School

Puppies
I like puppies, they're really cute.
They are more valuable to me than loot.
They are so very smart,
They have a very big heart.
I like the way they love to play,
They could play all through the day.
I don't want a cat or a snake.
Just a puppy, for goodness sake!
Braden Ward, Grade 4
W R Croman Elementary School

Life
Life is more special than anything
It's more complicated
And less complicated
Than you think
And is as lovely as the song of a bird
And as terrible as fire
So that's why many ask,
"Why are we here?"
Kelcey Flowers, Grade 6
State Street Elementary School

Saturn
S torms
A planet
T itan's the largest moon
U nder a magnetic field
R ings
N o craters
Andrew Bowman, Grade 4
St Joseph School

The Hero in Me

I know there's a hero in me
Somewhere, deep down, I can see her
I know there's a brave person within me
I just need to find her
I have to find her
She's in there somewhere
I'm pulling out my hair because
She's trying to hide
She didn't go deep enough inside
Me.
I think I found a trace of her, somewhere in my soul.
Was it her? Was it me? I cannot pay the toll much longer
The toll of not knowing the hero in me
I looked in my brain, she's not there, either. She's smarter than that.
The last place to look was my heart.
I took a peek, nothing, but I ventured in. I dug deep, looking. I found her. She was hiding, hiding, tucked deep into a remote corner of my heart. I didn't recognize her.
She didn't recognize me. Then I knew: she wasn't the hero in me. The hero in me wasn't in me, it was me. All I had to do was look. And after I searched my heart, I found her.

Aislinn Slaugenhaupt, Grade 6
Commonwealth Connections Academy

Real Beauty

A beautiful sunset,
The clouds as orange as a pumpkin,
The sky the color of lavender,
I stared at the sunset wondering about the beauty here,
Nothing was ever ugly,
A big field of flowers, roses and daffodils, lavender and daisies, golden rods and mistletoe,
The trees greener than emeralds, green grass, green trees,
Rainbow colored flowers,
A sunset, not to mention the waterfall and lake,
Crystal clear water as blue as the sky,
The water was sparkling,
Inside the water were all kinds of fish, boxer fish, rainbow fish, angel fish, goldfish, even fish that were so clear you could see right through them,
Dolphins were jumping in and out of the water, golden dolphins, they were sparkling and winking at me,
Soon there was a full moon,
The stars were shining like little pearls in the sky,
This place is amazing,
This place is real beauty.

Sarah Trebicka, Grade 4
Southern Lehigh Intermediate School

Thanksgiving

I see my well dressed and friendly family patiently waiting for the chocolate brown turkey
   to travel onto the fabulously decorated table.
I can smell all of the food my wonderful mom-mom made for everyone to enjoy: mashed potatoes, gravy, biscuits, and more!
I can hear my excited dad bellowing at the action packed football game
I can feel my stomach rumbling as hard as a volcano about to erupt!
I can taste all the great desserts: scrumptious pumpkin pie, frigid ice cream, vanilla cake, and more!

I LOVE THANKSGIVING!

Sarah Forchielli, Grade 4
Colonial Elementary School

Our Beautiful World

Magnificent colored leaves glide in the air
Waving and swirling without a care
Gorgeous flowers sprout in grass
While bees and butterflies happily pass.

Everyone playing in the flowers
Acting like they have special powers
Don't forget the flowers for the teacher
Wait, I think I see a creature.

Alaina Cottage, Grade 4
Fairview Elementary School

Our Beautiful World

Hot wide grainy deserts,
Where sand blows fiercely,
Magnificent Arabian horses thrive,
Manes flowing in the whispering wind.

Desperately looking for water,
Escaping the dreadful heat,
Full of stamina,
Eager to dash over the dunes.

Megan Claerbaut, Grade 4
Fairview Elementary School

Brand New Coat

Cozy, warm
Black design
Favorite coat
Favorite type
From Marshalls
Comfortable coat
Always wanted
Mine forever
Almost winter

Ibrahim Yarow, Grade 4
Wickersham Elementary School

Enchanted Forest

T owering
R ed oaks
E erily
E nchant
S mall forests

Mahima Reddy, Grade 5
Trinity East Elementary School

Friends/Bullies

Friends
Kind, trustworthy
Special, awesome, mean, fearful
Fighting, frightening, disliked
Bad, terrible
Bullies

Sarah Heller, Grade 5
St Sebastian Elementary School

Friends/Bullies

Friends
kind, sociable
loving, caring, giving
special, heart, devil, discouraging
harming, hating, disliked
evil, mean
Bullies

Marty Kenny, Grade 5
St Sebastian Elementary School

Friends/Bullies

Friends
helpful, nice
loving, comforting, liked
star, angel, criminal, monster
demanding, hated, disliked
hurtful, mean
Bullies

Olivia Hite, Grade 5
St Sebastian Elementary School

Friends/Bullies

Friends
safe, awesome
loving, caring, calming
buddies, winners, monsters, losers
harming, hated, disliked
hurtful, dangerous
Bullies

Brandon Hager, Grade 5
St Sebastian Elementary School

Snow

Snow is here,
Snow is there,
Snow is everywhere.
From the rooftops above,
To the ground below.
Snow brings great joy,
To every girl and boy.

Calvin Affinito, Grade 5
East Union Intermediate Center

Friends/Bullies

Friends
awesome, trusting
loving, helping, comforting
kind, funny, sinister, rival
disgusted, disrespecting, angry
mean, bossy,
Bullies

Dominic Hite, Grade 5
St Sebastian Elementary School

I Won't!

"I won't eat the peas,
They're too squishy.
I won't eat the chicken,
It's too crispy.
I won't drink the soup,
It has fish in it.
I won't eat the corn,
It's too hot.
I won't eat the lettuce,
It's too juicy."
"Well, would you like some dessert?"
"Yes, please!"

"Then you'll have to eat the peas,
and eat the chicken, too.
You'll have to drink the soup,
And you'll have to eat the corn,
You'll have to eat the lettuce, too.
Then when you're done,
You can have dessert."

Cindy Li, Grade 4
Middle Smithfield Elementary School

Rain Forest

Rain
Forest
Animals
Tarantulas
Life
Birds
Flowers
Weather change
Different sounds
Fish
Noise
Crickets
Chirping sounds
Howling hoot owls
Trees
Water
Tadpoles
Wet dirt squeaks
Evaporate
Moss

Alex Visan, Grade 6
Nazareth Area Intermediate School

Star

tiny, bright
twinkling, sparkling, shining
space, time, gem, ring
glittering, enchanting, alluring
gorgeous, rare
diamond

Shelby Dolan, Grade 6
Ross Elementary School

Soaring Through the Sky

I soar,
  I fly,
    I see the world,
      Through my eye,

I dance in the sky,
  I prance in the trees,
    I fly through noon to night,
      With my magnificent flight,

I twirl around clouds,
  With my long, large wings,
    And after a great, long day,
      I perch myself on a branch and sing,

I am a hawk,
  I can fly anywhere,
    I have unlimited boundaries,
      I am a hawk.

Samantha Schatten, Grade 5
Falk Laboratory School

My Mom and Dad

My mom and dad are so nice and sweet.
They help me through what is hard,
And if something wasn't clear to me,
They would say it slower so I would understand.

But when I would do something wrong,
They would get mad.
When they are mad,
They are also sad.

When they are sad,
I get mad.
But I get over it.
And they will have to, also.

When we are all happy,
We all say we love each other so very, very much.
When we are done,
We give each other hugs.

Gianna Azcona, Grade 5
McKinley Elementary School

When War Strikes

When war strikes
We all flee
But sometimes you will see
Mother or father, brother or sister
Leave the country
When war strikes
Ordinary fighters turn into heroes
The families hope, care, love, and pray
For the ones who suffer every day
When war strikes
People fall
Grass is coated in red
But the fighters forever stand still
Even when bullets tear, shatter, break, and shred
When war strikes
We all wait
To pay our respects
On this very special date
That we call Veteran's Day

Carley Ann Wingate, Grade 6
Pennridge North Middle School

A Christmas Day

Crackling in the hearth a lively fire grows,
It spreads me with warmth, down to my toes.
The mantle glitters with small white white lights,
It really is such a wonderful sight.
All along the rails, the garland is hung,
Outside the house, carols are being sung.
Cookies are baking, lovely cake too,
The icing, all spread, is a nice baby blue.
Snow covers everything with a beautiful glimmer,
Sometimes it even seems to shimmer.
The cookies are done, set out on a plate,
Darkness creeps up, for it is so late.
In bed I crawl, hoping for him,
To eat all the cookies and drink all the milk,
To leave some presents, all wrapped up in silk,
Then leave until next year while I open my gift,
Excited, out of the box I lift,
The best gift of all…
Life.

Lauren Trimber, Grade 6
Hopewell Memorial Jr High School

School

Ringing goes my alarm clock, it's time to go to school
Sometimes school can be cool, it's a learning tool
School isn't always fun
There's homework for everyone
Math is more than one plus one
There is lots of work to be done
Three o'clock, oh what joy!
No more teachers to annoy!

Manasi Deorah, Grade 5
Saint Theresa School

Thanksgiving

Thanksgiving is coming together with my family.
Playing football when the air is cold and crisp.
Getting to eat all I want (especially grandma's mashed potatoes.)
Thanking God for all he's done for me.
Watching sports on TV with my crazy family.
One of my favorite holidays.
A holiday I have off from school.
A very lovely day.

Sabrina O'Connor, Grade 6
Moravian Academy Middle School

Our Veterans

Every day they train for us, every day they push themselves for us,
Every day they prepare themselves for us, each one fighting for different motivations,
But all of them serving for one single nation,

When they get the call to go, they will be ready from months of preparation,
As they walk out the door they will leave one quotation,
"If I don't return it was for you, and the rest of my nation."

As they take another step, their wives will sob and cry,
But a soldier's eyes — a true hero's eyes are always dry,

As the hero steps forward, to see the moment he has waited for with such anticipation,
He sees the enemy's eyes and realizes, "Man, I'll kill for this nation!"

In the final moments through a true hero's eyes,
He sees the enemy's lines of perfect formation,
As he feels the sting of a bullet piercing through him,
Hears its shot penetrating his ears,
Tastes the blood running down his mouth,
He manages to speak his very last words, through the same bloody lips,
"I've come this far, why not die for my nation?"

I would like to thank my father, and my grandfather also, a gratitude I've owed since the day I was born,
Because when they weren't home taking care of their family, they were serving our nation instead.

Erin Everdale, Grade 6
Pennridge North Middle School

What Is Purple?

Purple is the color of my Christmas lights. In the city purple is night time bright.
Purple is my best friend's shoes. Purple is a combination of blues.

I hear purple on Halloween. Purple are ghosts unseen.
Purple tastes like grape soda. Purple tastes like jelly donuts.
Purple also is a sticker on a test bonus.

Purple smells like purple hyacinths that bloom in the spring. Purple are amethysts that go bling, bling, bling.
The feeling of purple is static electricity. Purple is the dress of a doll Felicity.
Violets are purple they smell really sweet. Purple is lavender swaying in the breeze.

I love purple, it's really true, I love purple, how about you?
Purple is the color of Lent. Purple is the color of a birthday present.
Purple is dark, but true. Purple reminds me of you.

You like purple, so do I. Purple makes your eyes grow wide.
Purple looks like a prom dress. Purple looks like a fairy princess.

Purple sounds like a girl's sweet dream. Purple is a cat's eyes gleam.
Purple is my cousin's room, it's really neat.
Purple is a candy wrapper covering a sweet treat.
Purple, purple I love the sound of purple.

Victoria Iannarelli, Grade 6
St Hilary of Poitiers School

Safety Net
I will keep you safe
As safe as I can
But you are only as safe
As your safety net can
That you put out for yourself,
But I'll always be there if you need help.
Jackie Wheeler, Grade 6
State Street Elementary School

Polar Bear
Bear
Furry, huge
Lives in the Arctic
White, awesome
Polar Bear.
Sean Mahoney, Grade 5
Russell Elementary School

Swimming
Splash!
Freestyle, backstroke,
Swim really fast!
Butterfly, breaststroke,
Swimming!
Paige Benasutti, Grade 5
Russell Elementary School

Love
Love
sweet as a million cherry pies
it never goes away even when someone dies
it's a fragile piece of broken glass
but when put back together, it's repaired
Da'Jour Moss, Grade 6
John G Whittier School

Thanksgiving Is…
The fly from PA to Texas
The dinner on the table.
A freshly baked turkey.
A late night watching TV
Spending time with my family.
Alex Damjanovic, Grade 6
Moravian Academy Middle School

Thanksgiving Is…
Time to celebrate.
Playing with my cousins.
Eating turkey.
A day full of joy and love.
Spending time with my family.
Emily Holt, Grade 6
Moravian Academy Middle School

Wickedness
Wickedness is a dark maze with no way out
Wickedness is a crushed onyx under a full moon
Wickedness is a jet black alleyway filled with graffiti
Wickedness is ebony spears glinting in the light
Wickedness tastes like acid burning through your tongue
Wickedness smells like bittersweet blush red roses
Wickedness sounds like a thousand nails screeching against a chalkboard
Wickedness feels like razor sharp thorns piercing your skin
Wickedness makes me feel paralyzed with fear
Wickedness makes even animals cringe
Wickedness spreads terror throughout the universe
Alyssa Placha, Grade 6
West Allegheny Middle School

Love
Love is the pink ribbon on your wedding bouquet.
Love is the marathon you're running for cancer support.
Love is the first splash into the pool, with your best friend after the last day of school.
Love is a red rose on your loved one's casket.
Love tastes like fruit punch at your first dance.
Love smells like home-baked cookies with your mother.
Love sounds like a harp being played for you, and you only.
Love feels like a monarch butterfly landing on your nose in spring.
Love looks like your friends cheering you up after your very worst day.
Love makes me as giggly as a 3 year old on her birthday.
Love is a nurse, holding her patient's hand in the recovery room.
Julianne Buterbaugh, Grade 6
West Allegheny Middle School

Excitement
Excitement is an overload of happiness and joy.
Excitement is someone hitting a home run in softball.
Excitement is a person winning the lottery.
Excitement is happy, vibrant lime green.
Excitement tastes like cool creamy ice cream on a hot summer's day.
Excitement smells like sweet snicker doodles on Christmas morning.
Excitement sounds like the crowd cheering at a football game.
Excitement feels like petting the soft fur of a new puppy.
Excitement looks like my cousins when I go to visit them in Michigan.
Excitement makes me radiate with happiness and joy.
Excitement is like nothing else in the world.
Ali Williamson, Grade 6
West Allegheny Middle School

Joyfulness
Joyfulness is baby blue like a plopping waterfall in the hot July summer at Niagara Falls on a cruise ship drinking strawberry splat smoothies.
Joyfulness looks like a cozy pillow you're lying on, while the whole city is watching the Phillies win the World Series of 2008.
Joyfulness tastes like a chewy Laffy Taffy in your candy bag.
Joyfulness smells like a beautiful yellow daisy that just grew out of the ground.
Joyfulness sounds like a chirping blue bird waiting for its food.
Joyfulness makes me feel like shooting the last free throw and the whole team is cheering because we just won the championship.
Chris Laskowski, Grade 6
Our Lady of Ransom School

High Merit Poems – Grades 4, 5 and 6

Frozen

Frozen in time.
Everything else around me is going about,
Moving, talking, laughing.
Life. La vie. Vita. Chava…
My sister tearing through her last precious present.
My grandma touching lightly my aunt's stomach,
Feeling her baby kicking about.
My cousin, secretly jumping on the bed,
Going unnoticed.
My beloved dog,
With snow on her nose, and snow on her paws.
Little Alexis,
Hanging up the final ornament on the fresh Christmas tree.
The baby, speaking her very first word "Ma!"
Parents, aunts, uncles, laughing, at child's first joke.
Neighbors throwing snowballs,
Flying across our window.
These snowballs,
These memories,
Frozen in time,
Frozen in my mind.

Lainey Newman, Grade 5
The Ellis School

Softball

It's about 75° weather
Our gloves made of leather
And the whole team working together

It's about all the athletes
With dirt on their cleats
And the team we hope to defeat

It's about going up to the plate
The score five to eight
And hitting the ball over the gate

It's about running the base
The left fielder in a chase
And the other team in disgrace

It's about more bats cracking
The ball the first baseman is attacking
And afterwards the whole team ice cream snacking

It's about the sport I like best…Softball!

Eileen Sam, Grade 5
Pocopson Elementary School

Basketball

The basketball is as soft as the bed.
The basketball is as round as a globe.
The lines on the basketball is as dirty as the floor.
The words are as are big as me.

Devonte Thomas, Grade 4
Wickersham Elementary School

Chachoute

C ompassionate
H onest
A wesome
C ourageous
H ow smart we are
O utstanding
U nique
T alented
E normous family

Brianna Chachoute, Grade 4
Philadelphia Performing Arts Charter School

Fin Whale

F ound in all oceans of the world
I ts flippers are small and tapered
N ickname is "greyhound of the sea"

W eight is between 50-70 tons
H ave a dorsal fin
A mong the fastest of the great whale
L ong, sleek, and streamlined
E ats small shrimp-like creatures called krill

Alyssa Amadore, Grade 6
Nazareth Area Intermediate School

Books

Open a book to see what's inside it,
it might have a dream or a nightmare beside it.
It could be an adventure with a lesson or two,
or it could be a story about something new.
It could be about kids who found something to do,
or tell about something that you never knew.
It might be a pencil that always could bend,
just open a book and read to the end.

Jennifer Greenleaf, Grade 6
Hopewell Memorial Jr High School

A Special Day

Oh, what a special day, a holiday
A chance to say "thanks" in a special way
While many holidays come then go,
This one seems to have more to show,
It may be thought of as a silly little feast
But it is more for the humans than the beasts,
If you have not guessed yet, this day is quite clear
It is Thanksgiving, so please do not fear.

Margaret-Mary O'Brien, Grade 6
St Joseph School

It Is the End of the World as We Know It

Cities are under siege
Ladders board houses
The dust is blinding
War and battle are only for gold 'n glor'

Ben Fugaro-Thompson, Grade 5
Nether Providence Elementary School

Clouds

Clouds dance by my window
Like cotton candy, big and fluffy
Like my pillow, extra puffy
They can't stay they must go

I see a bunny, I see a bear!
With clouds you can let your imagination run wild
It doesn't matter if you're an adult or child
You can just look up, and they're everywhere

If you are having a bad day
Just look in the sky
You will feel like you can fly
Because clouds will make your stress go away!

Jessa Ryan, Grade 6
St Jerome Elementary School

The Moon

The moon is very bright,
An amazing glittery sight.
Truly terrific lively light,
Brightly beaming, sparkling in the night.

Delightfully dreamy gleaming glow
Peaceful, patient, perfect pizzazz.
Sweetly shining, brightly blinding
Beautiful, glorious, glamorous light.

Wonderful, dazzling, silvery light
Crater covered and shines through the night.
Sweetly shining along with the stars
Till the morning when the moon departs.

Olivia Weaver, Grade 6
Linville Hill Mennonite School

Jimmy Schule

Jimmy is my older brother
He has brown hair and rosy cheeks
He is as tall as a light post on a street corner
He's very skinny but strong

Jimmy plays basketball for Kings College
Squeak! the sound of his basketball sneakers hitting the court
When Jimmy's off the court
He reports for his school paper

Jimmy is the brother I look up to
He can always make me laugh
Even though he teases me
I will always love him

Elizabeth Schule, Grade 6
St Jerome Elementary School

A Dog Named Cady

There once was a pup named Cady
Her best friend was a boy named David
She was a fine gentle little lady
And was devoted to her master David

Chewing, barking, running and leaping
Playtime was a favorite place to be
In piles of leaves that's heaping
Chasing as far as you can see

At night she becomes a lazy daisy
As she cuddles and lays next to me
The fireplace sparkling and crackling like crazy
As she wanders into her peaceful glee

David L. Fleming, Grade 5
East Union Intermediate Center

Books

Books, books, there are a lot
They have characters, settings and a plot
Some are for learning, some are for pleasure
Some are even considered a treasure

Biographies, mysteries, sports and fiction
All of these can expand your imagination
A novel is a journey traveling through time
Sports stories are a favorite of mine

Barnes and Noble, the library or the book fair
Keep them for yourself, but it's always nice to share
Books are like candy, there are many kinds
Read books to stimulate your minds.

Connor Vogt, Grade 6
St Jerome Elementary School

The Approaching Holidays

The fall is finally here
We all start to cheer
For the holidays are coming near
There's nothing to fear

We gather here to eat our main meal
Of turkey and gravy, which is a good deal
As we eat our dessert of pumpkin pie,
Our family and guests finish up and say good-bye

As the winter approaches and the cold weather arrives,
We leave cookies and milk for the big guy
As Santa hops on his sleigh and hits the sky,
The children look up and say good-bye

Emily Lorimer, Grade 6
St Jerome Elementary School

High Merit Poems – Grades 4, 5 and 6

Anger
Anger is cruel
Anger is madness
Anger is a dark abyss
Anger tastes like rotten moldy emerald cheese
Anger smells like sewer mixed with saltwater
Anger is the devil burning your soul
Anger sounds like a mountain lion growling
Anger feels like a volcano erupting
Anger looks like a cat running after a mouse
Anger makes me furious inside and makes me want to explode
Anger is World War II all over again
Michael Siwula, Grade 6
West Allegheny Middle School

Fear
Fear is a boy lost in the hazy woods
Fear is when you are in a haunted house
Fear is a deep onyx black
Fear is like a terrible nightmare
Fear is like someone chasing you
Fear looks like you are in a pitch black room
Fear smells like smoke
Fear tastes like a sour lemon
Fear feels like you are in an icy room
Fear sounds like ghosts screaming
Fear makes me want to cower in a corner
Mason Bynum, Grade 6
West Allegheny Middle School

It's a Dirtbike Day
It's a dirtbike day
Feel the gummy handle grips
Hear loud pitched sounds that pound against my ear drums
See mud, dust, and speed
Taste bugs going into my mouth from riding
Speed is my favorite thing
Like the air when it hits my face
When I jump it seems like I'm flying
Like riding threw mud and water
The smell of gasoline when the exhaust comes out
That's dirtbike day
Hunter Joseph Dyer, Grade 6
Pennridge North Middle School

Santa Claus
I wake up to a squeaking noise
Then I hear a shout
Who could it be?
Santa Claus without a doubt
I grab my robe and slip on my slippers
And run swiftly down the hall
I quietly go down the stairs without a sound at all
When I got to the bottom I looked around the corner to see
A big fat jolly man staring back at me!
Nicole Grimm, Grade 6
Hopewell Memorial Jr High School

Character Traits
Responsible is doing what you have to do
Respect is being nice to others
And being nice to you
Caring is helping others — it means a lot to me
But not nearly as much as accountability
Accountable is standing up
And saying what you'll do
Trustworthiness is keeping secrets
When people want you to
Fairness is saying "I don't cheat"
Loud and very clearly
Citizenship is helping out
People and your community
Shine bright!
And you will succeed,
Doing good things and doing good deeds.
Sedona Sowell Wilson, Grade 4
Lincoln Elementary School

Autumn
A gust of shivery wind
Shimmer on the red car
Cold and breezy
Red, orange, yellow, brown
Heart shaped leaves
The tree losing his hair
It falls slowly
It's like an animation slideshow
Until it hits the ground
Scraping sounds from a rake
A pretty collage of multicolor leaves in a pile
Children scampering through it
Until a call of the mom is heard to go
The children put up a fit like tea on a pot
The still leaves are now safe
Autumn
Taylor McGrath, Grade 6
Jenkintown Elementary School

Marc-Andre Fleury
The Penguins are the one to choose
Even when they lose, lose, lose.
Marc-Andre is called "The Flower"
Because he always shows his awesome power.

He always tries to block the goal
Because he plays with heart and soul.
Fleury's number is 29
And his playing is always fine, fine, fine.

He loves it when you chant his name
It always helps him win the game.
So next time you see him play,
Remember to cheer for Marc-Andre.
Madison Baker, Grade 5
Foster Elementary School

Good Old Dogs

I had a dog, who ate like a hog.
His name is Spudz, he's very fluffy but is still a puppy.
His nose is flat and very stuffy.
He loves to run, jump and play.
He chews on everything, but I love him anyway.
He is part mutt, with Shitzu,
and part Pekinese too.
My cat does not like him yet,
but in time they'll be friends I bet.
I love my cat, and dog the same,
but when there's poop in the house I know who to blame!
But, I also have a dog now that weighs a ton
he's very fun for everyone,
but he's very super-duper.
The part I don't like, involves his pooper-scooper!

Amanda Forgie, Grade 4
St Joseph School

Poetry

This poem is about poetry,
So it will be short and sweet.
It'll have that tingly jingle,
And make you tap your feet.
The author is not responsible for any unforgettable words.
She hopes this poem can be sung,
By all the neighborhood birds.
So, here's to lovely poetry,
So enjoyable and sweet.
You can have all of the wonders of the world,
Packed in one short sheet.
So go ahead,
Write a poem and be just like me.
You may not really know,
How surprised you'll be!!

Ricki Levitus, Grade 6
Hillcrest Elementary School

What Is Green?

Green is Ellis uniforms
Swinging on the swings or kicking the ball on the
Green top.

Green is when the game is over,
Getting mint chocolate chip ice cream.
Green is a shady tree on grass tickling our feet.

Green is an island with bright
Green palm trees swaying in the breeze with
Green cars driving to the beach.

Green is bathing suits swimming in the ocean waves,
Green is towels lying in the sand feeling the morning sun
Green is happiness…

Julie Missry, Grade 5
The Ellis School

I Love Fall

I wish the leaves always changed their colors.
I wish it wouldn't be so cold in the fall.
I wish the leaves wouldn't fall everywhere.
I wish the leaves spelled my name.
I wish pumpkins could come alive.
I wish you could get free candy in the fall.
I wish the sky would turn orange.
I wish pumpkins grew on trees.
I wish every fall it rained candy
I wish it would always be fall!

Kaitlin Collins, Grade 5
Clearview Elementary School

Harvest and Halloween

I wish pumpkins would carve themselves.
I wish apples were blue.
I wish turkey would be a chicken.
I wish leaves would float too.
I wish gourds would be a pie.
I wish candy was good for you.
I wish scary monsters won't haunt me at night.
I wish crows would not eat corn.
I wish candy was in my mouth.
I wish pumpkins would have no seeds.

Taryn Nemesch, Grade 5
Clearview Elementary School

Green the Color of the World

Green is the color of growing grass,
The color of an evergreen tree,
The color of spring leaves growing on the trees,
The color of spring bulbs pushing their way through the ground.

Green is the color of the recycling bin,
The color of a Philadelphia Eagle's helmet,
The color meaning "go" on a stop light,
The color of the boy's polo shirt for Holy Child Academy,
The color my teacher uses to correct my work.

Luke Radich, Grade 5
Holy Child Academy

Me

Me
Two sisters
Three dead pets
Four amazing, awesome teachers
Five broken toys unplayed with
Six functional TVs in the house
Seven family members living with us now
Eight older cousins that love me so much
Nine Halloween costumes that we want so so much
Ten people who have the swine flu and are sick

Norah Arias, Grade 5
Clearview Elementary School

High Merit Poems – Grades 4, 5 and 6

The Sorrows of Pearl Harbor

One hand in another's
Tears falling down
Men lying silently
Dead on the ground

So many people have died on this day
December 7th, so we pray

People try to comfort
They don't know what to say
Pearl Harbor was vicious
A most tragic day

Oahu, an island of beauty and grace
Show scars from the attack
Of hatred and disgrace

As the Japanese were bombing the shore
The planes kept coming, we could stand no more
America had thus, entered a war

Ashlin Brooks, Grade 6
Pennridge North Middle School

Christmas

Christmas is the time of the year,
When people spread holiday cheer.

Everyone decorates their Christmas tree,
They hang their stockings for all to see.

Christmas smells like cookies baking,
Gingerbread houses that children are making.

The sight of candy canes and mistletoe,
Oh! If only it would snow!

You can feel the excitement of the girls and boys,
As they wait anxiously for Santa's toys.

The voices of the carolers can be heard as they walk along,
While dancing and singing to each and every song.

Laughter dances in the air among family and friends.
I hope the joy of this season never ends!

Erica Fuss, Grade 6
St Jerome Elementary School

My Dog

I feel as sad as my dog being abused when he was little.
And I feel as mad as my dog wanting to chase that kitty cat.
I feel as hungry as my dog wanting to be fed.
I feel as sad as my dog not going in the car.
I feel protected when my dog is around.
Someday my dog won't be with my family and that will be a sad day.

Mike Fedel, Grade 5
Foster Elementary School

Christmas

Christmas
As kids rush down the stairs
Eyes wide with joy and pleasure
The birds chirp outside
Making a loud, but comforting hum
It's like they're saying, "It's Christmas! It's Christmas!"
Awaking all the neighbors, the kids, the parents, the pets,
Everyone thumps down the stairs, grinning ear to ear,
As they gather around the Christmas tree,
Which is decorated head to toe;
Pictures, reindeer, Santa, bulbs, and ornaments of all types,
Each hung delicately in its own place,
They wrap the tree in a dress with glitters and ribbons
The tree is still as the family scrambles around,
Finding presents, taking pictures, having fun,
Once all the presents have been opened and set into piles
The families sit around with hot cocoa and Christmas cookies
Laughing and thanking each other for all the presents
Celebrating the most joyful time of the year,
Christmas.

Rachel Westhoff, Grade 6
Hillcrest Elementary School

Why

Why do they keep me in a cage?
They clip my wings so I cannot fly
They tie my legs so I cannot crawl
They spill oil on my wings till I do not shine
Why have they crippled me so?
They accuse me, though I did nothing wrong
They make me feel like a fish on a hook
I am the fish, they are the fisher, the worm my grandfather's death
They restrict me from telling them my thoughts
Not letting me be as I please.
Everything is plain and dull
Otherworldly compared to Barbados
The rule sits like an ugly monster
On the path to happiness
Blocking my way
Why have they enforced such brutal rules?
Why are their minds so narrow and meek?
Why do they keep me from blissful freedom?
Why do they make me work so hard?
Why have they done this at all?

Vicki Wang, Grade 5
Boyce Middle School

Shy

Shy is violet
It sounds like a very small chick
It smells like a daisy with no bloom
It tastes like a muffin that is soft and smooth
It looks like a small peach
Shy feels like a little pearl

Kaylee Vega, Grade 4
Anne Frank School

Winter

Winter will be here so soon
Along with the snow
And the white shimmery moon.

The beautiful snow sparkles
From the sun's ray.
I can't wait for the
Very first snowy day!

Sledding and snow angels
Made in the snow
Winter is magical,
That I know.
Samantha Flor, Grade 4
Middle Smithfield Elementary School

Spring

The season earth wakes up
Trees open their eyes
Grass reaches for the sky
In a rainbow flowers bloom
Everything is fresh and new
Snow is gone for a bit
Earth is happy with a smile
Animals come out to play
Squirrels run up and down
Bees buzz to and fro
The sun warms all the ground
Spring smells fresh and clean
I love when it is here.
Arianna Yanovich, Grade 5
St Joan of Arc School

Better Future

I'll save the trees
And help the bees

I'll put out recycling cans
And make nonpolluting vans

I'll find trash on the beach
And put it where it is out of reach

I'll look for live animals
And help them strive

When I grow up I'll help the planet
Shannon McNeely, Grade 4
Fairview Elementary School

Blue Is…

As sad as one million teardrops
As happy as one thousand smiles
As quiet as a ladybug
Samantha Arnone, Grade 4
Jefferson Elementary School

Oregon

Many months of memories
Move my mind mightily
I see the mountains
Sparkling and white,
The sunshine's reflection
Oh, what a sight!

I hear the rivers
Gurgle and speak
That swiftly flow off the mountain peak.

I see the elk that roam
Each and every day
And the little calves who love to play.

I hear the sounds
Of whooshing wind in my ear
And I hear the winter breeze
Coming near.
That's the end of a marvelous year!
Brooke Lyn Nissley, Grade 6
Linville Hill Mennonite School

Stars

On a very starry night,
if you look up high,
you'll see the Big Dipper in the sky.
With bright stars surrounding it,
the Little Dipper's right by its side.
But on a cloudy night,
you won't see a star in sight.
If you're up high,
in the sky,
all of the stars will be nearby.
Also in the air,
if you give it a stare,
you may see the brightest star up there.
If you see that star,
you can make a wish,
and see a big flying dish.
Also in the air,
just like candy,
you may see the Milky Way and
many, many stars!
Alyssa Berrios, Grade 4
Middle Smithfield Elementary School

Fall

Leaves falling to the ground
Crunching sounds all around
The breeze is blowing
Through the trees
With colors so bright
Oh, what a beautiful sight!
Elizabeth Heller, Grade 6
St Sebastian Elementary School

Nature

It's about life and air
trees and grass
and flowers everywhere

It's about shining ponds
life in them too
all searching for food

It's about peace and quiet
it has noise too
when animals have a riot

It's about when flowers bloom
and fade in the winter
It's simply amazing!
Joshua Ciccarelli, Grade 5
Pocopson Elementary School

Cheerleading

Cheerleading is fun, cheerleading is cool
I'd rather be at cheerleading than school.
Flexible and athletic girls
Doing flips looking like ice-cream swirls.
Screaming loud like crazy men
The judges will give us a ten.
Go! Crispin Cougars we're number one
We get beat, by none.
Cougars on top
This team will never stop.
The blue, white, black
Crispin will attack!
The cougar knows were not afraid to fight
When we fight are motions are tight!
Julia Vizza, Grade 6
St Jerome Elementary School

The Statue of Liberty

The Statue of Liberty,
Her copper color stands out,
A lovely gift from France,
A gift for us to admire.

Her power and her pride,
Standing by the city's side,
Looking over all of us,
With her book and torch in hand.

The tourists are taking time,
As they're walking by,
In the camera lens I see,
The Statue of Liberty looking back at me.
Samantha Stopyra, Grade 6
St Jerome Elementary School

High Merit Poems – Grades 4, 5 and 6

Having Fun
Put my ball on the tee
Took some practice swings
Lined up on the ball
Swung the club back
Hoped for the best
Sat on a tee
Soaring through the air,
Landed with a thud
It hurt my white shell.
Ricky Poillon, Grade 5
St Anne School

Green
Muggy
Soothing sounds
Bright butterflies
Earth
Trees
Insects
Warm weather
Deep brown soil
Wet
Brenna Mertz, Grade 6
Nazareth Area Intermediate School

October
It is October,
Let's run and scream.
Halloween is here!
Get your costumes.
Time to get some candy.
Let's go party,
Have some fun.
Who cares?
It is October.
Bryanna Hamm, Grade 6
Chichester Middle School

Sam and Pam
There once was a boy named Sam
Who had a girlfriend named Pam
They went on a date
When they were only eight
And he made her a sandwich with jam
John David Lane, Grade 4
St Joseph School

My Dog Jazz
My dog Jazz is crazy.
She loves to bark daily.
She sleeps all day and never wakes.
She may be crazy but she is the dog for me.
There is no other dog like her in the world.
She is the best, unlike all the rest.
Kristin Rudy, Grade 5
East Union Intermediate Center

Brothers
Brothers
Nosy, mean
Snoring, skateboarding, sleeping
Cute, personalities, beautiful, nice
Talking, texting, shopping
Pretty, nosy
Sisters
Kendall Smith, Grade 5
Saint Theresa School

Sports
Football
Fun, energetic
Kicking, hitting, throwing
Helmet, safety, point guard, hoop
Dribbling, shooting, running
Exciting, competitive
Basketball
Tyler Dorcon, Grade 5
Central Elementary School

Football/Soccer
Football
Fast, physical
Running, kicking, throwing
Players, coaches, ball, goalie
Passing, blocking, scoring
Quick, active
Soccer
Tyler Girvin, Grade 5
Central Elementary School

Christmas
Christmas is awesome
You get presents on the day
That Jesus was born

December 25th
We get time with family
Christmas is so fun
Joel Cammarota, Grade 4
McDonald Elementary School

Harvest Day
H appy days
A corns for squirrels
R unning in the leaves
V ase for the table for Thanksgiving
E ating with your family
S tuffing in a turkey
T ablecloths made out of mini turkeys
Lessly Luna Raposo, Grade 5
Clearview Elementary School

Fall to Winter
Fall
breezy, dark
dying, blowing, sweeping
pumpkins, leaves, wind, snow
shoveling, sledding, freezing
dead, cold
Winter
Aron Bair, Grade 5
Hamilton Elementary School

Gymnastics
Gymnastics is so fun,
But there's a lot of work to be done.
Gymnastics rule!
They're very, very cool!
My friends and I all go and do backbends.
When all is said and done,
Gymnastics make me want to run!
Lanaya Kenyon, Grade 4
W R Croman Elementary School

Fall
Pumpkins
Orange, bumpy
Carving, lighting, eating
Jack-o'-lantern, candles, trees, leaves
Raking, jumping, crunching
Brown, orange
Fall
Elijsha Sanchez, Grade 5
Hamilton Elementary School

Fall
Fall
Windy, breezy
Swinging, dancing, rolling
Leaves, Halloween, Thanksgiving, holiday
Slumping, falling, dropping
Cold, freezing
November
Ruhama Lamure, Grade 5
Hamilton Elementary School

Peace
Peace is like a can,
It can be crushed;
but takes years to decay.
It can be shipped to a factory
and transformed into liquid,
only to be born to the world
in a new form.
Anna McDonough, Grade 5
Copper Beech Elementary School

Thanksgiving Is…
Spending time with family.
The extra stuffing on my plate.
The smell of turkey in the oven.
Conversation with relatives.
Falling asleep on the couch.
JJ Grencer, Grade 6
Moravian Academy Middle School

Thanksgiving Is
Spending time with friends and family.
Sharing meals on Thanksgiving.
Playing football in the backyard.
Talking and laughing with friends.
Stuffing turkey and pie in your mouths.
Grace Marmaras, Grade 6
Moravian Academy Middle School

Pirates
Pirates
Mean, rude
Fights, duels, battles
They are gold robbers.
Buccaneers
Luke Milhimes, Grade 4
Lincoln Elementary School

Walking Through the Woods
Going on a walk
Through the wonderful, cool woods
Close my eyes to think
Happy as the breeze goes by
Relax, I feel the wild life.
Claire Schumann, Grade 6
Ross Elementary School

Grandparents Are…
Another source of love.
Another source of influence.
Another source of happiness.
Another source of support.
The primary source of wisdom.
Avani Gandhi, Grade 6
Moravian Academy Middle School

Thanksgiving Is…
Inviting family members over to eat.
Playing football in the backyard.
Watching the Macy's Thanksgiving parade.
Eating the best turkey ever.
Cooking with my mom.
Cory Haldeman, Grade 6
Moravian Academy Middle School

Happiness
Happiness is fireworks booming on the 4th of July
Happiness is a rainbow that comes out after a storm
Happiness is running through the finish line in a race
Happiness is yellow like the sun when it comes out
Happiness tastes like burgers that are so tasty they are chocolate in your mouth
Happiness smells like fresh gingerbread cookies
Happiness sounds like fireworks in the sky
Happiness feels like a pile of confetti
Happiness looks like a huge explosion of joy
Happiness makes me want to jump as high as a mountain
Happiness is a big brass bass drum that bangs in a marching band
Alexander Britt, Grade 6
West Allegheny Middle School

Creativity
Creativity is a colorful candle on your birthday cake
Creativity is the sun shining through the clouds on a warm summer day
Creativity is the friendly 'tweet' of a canary
Creativity is yellow like a flower in full bloom
Creativity tastes like a strawberry dipped in pure sugar
Creativity smells like a wisp of imagination, entering your nostrils
Creativity sounds like the tiny 'yip' of a puppy on a lonely day
Creativity feels like a tiny little river rock, polished by the stream
Creativity looks like a butterfly spreading its wings to fly
Creativity makes me feel as colorful as a chameleon
Creativity is a rainbow of imagination
Tori Volk, Grade 6
West Allegheny Middle School

Happiness
Happiness is a big bag of cotton candy
Happiness is a gold medal winning in gymnastics
Happiness is lights shining down from Heaven
Happiness is like a wonderful strawberry, red and bright
Happiness tastes like sweet apples off of an apple tree
Happiness smells like fresh cookies out of the oven
Happiness sounds like squeaks of mice in my house
Happiness feels like a soft, silky, smooth blanket
Happiness looks like smiles on people's faces when they win the lottery
Happiness makes me joyful and energetic
Happiness is like nothing you have ever seen
Kayla P. Shoup, Grade 6
West Allegheny Middle School

The Eyes of a Liger
I am a liger, with the eye of a tiger.
I have big feet with claws like teeth.
Living in the jungle is fun, there many fields for me to run.
My favorite food is meat, it's such a healthy treat.
I am unique and very rare, hunting me would not be fair.
I stand to be very tall, in the cat family I am bigger than all.
My eyes allow me to see without light, this keeps me safe all through the night.
Some say the lion is the king, but I am grateful for everything.
Kayla Remshard, Grade 6
Interboro GATE Program

I Dreamed
I dreamed
I was Shane Victorino
Playing center field
Hitting second in the line up
    happily
Nolan Updegraff, Grade 4
Fishing Creek Elementary School

Christmas Time
Jingle bells ringing
Chopping down the Christmas tree
Tasty hot cocoa
Homemade cookies for Santa
Choosing, wrapping special gifts
Madison Regan, Grade 5
Holy Martyrs Elementary School

Old Orchard Beach
Pebble colored sand
Clear blue sky, fluffy white clouds
Riding boogie board
Picnic lunch with grandparents
Surfing the waves 'til sundown
Joseph Quinn, Grade 5
Holy Martyrs Elementary School

Tuna
Tuna
Fast and vicious
Cousins to albacore
Nothing can escape its strong clutch!
Tasteful
Bernard Lindinger, Grade 4
McKinley Elementary School

Ladybug
I dreamed
I was a lady bug
On a bright, green leaf
Eating aphids
Quickly
Morgan Wagner, Grade 4
Fishing Creek Elementary School

5 Things I Like About Christmas
Joyous carolers
Decorations glowing bright
Festive Christmas firs
Gift-giving, sleigh bells ringing
Savory roasted turkey
Corey Lavery, Grade 5
Holy Martyrs Elementary School

Snow
Silent, watery flakes,
Falling to the Earth's surface,
Silently falling down, down, down.
No one could ever hear it falling,
Unless you see it yourself.
It comes unexpectedly,
Unless you watch the Weather Channel.
It's relaxing to see it come down,
While the kids are waiting at doors,
Getting ready to play.
It's always fun to catch them on your tongue,
Letting it melt as if drinking fresh water.
Snowflakes,
Covering the rooftops of cars and grass
Forming a white, fluffy pillow
On the ground and on houses.
It's over after a few days.
Gone, just like that!
Forming little, wet mud puddles from melted snow.
Although, kids are waiting for next year for more snow to come and fall.
Sabrina Vicente, Grade 6
Hillcrest Elementary School

The Dreads of Wethersfield
I'm a macaw with color, but, they paint me gray.
I'm the odd one out and they make me fit in.
I'm an elegant ixora and they make me wither.
I'm a fish that swam out of ordinary waters.
Wethersfield has pulled me in and there is no way out.
    I do not belong here…
I'm the ground and they step on me.
I try to find the light but, when I do they pull me back into the darkness.
If I find something I like they destroy it.
Everyone stares at me, as if I turned orange.
I'm in an atmosphere of weariness.
Wethersfield swallows me into it's dullness.
    I should not be here…
They are trying to make me just like them…
    Just like them…
    Dull and gray…
    Dark and weary…
    All the same…
Wethersfield is not where I should be.
    This is a nightmare.
Alyssa Perry, Grade 5
Boyce Middle School

Autumn
I can hear the wind swirling in the towering majestic pine trees.
I can smell the damp decomposing leaves settling around me.
I can feel the green mossy carpet under my frosty feet.
I can taste the chilly fresh water from the old-fashioned pump house.
I can see the calm beauty of the Pocono Mountains.
    Autumn is here!
Hope Wallace, Grade 4
Colonial Elementary School

Blue

Blue is more than a color, it is a constant inspiration.
I know blue as a feeling — it makes me feel the tear I shall not shed.
When I look upon blue, I see an ocean of possibilities, and obstacles.
Blue is complicated, yet simple.
It is happy and sad.
It is life, death, everything and nothing.
One of the simple things of blue is the aroma — it's so it has me wonderfully dismayed.
It has the scent of the first drop of spring rain floating gently down into the grass, waiting for the morning dew.
However, in blue there is jealousy that comes from RED! RED is evil blood you may call it.
Blue goes around righting its wrongs and keeping it bottled up with the rest of the scumbags that threaten Blue's peaceful world.
However, Blue cannot do this without a partner and that is green. Blue makes green grow. Blue gives green life, and green gives blue a purpose — a purpose to be everything, a purpose to be BLUE!!!!

Leah Franklin, Grade 6
Reiffton School

Joy

Joy is coming down the stairs on Christmas morning — knowing there are many gifts under the tree.
Joy is the feeling you get after receiving a good grade on a test.
Joy is knowing you have one more week of school before summer vacation starts.
Joy is the orange color of the warm sunshine.
Joy tastes like the soft sweetness of cotton candy at the carnival.
Joy smells like an apple pie cooking in the oven.
Joy sounds like the beginning of the day as the sun rises and the birds are chirping.
Joy feels like the soft fur of my two rabbits as I pet them.
Joy looks like the soft fluffy clouds on a spring day as I look up.
Joy makes me very happy.
Joy is one of my favorite words and names, as it is my sister's middle name.

Armand W. Petito, Grade 6
West Allegheny Middle School

Beauty Is a Baby

Have you ever stopped and noticed a baby's joy?
Everything makes them smile, even the simplest toy.
From a rattle to a doll, to a cooking pot, everything makes them smile a lot,
You can't help but blow on their belly, or give them a kiss even when they're covered in jelly.
From their delicate cheeks, to their soft, smooth hair, you just can't help but stare.
From their hands to their feet, to their eyes so small, nothing in the world could beat that at all.
And now guess what? They're starting to walk.
And before you know it, you hear them talk.
They used to drink out of a baby cup, but now they're starting to grow up.
They are getting so very smart, but you know they'll never leave your heart.
There's lots of words that describe beauty, but the one that does it best is BABY.

Chloe Bock, Grade 5
Chestnut Hill Elementary School

The Rain

A cloud is overhead as I head for home.
I sit in my room as the rain starts to knock at my window.
Hours pass.
I watch the barren streets.
Now I listen to the rain a little closer…
It sounds like a percussion band on my roof!
I look at the rain and see that it is dancing to the sound of thunder and the flashes of lightning.
So I sit watching closely, and listening attentively to what the rain has to say.

Jarod Wingert, Grade 6
Infinity Charter School

High Merit Poems – Grades 4, 5 and 6

The Season of the Year
Winter is the season that starts and ends a year,
It is gonna be cold so don't be bare.
Christmas is in winter so get some wrapper,
Christmas is not a time for an ear of corn,
But it's the time that Jesus is born.

Spring is next and the flowers bloom,
It's getting warm so get out of the room.
Birds start singing and the river starts flowing,
The tree is full of leaves and the snow takes its leave.

Summer comes and the school leaves,
Time to go swimming and have some fun.
The woods are green on the way to Kennywood,
It's gonna be a blast you know it would.

Fall comes next so be prepared,
It's gonna be cold so don't be bare.
The leaves' colors change and the critters hide.
The wind is blowing and Thanksgiving is coming,
So go eat a turkey with your family.
That would bring us back to winter.
Ken Lin, Grade 6
Immaculate Conception School

Happiness
Happiness is straight A's at school
Happiness is an aquamarine, cloudless sky
Happiness is a little kitten being helped off the streets
Happiness is the color violet
Happiness tastes like a sweet, delicious candy cane
Happiness smells like a fresh, fragrant flower
Happiness sounds like the hushed river in the distance
Happiness feels like my soft and furry dog
Happiness looks like a speckled sunset
Happiness makes me very excited
Happiness is the best thing in the world
Abigail Scheers, Grade 6
West Allegheny Middle School

First Day of School
It's about the one awesome first day,
With backpacks flopping,
Mothers sobbing,

It's about new pencils,
With new learning utensils,
To start the year,

It's about a new grade,
With children afraid,
Of having no friends,

It's about the best day ever…First Day of School!
Dina Spyropoulos, Grade 5
Pocopson Elementary School

Fall Time
An eruption of changing colors appear
Green, red, yellow, and orange all around me.
I hear around me a chorus of birds chirping with their souls.
I walk through the path and hear the rustling of leaves.
STOMP! STOMP! CRACKLE!
The wind blows on the tree leaves and make an excellent noise.
I smell the rain.
The clouds were in the sky and it was damp,
so I knew it was going to rain.
It always smells like that before it rains.
I wonder when the rain will come?
I cannot wait till next fall!!
Ashley Tarnoff, Grade 6
Pennridge North Middle School

Beachy Days
The sun is beating
The sand white and burning
The waves crashing and roaring
As if a lion controlled the seven seas
Little children scream and shout
When the cold, ferocious, ice blue waves come about
The shells in all different shapes, sizes, and colors
Laying on the ground with each other
Sand crabs nip at your toes
That's when I know
It's another ordinary day at the beach.
Stacy DiCandilo, Grade 6
E T Richardson Middle School

Sky
The sky is beautiful
It is cloudy and gray
Clear, blue and sunny
It renews the earth with water
Sometimes it booms and lights up
The sky sends us a cool breeze on hot summer days
It allows us to fly our helicopters and airplanes
Birds have enough space to fly freely and nest in trees
What else can the sky do for us
Maybe the future holds a key I am not sure
Looking up! I wonder what's beyond the sky
Joseph Popp, Grade 6
St Jerome Elementary School

Do You Ever Wonder?
Do you ever wonder
If winter and summer are friends far apart
I bet they are
Because they have lots of heart
Even though they're different
Winter snow falls on the ground and summer kids run all around
Yes, they're different
But friends I know for sure that they're friends far apart
Rachel Larkin, Grade 5
Saint Theresa School

Bells
Some bells are big
Some bells are tiny
Some bells are very sparkly
And sometimes they are shiny
Some ring on a door
And some wake you from a snore!
Some bells sing a song
And sometimes they gong
Some ring the phone
And others tell you when it's time to go home
But the best of all, whether big or small,
Is the one that brings you in for dinner y'all!
Blake Thomas, Grade 5
East Union Intermediate Center

Soccer
I love to play soccer, it's a great game.
Once you give it a try, you may feel the same.
It's a challenging sport, where you can't use your hands
Except if you're the goalie, then you can.
You must use your feet to dribble the ball,
And hope that the ref doesn't make a bad call.
Everyone works as a team to protect their goal,
But you must stay in position and block all the holes.
This sport takes real skill and endurance, too,
I'm sure that is something you already knew.
But the best feeling is when you score on the other team.
That is the greatest feeling in the world.
Parker Waynar, Grade 5
East Union Intermediate Center

Cheerleading
C hichester competition cheerleading is the team for me
H igh, yes I soar when I toe touch and pike
E xcellent sweet; that routine was a treat
E mbarrassing, omg…it's so embarrassing if you mess up
R emember the routine to help the team
L oud — the crowd and the music sound so loud
E nergetic is the only way to be
A mazing if you win first place
D efeat the other teams
I ncredible roars the crowd
N ever give up
G reat — it's over and we won!
Monique Oliver, Grade 6
Chichester Middle School

Love
Nobody knows what love really is
all we know is love is really big
there are lots of ways to say you love
but the only one who knows is the one above
love is pain, lust and trust
love is really big
Jamil Sessoms, Grade 6
John G Whittier School

October Joys
Showers of fireballs flutter off the tree,
praying to God and hoping to be free.
In the silvery light of a moonlit night,
the leaves will come and go, in the wind's crisp blow.

The old spider is in the corner, what a shock,
looking over the house like a grandfather clock.
His masterpiece comes to life as he weaves,
but he soon knows he will have to leave.

The bats fly by and all around,
then abruptly diving towards the ground.
They fly to a tree and hang upside down,
their faces looking horrific with a frown.

October is fun and full of joy,
for anyone girl or boy.
With celebrations and special occasions,
October my favorite season.
John Werynski, Grade 6
Pennridge North Middle School

Season Fun
WINTER, SPRING, SUMMER and FALL
I don't know which one is the greatest of all but let's start with FALL.
Leaves start to change color and fall on me with a simple breeze.

WINTER is next, the cold has come,
A snowball fight could be a ball,
Building a snowman can make you feel alive.

SPRING is here and it's a real down fall,
So stay inside and run around,
Play a game; all of them are the same,
On a rainy day.

The best season is here,
SUMMER is the best part of the year.
Let's take a big breath and cheer
Doing a cannonball in a pool under the sun.

That's why this poem is called 'SEASON FUN.'
Brandon Lawryk, Grade 6
Immaculate Conception School

Friendship
Friendship…the angel on your shoulder,
the everlasting God…in your heart.
Friendship…the song that you hear,
the song that remains the same, the melody of the soul.
Friendship…the chorus of the well being,
the band of the psyche.
Friendship…as we live our sometimes troubled lives,
our friendship lives on.
Declan Ayala, Grade 5
Copper Beech Elementary School

High Merit Poems – Grades 4, 5 and 6

Thanksgiving Time!

I hear chuckles and my bellowing family fighting over outstanding food
I can smell smoky, strong turkey with rice white mashed potatoes and crimson red sauce
I see my family splashing food over our stained table
I taste the fresh home made blueberry pie as it boils in my fruity mouth
I feel the smooth, steamy turkey as I pull the sticky, slimly wishbone trying to pull the largest piece

Nicole Esposito, Grade 4
Colonial Elementary School

Flippers

penguins slide on their stomachs and they don't fly. into the water they go diving diving to get some fish, no not trout. when the fun is done they get up get out. they go to bed with a sleepy head and get up and do it again, but this time a little different. they do it for fun they play and run. this time when they go to bed they jump. then they say good night go to bed.

Alexis Graef, Grade 6
Hopewell Memorial Jr High School

The Sports I Play

I play sports all the time even when rain clouds cover the sun. I always try to score a few points to help my team out so we can win the game. When I score a goal or two, the crowd, my team, and the coaches go wild. If we win the game, the team gets excited so we are all happy because we are still undefeated.

Devin Wayne, Grade 6
Hopewell Memorial Jr High School

That's Just Me!

In football I have no talent or taste,
But in a footrace, I can win first place.

If you give me a book, I'll read it front to end
For every book is my faithful friend.

In folding paper, I have a knack.
Soon for my origami, I'll need a rack.

I love it so when flowers bloom
For they take away the winter gloom.

I am full of art and creativity.
And questions fill inside of me.

If I read about Albert Einstein
I, unlike others, would not cry or whine.
For I think what he does is quite fun
Even though people doubted him when he was young.

Leonardo da Vinci was a great Renaissance man,
And for his artwork, I am a great fan

If the universe can go on forever, how?
I doubt anyone will know, not ever not now.

Those are my feelings, and you can't make me change any.
And to change them all would be hard, considering there are many!

Amir Gold, Grade 5
Southern Lehigh Intermediate School

Happiness

Happiness is joyful jolly yellow on a sun shining day
   in South Carolina with the family
   in Sunny Dale Park singing
   spontaneous special songs.

It looks like a sunflower on a spring day in June
   while playing jump-rope
   on the sidewalk with friends.

Happiness tastes like sweet small Snickers on an island
   covered with palm trees
   with the family on Miami beach.

It smells like fresh baked warm cookies
   right out of the oven
   while baking a pound more in the kitchen.

Happiness sounds like beautiful boiling music to my ears
   on the Fourth of July
   at my grandmother's house.

It feels like a magnificent day on a happy hill
   that can make anybody feel
   like a wonderful person.

Nicole Galvis, Grade 6
Our Lady of Ransom School

Blue Is…

as drippy as the rain falling down from the sky.
as salty as the ocean's blue waves.
as soft as a fluffy stuffed teddy bear.

Alice Tremblay, Grade 4
Jefferson Elementary School

Five Kittens

Five kittens, two weeks old.
Eyes not open, but bold.
Two are tan, one is black.
Two are gray, that's a fact.
They all pile on each other.
Which one's a sister? Which one's a brother?
The kittens are tiny, they fit in your hand.
Why someone left them, I don't understand.
They're in a box in the barn,
But they don't have a toy ball of yarn.
They're cute, they're soft and lots of fun.
Too bad my dad won't let me have one!

Megan Monteforte, Grade 4
Lathrop Street Elementary School

Snow

I am glistening drops of white happiness,
the sight of me makes children happy
they want to go get sleds
and drink hot chocolate,
yes yes it is true that when I come
the children hum nice tunes
oh yes very soon Santa Claus will be coming
but until then we will watch cartoons on TV,
he will be there when you are tight asleep
he will leave presents for you when we say please.

Can you guess what I am?

Jorge Reyes, Grade 6
Immaculate Conception School

On a Cold Morning

If I were green,
I would be an evergreen tree waiting to be a Christmas tree.
If I were green,
I would be rich, green grass with dew on top.
If I were green,
I would be leaves swaying in the wind.
If I were green,
I would be a praying mantis sitting on a flower petal.
If I were green,
I would be a frog waiting to catch flies.
If I were green,
I would be Mother Nature's favorite color.

Nichole Heller, Grade 5
Holy Child Academy

Halloween Is Such a Fright!

My Halloween favorite is apple bobbing,
Also when the ghosts come out and start popping.
The Jack-o'-lanterns glow in the night,
Some of them are such a fright.
All of a sudden I jump in the air,
Standing in front of me is a witch with green hair!

Megan Dano, Grade 4
Cathedral School of St Catharine of Siena

Football

F is for football, my favorite sport to play
O is for out of bounds
O is for the "oohs" and "ahhs" when the big plays happen
T is for the TOUCHDOWN!
B is for blowout games
A is for the AFL
L is for the laces on the ball
L is for an unexpected loss

Michael Lo, Grade 6
Chichester Middle School

Football

F riends join to play the game
O utstanding fans cheer as I run the touchdown
O ld men showing up to watch the game
T ackling people left and right until they fumble the ball
B all flying over your head as a touchdown pass was thrown
A ll players groan after the touchdown pass
L osing or winning — it's always fun to play
L ucky catches, lucky runs, scaling touchdowns.

Billy Whelan, Grade 6
Chichester Middle School

Yellow in Nature

Yellow is the sun shining down on us.
Yellow is the lemons on the lemon trees ready to be picked.
Yellow is yellow birds chirping in the sunset.
Yellow is bees buzzing in and out of flowers.
Yellow are the leaves in autumn falling to the ground.
Yellow is people eating ripe, soft bananas.
Yellow is little kids picking bright yellow flowers.
Yellow is sunflowers growing in a meadow where people picnic.

Gillian Chestnut, Grade 5
Holy Child Academy

Pumpkins

P umpkin pie
U sing a rake to rake up leaves
M ums blooming
P laying kickball with my friends
K ids jumping in the leaves
I n the oven, a yummy pumpkin pie is cooking
N asty goo when you are carving pumpkins
S chool is starting.

Natalie Weston, Grade 5
Clearview Elementary School

Love

Love is like another world to me
where everything is free
no problems, no drama
an everlasting life that's yours to keep
it's like a roller coaster, up and down, side to side
but it can be anything you want it to be.

Theresa Council, Grade 6
John G Whittier School

It Is a Boneless Buffalo Wing Day!
It is a boneless buffalo wing day
Going to Mad Mex
Smelling the spicy sauce
Nice, crispy, sizzling from the grill
Blue cheese and ranch sauce
Healthy green celery
Taking a bite, bringing it to my mouth…
"BAM"
Dropped on the hot wing
Bone dropped vibrating the floor
Take the next one
Put the wing in my mouth…
It is a boneless buffalo wing day!
Toriah Morea Hannah-Lee, Grade 6
Pennridge North Middle School

Movie Day
Today is a movie day
Feeling tired and lazy
Smelling the buttery popcorn
Tasting the sweet and sour candy
Touching the ice cold coke
Snuggling up to the fuzzy PJs
Hearing pats of rain hitting the window
Watching the TV screen different colors
Thinking about the next movie
Cuddling up to the warmest blanket
Listening to the action-packed movie
Feeling your eyelids closing slowly
And that will end another movie day
Kellyn Nicole Puchalski, Grade 6
Pennridge North Middle School

The Happy Thanksgiving
At Thanksgiving
everybody comes around
walking, talking in the kitchen
watching TV, playing around,
helping cooking, making vegetables,
chicken, rice, mac & cheese
walking around
talking about what you are thankful for
your stomach is growling
you circle around the table
pushing yourself in the chair
sharing the food,
it is delicious.
Tinijia Witherspoon-McClam, Grade 4
Wissahickon Charter School

Sharks
Swimming in the sea,
Very beautiful to watch,
Have razor sharp teeth.
Noah Freeman, Grade 5
East Union Intermediate Center

Apple Pie
The apple falls,
From upon the tree.
And who it seeks?
Oh, look it's me!
In my hand,
I run hard and fast.
To the land of Thanksgiving,
And have a pie at last.
Shannon Shawgo, Grade 6
Hopewell Memorial Jr High School

Thankful
T hinking things through
H elping our free country
A lways being safe
N ever thinking negatively
K nowing what's best
F looding with pride
U nforgettable wars
L oving and caring
Alexis Halvin, Grade 4
Fairview Elementary School

Softball
S portsmanship
O utfield
F ast pitch
T eam
B atting
A ll star
L eading
L ove for the game.
Brittany Dengler, Grade 5
East Union Intermediate Center

Faithful
F ighting for our country
A ll are tough
I n our hearts
T ruthful
H aving good intentions
F ull of pureness
U nable to lose
L et the war be over
Kody Todd, Grade 4
Fairview Elementary School

Blue
Blue is peace
Blue is the tear coming out
Of your eyes
Blue is a heart broken
Blue is someone who cries
Blue is someone who you think of that died
Jelissa Brown, Grade 4
Wissahickon Charter School

White Thanksgiving
Cold
    white
        frozen
winter wonderland
sparkles in the sunlight.

Tiny
    cold
        specs
of white make the sky
look blank.

But
    inside
        we
sit by the fire
warming our hands.

A delicious
    turkey
        smell
fills the
humid air.
Maggie Mayer, Grade 5
Falk Laboratory School

Three Wonders of Nature
The Sea
I wash the ocean shore,
I lay on the ocean floor.
The waves are my beauty,
The current is my duty.
The sea life is within me,
The sea — that's what they named me.

The Night
The king of my land, the moon,
My songster, the midnight loon.
With me one sees the North Star,
My beauty's the fairest by far.
When you can see starlight,
You'll know it's me, the night.

The Winter
A blanket of white I bring,
The snowbird is here to sing.
A season of cold and frost,
The warmth of summer lost.
I am winter as you see,
A wondrous filigree.
Molly Wells, Grade 5
The American Academy

Thank You

You make fear go away
You see people die and have a straight face
You kill people without a second thought
You see blood and don't faint
You look at death in the face and say, "Hello"
You watch people fall and step over them
You want to make a difference
Thank you for doing this

When do you sleep?
When do you eat?
Are you scared of dying?
You do this for a reason, Thank you.

When you do this, you have appreciation
I thank you
For the things you do
For one last time, Thank you.

Madeleine Whitmore, Grade 6
Pennridge North Middle School

Candy for One Quarter

As I get my allowance for the week
My mother gives me one little quarter
But one little quarter gets me
one glamorous piece of candy
I walk to the candy shop with my coin
As I walk into the shop
I look at all the candy
My mouth starts to water with the taste
My mind gets overwhelmed with what type of candy I should choose
Should I buy some Jolly Ranchers?
the small Hershey's chocolate bar?
I scoop a quarters worth of Skittles
and pay
Each piece tastes like heaven
I go home and wonder
which kind of candy
I will choose
next week.

Garrett Green, Grade 5
Lincoln Elementary School

The Cockatoo

He sits on the morning prowl,
Awaiting his gourmet French toast.
He will wake with the loudest screech.
It sounds like nails scratching on a chalkboard.
And if he's missing he's probably playing,
Under his mile high stacked papers.
How does he do it?
He makes it out of paper.
We say the Tent o' terror.
That's my cockatoo Sinbad.

Dylan Brown, Grade 6
William Penn Middle School

Love

Love is the scent of fresh cookies in Grandma's house
Love is a soothingly warm walk on the beach
Love is a cup of simmering hot cocoa on a winter day
Love is florid like a shiny new ruby
Love tastes like chocolate in a s'more while you're camping
Love smells like fragrant, fresh cut flowers
Love sounds like a kitten's purr, nestling in a warm fuzzy blanket
Love feels like a fluffy puppy cuddling a new toy up next to you
Love looks like elegant swans dancing around a fountain
Love makes me smile as if I was on a roller coaster upside down
Love is bright and cheery like a rainbow
Love is the first smile of a newborn baby
Love is the joy of having a new pet

Allison Banas, Grade 6
West Allegheny Middle School

Invisible Friend

I am the wind,
I am your friend tapping you on your shoulder.
I am the wind,
You can't see me, smell me, taste me, but you feel me for sure.
I am the wind,
I'm chilly but my heart is warm.
I am the wind,
I call your name, whoosh…
I am the wind…
Fierce,
Loving,
Gentle,
Wind.

Taylor Brown, Grade 5
The Ellis School

The Sea

The sea is a cruel thing
Swoosh it goes as it slams into a rock like a hammer
Making foam like a snarling dog
It floods coastal areas destroying houses and buildings
Its waves are horses racing for dry land
Only to trip on each other and crash into the sand
Even though it is violent, it is a home for creatures, big and small
The sea gives me a sense of peace
I'm in awe at its majestic sight
The sea, the sea
How dangerous it may be
It is a home for creatures with life
Just like you and me.

Adrian Toledo, Grade 6
St Jerome Elementary School

Bright Yellow Sun

The stone bounced down the hill.
It had fallen from the mountain above.
Splash! It carved the water in the bright yellow sun.

Casey Fox, Grade 5
Nether Providence Elementary School

High Merit Poems – Grades 4, 5 and 6

Halloween

Jack-o'-lanterns, lamp of light,
Trick-or-treat through the night.
Be as sneaky as a cat,
But please don't chase a rat!

Creepy crawlies, quiet as a breeze,
But please don't feel at ease.
Goblins at a fire, bright as the sun,
Through the crackling of the flames,
You can hear the witches hum.

Marissa Herzig, Grade 5
McKinley Elementary School

My House at Night

My house at night is such a fright!
Once you open the doors there is no light.
The first step you take will be your last.
Do not run so fast.
If you dare to go in my house,
It's as frightening as a gigantic mouse.
When you go into the un-living room,
You will see me, and face your doom!
So take it from me,
Do not go into my house!
EVER!

Hannah Corson, Grade 5
McKinley Elementary School

World Peace

Everyone holding hands,
No more wars,
No more fighting,
Drop your weapons,
Step away from them,
Go across the battlefield,
Embrace your opponent,
Love,
Peace,
Happiness,
The war has ended.

Isabella Roll, Grade 6
Ross Elementary School

Confident

C oming for victory
O n the ball
N ever giving up
F all down with pride
I n positive moods
D oes it the right way
E veryone does their best
N ever want to lose
T he best at what they do

Collin Olash, Grade 4
Fairview Elementary School

Skateboards

S ummer is the best time to skateboard.
K ick-flipping all day.
A wonderful lifestyle.
T otal control of the board.
E very day is a blast.
B ring your boards.
O pen skateparks all day.
A lways wear a helmet.
R ushing to the skatepark.
D oing railgrinds.

Vincent Sammartino, Grade 5
East Union Intermediate Center

Candy Cane

C heery
A shepherd's staff
N aughty or nice
D elicious decorations
Y ummy

C hristmas traditions
A lways different
N ever the same
E nough is never enough!

Nicole Stepp, Grade 5
Saint Theresa School

Scott O'Dell Books

Makes you see
What you read
Funny things here and there
Makes me laugh
Are you aware?
Imagination fills the air
Can't stop reading
It's too amazing
Can't believe everything
That I read

Alexis Wilson-Ussack, Grade 5
East Union Intermediate Center

The Argument of My Book

I sing of soccer and softball,
flowers and nature,
of holidays and my birthday,
animals and bugs,
I sing of school and college
of my family and friends,
baseball and football,
and also care and respect,
empathy and cooperation,
and also LOVE and HAPPINESS.

Emily Cantrell, Grade 5
Copper Beech Elementary School

Candy Corn

C andy corn is as bright as the sun.
A wesome and the best treat,
N ever have enough,
D ancing on your tongue,
Y ellow and orange,

C andy corn tastes awesome.
O utstanding treat you can ever get!
R ockin' in your mouth!
N ow I am going to get more candy corn.

Lindsay Fullerton, Grade 5
McKinley Elementary School

The Soccer Game

Friday night lights shining in my eyes
As I step on the field, I hear the cries
Of the hometown fans
As they cheer on their very own Rams.
As the whistle blows
I am on my toes.
I struck the ball,
I knew the goalie would fall.
I had scored
And my fans roared!

Jack Austin, Grade 5
Foster Elementary School

Dance Parties

As you dance across the floor,
tryin' to dance forever more.
As the disco ball spins around,
make sure you aren't on the ground.
As you rise to the top,
make sure you never stop.
You are up on the stage,
try not to let out rage.
Keep on dancin' never stop,
because you are on the top.

Luke Keyser, Grade 4
Lincoln Elementary School

Mariah

Mariah
Funny, shy, smart
Sister of Danny
Who feels happy about summer
Who needs books, family, and friends
Who shares toys, hugs, and friendship
Who'd like to see my cousin
Who dreams of teaching
A student of Miss Tadlock
Yah Yah

Mariah Santana, Grade 4
Wickersham Elementary School

A New Hope
A new hope is coming.
A new hope of peace, grace, and love.
A new hope that the wars will end and peace will prevail.
A new hope that everyone will get along.
A new hope that everyone will have a happy life.
A new hope that everyone will have a family.
A new hope that the world will be a better place.

Michael Petruccelli, Grade 4
Jefferson Elementary School

Friends
Friends and laughing.
You will find me laughing with my friends all the time.
We see them every day, and every day we laugh together.
The background changes all the time: her house, mine.
But no matter where we go together, we always share a laugh.
We will never be quiet whenever we're together.
Friends forever!

Tess Hallman, Grade 6
Hillcrest Elementary School

My Grandparents Are...
Willing to care for me when I'm sick.
Always volunteering to help with homework.
Cooking really great meals.
Greeting me happily whether it's at the bus stop or the airport.
So loving and understanding.
Always making me feel better!
Loving me no matter what.

Madeline Kirkwood, Grade 6
Moravian Academy Middle School

Christmas Dinner
At Christmas dinner,
They give us lots of good food.
And after that,
You will get lots of presents from your parents.
And after that,
You can open all your presents,
And have fun!

Gabrielle Buck, Grade 4
W R Croman Elementary School

Phillies
I went to the Phillies game!
I was as happy as a clown.
The sun went down
And the huge lights burst on like the sunrise.
Then the game began.
The fireworks were like shimmering stars.
What a wonderful, fantastic night!!!

Olivia Barbacane, Grade 5
McKinley Elementary School

Surprised
Surprised is strawberry pink
It sounds like red berries that are ready to be picked
It smells like a pink peach cake for a happy birthday party
It tastes like a white wedding cake with flowers all around it
It looks like a yellow world with horses
Surprised feels like love and joyfulness

Victoria Yujanova, Grade 4
Anne Frank School

Green
Green looks like some parts of the ocean,
Green sounds like leaves flowing in the wind,
Green feels like grass between your toes,
Green tastes like yummy string beans,
Green smells like fresh cut grass.

Shannon Kutos, Grade 5
Clearview Elementary School

Love
Love is what makes this world what it is now,
so let's all pitch in and make this world beautiful.
Why don't we stop all the fighting and arguing,
put aside our differences and make this world unstoppable.
Because love is what makes this world what it is now.

Diana Alvarado, Grade 4
Middle Smithfield Elementary School

Veteran
B old when fighting
R eliable all the time
A s tough as an animal fighting for freedom
V eterans are heroes
E very veteran is brave!

Zack Renda, Grade 4
Fairview Elementary School

The Fuzzy Little Duckling
The fuzzy little duckling
Following her mother through the glistening water
At the start of a warm summer day
On the surface of the shimmering pond
She knows she'll be a mom someday!

Alec Duquette, Grade 5
Ross Elementary School

Magical
Stars, stars
Shining so bright.
They will light up the night
And lead the way in a sparkling twinkling light.
Across the sky are beautiful stars.

Annie Iezzi, Grade 5
Maxwell Elementary School

No More War

You just heard a crack
You know you're under attack.

All you see is people on the ground
Your friend is nowhere to be found.

You yell, "Retreat!"
With a loud shriek!

Then you hear a boom
You think this room will be your tomb.

All of a sudden you see an open door
In walks a friendly soldier shouting, "No more war!"

You cheer, the smoke clears,
You're so happy you're in tears!

Nico D'Alesandro, Grade 5
Foster Elementary School

Thank You

Thank you for risking your life for others
For leaving your family
For leaving loved ones

Thank you for giving me freedom
To let me make my own choices
Freedom to make my own decisions
To choose my own way

Thank for great-grandfather
Thank you for fighting for my country
For standing in death's way just so we could be free

War is death
You fought for us anyway
You may be gone
You'll never be forgotten

Dalton Wayne Hunsberger, Grade 6
Pennridge North Middle School

Bravery

Soldiers are very brave.
They fight for our rights.
They show safety, seriousness and spirit.
They stay up through the dark, damp night.
The big guns they use go BOOM!
They feel tired, scared and worn.
They love their country like parents love a child.
The wonderful day it was born.
The soldiers are a wall.
They never will fall down.
They will fight till the war is won.
Our freedom is still found.

Ben Bruce, Grade 6
West Allegheny Middle School

Summer Days

Why do summer days fly by?
Like when you're having a dream that you're president
and then you just wake up and you can't get it back.
Or when you're waiting for a roller coaster forever and you get on,
strap yourself in and then it's already done.
That is how summer feels.
I love the feeling of the mud in your feet and you get that squish,
or roasting marshmallows in your backyard with laughter and fun.
Is it that time goes by faster or summer is something that we have
that's never meant to last?
Summer Days, oh Summer Days
Why they fly by.

Alex O'Brien, Grade 6
Hillcrest Elementary School

The Winter Season

The winter season,
I love it for more than one reason
It is very cold, it isn't warm
It is the season Christ was born
A lot of kids like this season, I know
All they want to do is play in the snow
Then there is Christmas, such a wonderful time of year
The sound of Christmas songs, "Boom! Boom! Boom!" in my ear
In this season the trees are bare,
Finding a tree with leaves is quite rare.
The winter season is like a wonderful day
I wish this season could just stay.

Peter Zawycky, Grade 6
St Jerome Elementary School

Anger

Anger is terrible.
Anger is horrible.
Anger is the worst.
Anger is red like a blazing fire.
Anger tastes like atomic hot sauce…YUM
Anger smells like a monkey.
Anger sounds like a huge lion singing.
Anger feels like rocks on a chalkboard.
Anger looks like someone having a bad hair day.
Anger makes me want to dive off a cliff.
Anger is the worst thing ever.
Anger is something everyone experiences.

Jeremy Scaccia, Grade 6
West Allegheny Middle School

Crazy

Crazy is nut brown
It sounds like some kid running around not knowing what to do
It smells like someone who puts on too much cologne
It tastes like someone who never took a bath
It looks like someone who does not know what he is doing
Crazy feels like someone annoying you

Bruno Campos-Santos, Grade 4
Anne Frank School

Excitement

Excitement is my baseball team winning the championship
Excitement is an Australian shepherd-lab mix rescued from a puppy mill
Excitement is a big bass that I battled and reeled in
Excitement is the hot orange sun at the beach
Excitement is ice cream on a cone
Excitement smells like flowers that grow in my Pappy's garden in the spring
Excitement sounds like the final buzzer blowing at the end of the Stanley Cup
Excitement feels like warm sand between my toes at the beach
Excitement looks like a sun setting over the horizon at the beach
Excitement makes me want to give hugs to my friends and family
Excitement is the Penguins winning the Stanley Cup and the Steelers winning the Super Bowl

Anthony Kriznik, Grade 6
West Allegheny Middle School

Love

Love is like a lightning bolt that spreads through your bones and talks to your heart
Love is an emotionally weird emotion that you feel when you have just been asked out
Love is still exciting even though it is romantic
Love has a wonderful color of hot pink and shiny red
Love tastes like fresh chocolate fudge brownies recently made
Love smells like when your grandma made your favorite type of cookie
Love sounds like a night by a romantic fire going crack, sizzle, crack
Love looks like a breathless sunset on a Maryland coastal beach
Love makes me have different emotion such as happiness, joy, excitement, and sometimes sadness
Love is probably my most important emotion I have yet to experience

Emily Mihaljevic, Grade 6
West Allegheny Middle School

Competition

Competition is sweat running down your face knowing you have done your best
Competition is fear in your opponent's eyes when you step up to bat
Competition is when you get so mad you want to fight another player
Competition is neon green like a policeman's reflective jacket
Competition tastes like blood from cuts on your legs and arms
Competition sounds like a softball cracking off the bat soaring out of the park
Competition feels like rocks being pushed into your spine making you vulnerable and mad
Competition looks like two hungry tiger sharks fighting for meat
Competition makes me angry my face turns beet red and I am like a lion ready to attack
Competition is strength, because competition makes you better in the mind mentally and in your self-belief

Spencer Sinclair, Grade 6
West Allegheny Middle School

Luckiness

Luckiness is a golden snowy frozen fluffy field of fluttering fuzzy snowflakes pounding earth
with blankets of snow on Christmas morning relaxing with my family opening gifts.
It looks like a large luxurious blooded blue sea on a midday sunset.
It tastes like delicious, ripe, fresh, foreign tropical fruits from a Caribbean island.
It smells like all the Thanksgiving Day food, freshly prepared by my grandmother.
It sounds like a deep depressing rain forest waterfall flowing through the jungle.
It feels like falling asleep on an enormous white cloud relaxing in the hot waves of the sun's warmth.

Anthony Cantando, Grade 6
Our Lady of Ransom School

Autumn

In autumn the leaves change colors
They can turn yellow, red, or brown
The trees seem so bare without leaves
But at the same time so pretty
In autumn it also gets cold and chilly
And it feels a little like winter
Another thing during autumn is Thanksgiving
This is one of the best holidays because of the food
Then before you know it is winter
All of these reasons are why I like autumn

Jake Nadorlik, Grade 6
St Joan of Arc School

All About Me

Eliza
Funny, nice, and fun
Sister of Javian and John
Who loves Giants, Yankees, and family
Who needs new pencils, alone time, and hot Nikes
How gives smiles, happiness, and fun
Who'd like to see Michael Jackson
How dreams of dancing
A student of Miss Tadlock
Eli

Eliza Trout, Grade 4
Wickersham Elementary School

Endurance

Endurance is the strength to continue on.
Endurance is serious, like saving someone's life.
Endurance is the blush red color of your cheeks.
Endurance tastes like the sweet victory when you win.
Endurance smells like the sweat running down your face.
Endurance sounds like a crowd cheering for you.
Endurance feels like the roughness of concrete.
Endurance is a hard game to beat.
Endurance makes me scream and shout when I win.
Endurance is endless encouragement for enduring energy.

Mara Petrone, Grade 6
West Allegheny Middle School

Red

Red is roses.
Red is a leaf falling to the ground.
Red is when I'm annoyed.
Red is a cut.
Red smells like freshly picked apples.
Red tastes like fruit punch.
Red sounds like blood rushing through my veins.
Red looks like a gleaming red cherry on top of a sundae.
Red feels like my heart beating.
Red is my favorite color.

Michael Scott, Grade 5
Lincoln Elementary School

The Things That I Love

I sing of birds and bees,
of full moons and sights to see,
I write of fiction, action, and distress,
And when I eat spaghetti I might make a mess,
I sing of after it rains and the smell of mint,
of snowing all day and presents, hint, hint,
even though I have scars on my elbows and knees,
and I don't like rotten cheese,
I still dream of happiness and awe,
and I wish to give some to all…

Robert Naylor, Grade 5
Copper Beech Elementary School

Marco Polo

Marco
Explorer, sailor, hard worker, honest
Related to Father Nicolo, Uncle Maffeo, and brother Maffeo
Cares deeply about his three daughters
Who needs to be let free from the Kahn
Who gives his silk clothes away
Who fears the next Kahn might not like them
Who would like to see China
Resident of Venice, Italy
Polo

Anthony Bond, Grade 5
Indian Lane Elementary School

Tonkey and Zazz

Tonkey and Zazz they are hard to see,
Invisible but friends to me.
Small and blue live in a tree,
And when I turned three I needed them no more.
So off they went to the boy next door.
I invite you to meet my sweet little friends,
And you will finally see they're not just nice to me.
If you have your own come see me,
A party we'll have,
With our best friends indeed.

Mark Lamendola, Grade 5
Foster Elementary School

Thanksgiving Is

Family coming together.
Passing a plate of mashed potato's around.
Giving of thanks.
Helping one another.
Making cake and treats for the whole family.
Being able to see family that does not live by you.
Hugging each other.
Seeing family members so happy to see each other.
Telling stories of when they were kids.
Playing video games with my cousins.

Jonathan Graham, Grade 6
Moravian Academy Middle School

Blue Is…
As constant as the ocean
As graceful as a deer
As beautiful as a butterfly
As young as a rose bud
As strong as our freedom.
Tatiana Williams, Grade 4
Jefferson Elementary School

Girls
G raceful
I ntelligent
R adiant
L oyal
S entimental
Debbie Fritch, Grade 5
East Union Intermediate Center

Leaves
Leaves
Crispy, dying
Dance in wind
Swirling, twirling, having fun!
Fall
Kaylani Hernandez, Grade 5
Hamilton Elementary School

Thanksgiving
Feast
Happiness, together
Giving, caring, sharing
November, night
Food
Feben Kebede, Grade 5
Hamilton Elementary School

The Man from Space
There once was a young man from space,
Who was scrubbing and scrubbing his face.
Soap went in his eye,
And he started to cry,
And he floated all over the place.
Noah Schultz, Grade 5
Foster Elementary School

Fall
Leaves
green, yellow
raking, kicking, playing
wanting to listen
Peaceful
Tiyananonsion Torres, Grade 5
Hamilton Elementary School

Fall Leaves
Leaves as crunchy as potato chips have fallen to the ground,
Smell the smell of old leaves absorbing the smells of the morning.
Look at the bright red, orange, yellow, and green colors of nature's painting,
Rake up each delicate leaf carefully so they don't break,
Count to three and jump into the mountain of leaves.

The next day the pile is smaller,
Some leaves have twirled and danced like little tornados and have left,
The leaves are broken, crushed, and shattered like broken glass,
Now all the leaves have twirled and danced in the arctic air and
    abandoned the pile.
Kaila Brown, Grade 5
McKinley Elementary School

Happiness
Happiness is the sun in the morning smiling down at the world
Happiness is winning the Stanley Cup Championship
Happiness is living life and enjoying it
Happiness is vermilion for love on Valentine's Day
Happiness tastes like sugar cookies in your mouth
Happiness smells like steak sizzling on the grill
Happiness sounds like the buzzer in hockey when you score going buzz-buzz
Happiness feels like a warm comfy blanket
Happiness looks like your dog wagging his tail when you get home
Happiness makes me want to jump up and down
Happiness is family on Christmas morning
Robert Carter, Grade 6
West Allegheny Middle School

Bravery
Bravery is a wrestler struggling for a pin on the wrestling mat.
Bravery is a fireman diving into a burning building to save a young little baby.
Bravery is a soldier going to Vietnam to fight for our country.
Bravery is bright orange in the hot summer sun.
Bravery tastes like spicy Italian sausage right off the grill.
Bravery smells like hot jalapeno peppers.
Bravery sound like the boom of a bomb just exploding.
Bravery feels like a strong stiff metal shield.
Bravery looks like a ferocious lion.
Bravery makes me feel like nothing can bring me down.
Bravery is scientists working to find a cure for cancer.
Alex Pichi, Grade 6
West Allegheny Middle School

Joyfulness
Joyfulness is sky blue like a beauteous sky on a summer day with my family and friends sitting in Pennypack Park for a picnic.
It looks like trees dancing in the Amazon rain forest on a summer day.
Joyfulness tastes like bubblegum cotton candy on a carnival night on the Fourth of July.
It smells like red ruby roses smiling at me on a warm spring morning.
Joyfulness sounds like roaring waves crushing onto the shores of Wildwood on May Day.
It feels like a bird flying and chirping in the air on the first day of spring.
Sylvester Inyang, Grade 6
Our Lady of Ransom School

High Merit Poems – Grades 4, 5 and 6

Elements
Water rippling,
Fires blaze without control,
Earth is impenetrable,
Air exhilarates senses,
Elements shape moonlit dreams.

Waves crash peacefully,
Fire, a weapon or peace,
Moist earth cools and soothes,
Air, a friend eternally,
It forms a beautiful sight.
Maria Clegg, Grade 6
Ross Elementary School

Fear
Fear is unwanted
Fear is terrible
Fear is the containment of your soul
Fear is ink black
Fear tastes like a bittersweet lemon
Fear smells like gunk
Fear sounds like the beating of your heart
Fear feels like the rippled back of a serpent
Fear looks like a house in flames
Fear makes me terrified
Fear is unwanted
Nicole Zanella, Grade 6
West Allegheny Middle School

Life
Life. A great surprise!
What is the meaning of life?
is it animals?
is it the people on Earth?
is there a meaning for life?

NO. Life is caring
life is the people you love
life is happiness
life is imagination
life is caring, love, and us!
Camille Traczek, Grade 4
Ross Elementary School

Halloween Is Fun
H arvest night
A cting like monsters.
L ollipops are tasty.
L oads of candy.
O ctober parties.
W eather is windy.
E verybody dressed up like monsters.
E ager for candy.
N ovember chills.
Mohamed Swaray, Grade 5
Clearview Elementary School

Rain Forest
Frogs
Bamboo
Grasshoppers
Alligators
Rain

Hot
Monkeys
Waterfalls
Extremely dense
Bugs
Gino Bonomo, Grade 6
Nazareth Area Intermediate School

Christmas
It's about setting up lights
When houses are bright
There are silent nights

It's about trees in the house
Full houses
Stars on top

It's about caroling
Hot cocoa
Watching holiday movies
Rayna Miller, Grade 5
Pocopson Elementary School

Friendship
F un together
R ead together
I ce cream
E at together
N ever stop being friends
D o things together
S leepover parties
H ave the same friends
I nto the same places
P arty together
Elyja Sanchez, Grade 4
Wickersham Elementary School

Friends
Friends,
isn't that what we are about,
through good times and bad,
we always work it out,
I just want to let you know,
I'll always be around,
and for any reason if you need me,
I'll never let you down,
because you are my friend,
and that's what we are all about.
Sami LaRusso, Grade 4
Middle Smithfield Elementary School

Halloween
H arvest
A pples
L eaves
L aughter
O ctober
W indy
E nchanted
E erie
N ippy
Kayla Valenti, Grade 5
Clearview Elementary School

Colors
Blue is the color of a little, sad kid
Orange is the hot, sweltering sun
Hot pink is a wonderful, loving heart
Green is the thick, spring grass
White is the smooth blanket of winter snow
Black is the darkness at midnight
Purple is a fresh, plump, ripe plum
Red is a shiny, healthy apple for the teacher
Brown is my puppy dog's fluffy, warm coat
Zha'Keirah Robinson, Grade 6
Chichester Middle School

Blue
Blue is the color,
Of a tear drop from a sad heart.
The color of our freedom,
And of our rights.
Is a little girl's shoes,
The boy who has the blues.
The power to lead,
The power to grieve,
It's the color, blue.
Melanie Anderson, Grade 6
Chichester Middle School

Koalas
Koalas
Kindhearted, diminutive
Climbing, swaying, working
Cute soft buddy
Adorable!!
Allison Stowman, Grade 5
St Anselm School

Anger
Anger is red
It smells like a pot burning
It sounds like a house on fire
It tastes like hot peppers
It looks like a ghost rider
Anger feels like sharks' teeth
William Walker, Grade 4
Anne Frank School

All I Am to Be
I am a superhero teacher who can grade papers faster than the speed of light.
I wonder what it would be like to have stayed up until 5 o'clock in the morning grading papers with my eyes half shut.
I hear my pen scribbling A's-F's all throughout the 2 poems 31 kids have done while they were in Language Arts.
I see my pointer finger going all over the paper pointing out different things to my eyes.
I want to be able to just write A's all over the paper without reading them, because they are so good.
I am a superhero teacher who can grade papers faster than the speed of light.
I pretend to be the slowest grader ever but my hand just keeps on writing A's and B's.
I feel unstoppable like a flower growing from a planted seed.
I touch the soft, thin paper and I grip my black, hard, and smooth grading pen.
I fear that the other teachers at the school, might become jealous and try to give me brownies which will kill away my powers forever.
I cry when I have to write more than 5 F's on people's papers; it upsets me greatly.
I am a superhero teacher who can grade papers faster than the speed of light.
I understand how bad it must be for the other teachers to not have any luck on a shooting star because that is how it used to be for me.
I say that the kids that are the best get the best, and the kids that are the worst will not get the best.
I dream that I could keep my powers forever, I know someday when I grow up I will forget about the brownies and lose my powers.
I try to be the nicest teacher but I think Miss Young outdoes me sometimes.
I hope the other teachers and I get to be friends for the rest of our lives teaching together.
I am a superhero teacher who can grade papers faster than the speed of light.

Leighan Patricia Herzberger, Grade 6
Pennridge North Middle School

To All the Soldiers
War is terrible even though so many people serve
The men and women that risk their lives are the greatest of all
Nobody deserves to go through the tragedies of war
Every soldier dedicates their lives to the USA
Each second someone dies to protect the land we live on and the future

The explosions, the bullets whizzing by your face, the heat of battle never ends
Screaming soldiers or silent soldiers, all in pain, suffering so we can be safe
Even though the pain is unbearable, they fight for freedom, and honor
Only one day a year we appreciate these brave heroes, although it should be every day
Veteran's Day is dedicated to every soldier, every family, who are lost, or have lost someone in war
Tears are shed by families with relatives in war, but they know it's for good
Proudly we stand red, white, and blue every single day
On this day I think of the brave men and women who died for our country

I thank all the soldiers for protecting me and everyone in this country
Willing to risk their lives for us
It is the best gift I could ever receive
Just thanking these amazing people isn't enough
When it's all over, soldiers say it was worth it, but we know they killed and have regrets for doing so

Mark Weichel, Grade 6
Pennridge North Middle School

Depression
Depression is smoky-gray like a storm cloud coming coldly in fall on a dark October night going past miles of forests.
It looks like a stormy Saturday night in the woods lost and alone.
It tastes like unwashed garbage trucks in summer on a hot and humid afternoon.
Depression smells like burning firewood in wintertime on Christmas night after finding emptiness instead of presents.
Depression sounds like a sigh of uneasiness when you have just been fired from your job.
Depression makes me feel like doing nothing at all.

Ashley Sanchez, Grade 6
Our Lady of Ransom School

High Merit Poems – Grades 4, 5 and 6

Hockey/Baseball
Hockey
fun, awesome
shooting, scoring, learning
stamina, endurance, strength, power
hitting, sliding, boring
long, tedious
baseball
Joe Nace, Grade 6
St Maria Goretti School

Summer/Winter
Summer
Sun, pool
Water, heating, shining
Humid, sunny, cold, windy
Snowing, freezing, blowing
Icy and cold
Winter
Ilya Golovin, Grade 5
McKinley Elementary School

Friends/Bullies
Friends
awesome, dependable
loving, dedicated, sharing
sisters, buddies, thief, enemy
hurting, unloved, threatening
ugly, powerful
Bullies
Anna Rutkowski, Grade 5
St Sebastian Elementary School

Glamorous/Plain
Glamorous
Colorful, one of a kind
Interesting, outgoing, shining
Amazing, perfect, dull, ordinary
Not frilly, boring, tiring
Regular, blank
Plain
Grace Kelly, Grade 5
McKinley Elementary School

Friends/Bullies
Friends
funny, kind
trusting, caring, loved
companion, ally, rival, enemy
hating, fighting, hassled
stingy, mean
Bullies
Savannah Renner, Grade 5
St Sebastian Elementary School

Life Is a Highway
Life is a highway,
Along the way you hit bumps in the road,
Carrying a load of pressure,
Then you come to a nice smooth road,
Having a good time,
Never looking back at the bumps,
Now you reach speed bumps,
Trying to slow you down,
You are now stressed,
Thinking of what you should do,
Should I keep going or stop right here,
KEEP GOING!
It doesn't matter which way,
RIGHT or LEFT,
Just as long as you keep moving forward,
Don't let things slow you down,
Make them fear YOU,
Just remember to keep moving forward.
Skyler Mason, Grade 6
Hopewell Memorial Jr High School

Snuggles, Our Dog
Snuggles, our dog,
As white as snow,
When you walk in the door
And step on the floor
Be ready to be greeted
By our hyper dog.

Snuggles, our dog,
Loves to run
And have a lot of fun,
Jumps in the flower bed
And rushes out filthy.
That's our crazy dog!

Snuggles, our dog,
Soft and silky
Smooth and fluffy
Snuggles, our awesome dog!
Jared Stoltzfus, Grade 6
Linville Hill Mennonite School

I Love You
With open eyes I see you.
With closed eyes I hear you.
When I don't see you I miss you.
When I'm bored I watch you.
When I'm sad you make me happy.
When I'm angry you are my joy.
When I am alone you are my friend
When I'm blue you make me colorful.
Someone asks who are you.
I love you…TV.
Lawrence Zmuda, Grade 4
Middle Smithfield Elementary School

Ode to God
O God, I love you evermore
You created me to have a good life
But not to take a life
When I am melancholy, I pray to you
Because I have nothing else to do
When I am in heaven with you
I will be happy and true
But never again blue
Jacob Nadonley, Grade 4
All Saints Catholic School

Cookies
Oh how I love cookies
And the way they make me smile
Cookies are like pillows
All soft and fluffy
Cookies are so chewy
And very, very gooey
Cookies are like heaven
I eat them 24-7!
Tyler Barnick, Grade 6
State Street Elementary School

Currency
C oins
U ndeniable
R ich
R esponsibility
E agle on back
N ickel
C ounted by cashiers
Y ou use it to buy things
Jordan Denish, Grade 4
McKinley Elementary School

Patrick the Penguin
Patrick the Penguin
Was swimming around.
He went so deep
Then he went into a mound.
He hit his head hard
And turned into a grump.
He was mean to everyone
All because of a little lump.
Leo Newman, Grade 4
St. Andrew School

Football
When you play football,
Of course, you need a ball.
You get a lot of touchdowns
In a lot of little towns.
Football is a good dream,
If you're not afraid to get creamed!
Hunter Benjamin, Grade 4
W R Croman Elementary School

I Wish

I wish for a puppy
I wish for a horse
I wish for a guppy
I would wish of course
If I had endless wishes
I would keep wishing
I would never stop
Until my room was full to the top
I would wish for ice cream
Because ice cream is yummy
But not so good for my tummy
Oh well
Then I would wish for my tummy to not hurt
So I could have more
Wishes are wishes
Mind would never end
I would keep on wishing until
I have no more words to say
And the world was full of my wishes

Ali Wessel, Grade 5
The Ellis School

Purple Inspirations

Purple flowers blowing
in the breeze.
The excitement getting ready to come out
Too excited to go to school
My excitement turns into fireworks
going into a purple patch of daisies.

Come home seeing sisters eating purple grapes
lips are dark purple
Put on never-before-worn purple p.j.s,
come down watch the Color Purple

Get in my purple bed
under my purple covers
Close my eyes going to bed
and sunset as purple as my lips
sun going down
as I snuggle under my covers.

Isis Truxon, Grade 4
Wissahickon Charter School

The Monkey

The monkey soon grows very old,
And swings on lots of trees.
And later he is solemnly told,
To watch out for killer bees.

The monkey didn't look close enough,
And got stung so very hard.
So his friend made him some tasty mush stuff,
And got him a "Get Well Soon" card.

Mark Roces, Grade 5
Foster Elementary School

Senses

The fun I see, the fun I see is when I see my friends.
The lights I see, the lights I see on the fourth of July.
The softness I feel, the softness I feel when I wrap up in a blanket.
The sourness I taste, the sourness I taste when I bite a lemon.
The hugs I get, the hugs I get when I see my family.
The cold, frosty bite, the cold frosty bite I feel in the winter.
The words flow, the words flow when I talk on the phone.
The music flows, the music flows when I hear the radio.
The happiness I feel, the happiness I feel when I see my dog.
The things I learn, the things I learn when I go to school.
The sadness I feel, the sadness I feel when I end this poem!

Madeline Noble, Grade 5
Russell Elementary School

Happiness

Happiness is a smile and a kind word.
Happiness is a gift of kindness and warmth.
Happiness is the present you wished for on Christmas Day.
Happiness is blue like the sky on a sunny day.
Happiness is ice cream on a hot day.
Happiness smells like candles on a birthday cake.
Happiness sounds like children playing.
Happiness feels like a soft, warm blanket.
Happiness looks like the first day of spring.
Happiness makes me glad to be alive.
Happiness is you, me, and everyone in the world.

Anthony Argiro, Grade 6
West Allegheny Middle School

Joy

Joy is a baby's laugh
Joy is a bonfire with all my friends
Joy is a brand new puppy
Joy is the color of a bright new rainbow
Joy tastes like a fresh baked batch of cookies
Joy smells like a garden full of fruit
Joy sounds like a forest full of birds
Joy feels like sleeping on a pile of cotton
Joy looks like a brand new mansion
Joy makes me want to bust out and laugh
Joy is the WORLD!!

Trevor Cogar, Grade 6
West Allegheny Middle School

Freedom

I like to soar through the sky and glide through the wind,
to go on adventures and find out new things.
I like to ride on my horse while galloping through the hills,
and racing the eagles flying so high in the sky,
having a great time at Gramma's —
eating chocolate chip cookies which are hot and delicious
like the great big sun wrapped in cotton candy in your mouth.
Loving to fly in the summer sky with the birds so close to me,
to feel like I could be the queen of all eternity.

Simone Qually, Grade 4
Lincoln Elementary School

What Is Green?

Green is my Christmas tree
Crisp money, green grass,
That is what I see.
Green is the sound of leaves in the wind,
And children jumping in piles of them,
When autumn begins.
Green is the smell of fresh mowed lawn, lollipops,
Dewdrops that form at dawn.
The taste of mint chocolate chip ice cream, tangy limes,
Dreams bursting at the seams.
A touch of green is smooth, sharp grass,
A Christmas ball, paint on the wall.
Green is a fish that swims in the sea,
St. Patrick's Day, maybe a stingray.
Green is laughter that comes from a joke,
A butterfly, a painted sky.
Green is the color of dreams,
When they all come true.
Green is the song of Christmas carols,
Loud and bright,
Like all the world, for me, and for you.

Julia Boyd, Grade 6
St Hilary of Poitiers School

What Is Yellow?

Yellow is the color of happiness,
Also the color of joy,
The color of a child's eyes
When receiving a new toy.
Yellow is bittersweet,
Never does what it's told,
Also independent and bold.
Yellow is a hot summer day,
The color of the flowers blooming in May,
It is kind but firm,
And always waits for its turn,
Yellow is the color of the sun,
But at night is the color of the stars,
And the color of some cars.
Yellow is a bird singing,
A church bell ringing,
Yellow is very bright, it can shine through the night.
It is different, but that's all right.
As radiant as the sun, as it dances in the light.
As it shines with all it's might.
It is very mellow, I love yellow

Maura Dimes, Grade 6
St Hilary of Poitiers School

The Heroes with a Place in Our Hearts

We look up at the clear blue sky
And then we remember
That deep feeling in our hearts we got
When you fought for our freedom

It was you who risked your lives,
You who suffered and had to watch others die
But you still fought
Even though we never did anything to help you

As the fire in your hearts blazed,
And you felt the stabs of pain
Just to keep us free was all you cared
For you we huddle safely together to pray

When you fall and take your last breath
And hear your last soft heartbeat
What you do not realize is that you have not failed
You have won because we give you our love, hope, and respect
We will never forget you
God bless you

Ashley Elizabeth Mathew, Grade 6
Pennridge North Middle School

I Am

I AM CARTER KROUSE
I am athletic and energetic
I wonder how much I will learn this year
I hear the bang of the soccer ball being kicked
I see children having fun
I want to be a baseball player
I am athletic and energetic

I pretend to be a real basketball player
I feel happy at school
I touch my World Series ticket that brings memories to me
I worry that someone in my family will die
I cry when my soccer and baseball games get rained out
I am athletic and energetic

I understand that people can make a difference in this world
I say that I will do my best in everything
I dream of being a famous sports player
I try to be a better soccer player
I hope I can accomplish my dream
I am athletic and energetic

Carter Krouse, Grade 5
Nether Providence Elementary School

Winter

In the winter there is snow so I have no grass to mow.
The cold wind will blow the snow.
I like to make snowmen and I always make ten.
My mom always helps me make a snow den.

Elizabeth Zacharias, Grade 6
Immaculate Conception School

A Shadow Life

As the summer light shimmers upon my face,
the beautiful artwork my mother gave me.
The path to heaven opens,
but the darkness of Earth still haunts me.

Matt Murray, Grade 5
Nether Providence Elementary School

Halloween
H appy kids buying costumes
A lways frantic mothers keeping track of their kids
L aughing children running around in their costumes
L oving all the candy they get
O ut all night knocking on doors
W hining kids that are scared of other costumes
E ating candy all night long
E xcited trick-or-treaters
N ow that the night's over and time to sleep from the frantic night
Serena Warner, Grade 5
Clearview Elementary School

The New School Year
The new school year is starting.
The smell of hot dogs and sauerkraut fills the air.
Teachers smiling, greeting the kids,
Annoyed bus drivers.

Papers fresh from the printer.
When I hear the last bus pull up and stop,
With its squeaky brakes,
I know that school is really here, and that summer is over.
Danielle Sharp, Grade 6
Chichester Middle School

Halloween Night
Halloween, Halloween, Halloween night
Witches and goblins you're in for a fright.

Halloween, Halloween, Halloween night
Candy, candy plenty in sight.

Halloween, Halloween, Halloween night
Don't be afraid to go outside for what is in store
Is a wonderful night!
Mazie Bradley, Grade 5
Central Elementary School

My Grandparents Are…
Like cookies and milk at sleepovers.
Like hugs and kisses when we have to leave,
Like parties with our family members,
Like presents around the Christmas tree filled
with happiness and joy,
The best!!!
Dana Turner, Grade 6
Moravian Academy Middle School

Red
Red looks like a cardinal flying through the air.
Red sounds like leaves falling off of trees.
Red feels like a soft red shirt.
Red tastes like a delicious apple.
Red smells like a big fire burning.
Adam Weiss, Grade 5
Clearview Elementary School

Summer
Summer is the best of seasons,
I can give you many reasons.

School is out, it's time for fun,
And most kids will play in the sun.

All the ice cream stores will open,
For about ninety days, no more pencils and pens.

On the Fourth of July, the fireworks fly
The fireworks fly, in the night sky

The water in some pools is very cool,
In circle pools, we sometimes make a whirlpool.

Summer can be hot or cool,
And it definitely wins by the majority rule.

Summer is the best of seasons,
And I gave you all the best reasons.
Matt Tutsock, Grade 6
Ss Simon and Jude Elementary School

Sense of Knowing
The sense of knowing someone is there,
Can give a person warmth of safety or the chilliness of a scare,

To know that a loved one has passed,
Can make you cry for a while, but it will not last,

The sense of evil in the air,
Can make a person go insane or make them say a prayer,

The sense of love in someone's arms,
Can make you cry tears of love or make you feel safe from harm,

Knowing that someone will be there for you,
Gives you a sense of relief to get you through,

Having known the pain someone has been in,
Doesn't make you laugh or shed a sly grin,

Sense of knowing the sadness in one's face,
Makes you open your arms to their embrace.
Katie Brosky, Grade 6
Ss Simon and Jude Elementary School

Red
Red
Red is the feeling in your stomach after drinking red soda.
Red sounds like red robins singing a song.
Red looks like bright juicy apples.
Red tastes like yummy strawberries in season.
Red smells like new bright cherries on a cherry tree.
Jenna Jimenez, Grade 5
Clearview Elementary School

People of War
War is a sad, sorrowful time
Full of sadness and pain
Many people sacrifice their lives
   to keep us safe
Like a lion protecting its young
BAM! BAM! BAM!
Gunfire, Bombs, Explosions
Killing our soldiers every day
The pain! The suffering!
Soldiers doing their duty
Protecting every American in this country
They do it for all people around the world
War takes our soldiers
War takes lives from us
Soldiers are our brothers, sisters, parents,
   aunts and uncles who love us
We must take their place someday
Then it will be us who defend our country
Hope is in our hands
Michael Schiavo, Grade 6
St Jerome Elementary School

Burning House
Strangely, I do not feel pain
Even as the
Burning orange flames
Lick the house
That I grew up in
Where I played
Where memories lived beside us
What cuts me beyond the bone
Is to hear a scream
A voice I know
But cannot place
Like an old forgotten friend
The voice drifts in and out
Of my mind
Until I can place it
And when I do
I do not like it
For I know I am as doomed
As the old house
Jordan Seroka, Grade 6
Rolling Ridge Elementary School

Halloween
Ghosts, goblins, ghouls, galore.
Reeses, Skittles, Hershey, and more.

Halloween's the best,
Although a scare fest.

Too much fun for you to believe…
It's already time for us to leave?!
Bridget Barry, Grade 5
McKinley Elementary School

Nervous
Nervous is stomach turning
Nervous is breathtaking
Nervous is a weird sensation
Nervous is navy blue
Nervous tastes like pure lemon juice
Nervous smells like a rotten cantaloupe
Nervous sounds like thunder pounding
Nervous feels like porcupine quills
Nervous looks like dark clouds
Nervous makes me sick
Nervous is a habit when worried
Emily Metz, Grade 6
West Allegheny Middle School

Anger
Anger is hot
Anger is mean
Anger is frustrating
Anger is bright red
Anger tastes like hot peppers
Anger smells like red hot sauce
Anger sounds like a sizzling fire
Anger feels like a cactus
Anger looks like a boiling pot of water
Anger makes me mad
Anger is ugly
Chris Giura, Grade 6
West Allegheny Middle School

Fall
Fall is a beautiful time of year.
Leaves dancing in the wind
Reds, yellows, oranges, and browns
Raking, arms aching
Carving pumpkins
Scary costumes
Itchy hay rides
Smelly animals
My hair blowing in the wind
Bundled up in my jacket
The best time of the year!
Jacque Vas, Grade 6
St Joan of Arc School

Baseball Fun
Baseball can be fun or sad
It can be fun when you score a run
You are sad when your team is bad
When you get into a jam
You might hope for a grand slam
If you get called out
You might scream and shout
You might be in the Hall of Fame
Only if you are good at playing the game.
Jarret Pipes, Grade 5
East Union Intermediate Center

BMX
I can ride a bike
I can bunny hop too
I can almost do a tail whip
How about you?
Tripping and falling, don't hold me back
Front flip and back flip
I am on the right track.

That's all I can do
Remember, you must try too!
Ryan Gist, Grade 5
Foster Elementary School

My Family's Trip
Last year I went to China
It was really great
I learned so much in two weeks
I really loved it
Although the plane ride was long
It was amazing
We adopted a baby
She is really cute
And soon our two weeks were gone
I want to go back
Annie Carne, Grade 5
McKinley Elementary School

Halloween
Bats are flying
  Spiders are climbing
    Black cats are running
    Pumpkins are shining
    Witches are flying
    Candy is sweet
     Vampires are crying
     Children are smiling
    Ghosts are scary
    Werewolves are hairy
Erika Duff, Grade 5
McKinley Elementary School

My Kitty
My kitty
Orange, white
Plays often
Eats mice
Meows crazily
Red collar
Scratches people
Drinks water
Drinks milk
My kitty
Karina Castilloveitia, Grade 4
Wickersham Elementary School

Happiness

Happiness sounds like ha, ha, ha
Happiness makes me feel good about the world
Happiness feels like a warm, cozy blanket
Happiness smells like a turkey roasting in the oven
Happiness tastes like a juicy, sizzling steak
Happiness is when I get an A in school
Happiness is the Steelers scoring a touchdown
Happiness is the color orange
Happiness is Christmas day
Happiness looks like cheerful children
Happiness is when everyone is healthy

Ty Morris, Grade 6
West Allegheny Middle School

The Thinking Thanking Elephant

I'm nice and big and very gray
I'm thankful for the grass and hay

My trunk can drink up lots of rain
I also love my thinking brain

I can hear soft things and swat away flies
My ears keep me cool even in the hot sunrise

My tusks keep danger far far away
And I can camouflage from enemies or prey

Amy Huddell, Grade 6
Interboro GATE Program

Great Man

M y kids won't be judged by the color of their skin
A n important man
R acism is wrong
T he reason why races get along
I have a dream
N on-violent man

K ept peace between blacks and whites
I n 1964 he was awarded the
N obel Peace Prize
G reat man

Donovan Ford, Grade 5
Hamilton Elementary School

Obstacles

No matter where
life takes you there
are always going to be obstacles.
Left and right wherever you go
they are always going to be there.
You try and avoid them and they get worse.
You try and get away from them and they just keep coming back.
So just keep going and don't let anything or anybody
get in the way of living your life.

Briana Losco, Grade 6
Hopewell Memorial Jr High School

Horrifying Night

Look in the haunted house
Look at that scary mouse

Hear the wolf howl over the moon
Halloween will be coming soon

Jack-o'-lanterns cackling in the night
Look at their terrifying light

Can't you hear the witches call?
Look at that scary spider on the wall

Natalie Perdue, Grade 4
Cathedral School of St Catharine of Siena

On Halloween Night

On Halloween night you get a treat.
If you're lucky they will be good and sweet.

Be careful, I hope you don't run into a ghoul.
For they always haunt the school.

The moon rose up so the werewolves howl.
Something scared me but it was just an owl.

When Halloween night ends all the kids sighed.
Finally everyone went inside.

Jacob Roma, Grade 4
Cathedral School of St Catharine of Siena

Keep It Clean

The world is such a special place.
See the big smile on my face.

If we want to keep it clean,
We will have to work together as a team.

Do no litter; pick up trash.
When you do it, have a blast.

Soon the world will be as clean as new,
All because of me and you!

Casey McKimpson, Grade 4
St John Neumann Regional Academy - Intermediate School

Fall Leaf

F olks drinking apple cider.
A turkey on the dinner table.
L eaves blowing in the wind.
L aughing kids that are playing.

L arge and small kids celebrating.
E xciting or bizarre costumes on Halloween night.
A nice fire in the fireplace.
F orce of the wind.

Jason Morales, Grade 5
Clearview Elementary School

High Merit Poems – Grades 4, 5 and 6

The Ultimate Day
If I had the best day ever, I would wish for:
brownies
cookie cake
peanut butter
mint ginger ale
sunny days
Florida
lime green
pajamas
California
my family
dogs
live concerts or plays
cookie dough raw
bread
my birthday
music
softball
Halloween
Christmas

Francheska Pokora, Grade 6
St Sebastian Elementary School

Why
Why do they cage me up, beat me,
Yell at me,
Treat me like a slave,
I am like a tropical bird with vibrant wings,
Trapped on a cold, dark, remote island,
I stand out like a sore thumb,
In the midst of nowhere,
But darkness,
Everywhere I look, I see unusual things,
Everyone looks down on me,
Like I was the mouse and they are the cat,
Like I was the land,
And they were the water,
Their stares seemed to crash waves on me,
And wash my soul away,
Even as I stay there,
My lush green fields,
Slowly,
Drifts away.

Yang Zhang, Grade 5
Boyce Middle School

Pets
Pets
Playful, soft
Fighting, eating, playing
Love to pet them
Barking, meowing, panting
Fast, big
Animals

Erik Musselman, Grade 5
Saint Theresa School

Ronnie the Raccoon
Ronnie the Raccoon
Wanted some cheese.
He climbed down from his tree
With a whole lot of ease.
Ronnie the Raccoon
Looked all around
Then Ronnie the Raccoon
Saw some cheese on the ground.

He scooped it all up
With a whole lot of care.
He ran back to his tree
So he didn't have to share.
Ronnie the Raccoon
Looked up to see
A small flying creature.
It was a yellow bumblebee.

Mary Majercsik, Grade 4
St Andrew's School

Ernie the Elephant
Ernie the Elephant
Was getting water from the lake
When all of a sudden
He saw a snake.
He got so frightened
That he started to shake.
Then he finally realized
That the snake was just a fake!

He wanted to find out
Who played such a trick.
Soon he found out
It was his friend, Rick.
Ernie and Rick
Had a good laugh.
Then they went off
To scare their friend, Gerry the Giraffe.

Serena DiLoreto, Grade 4
St Andrew's School

Summer
I love summer
It is very warm
The sun is shining
The sky is blue
The clouds are moving
While kids are watching
All the kids are running and jumping
Enjoying summer and having fun
All the kids love summer vacation
Hoping summer will never end
So they don't have to go to school
Summer is the best season

Cory Dinkfelt, Grade 6
St Joan of Arc School

Garfield
My cat is very very nice,
Although it is quite fat.

It always needs my attention
I know it has a nice intention.

It is extremely old,
I wonder if it's getting cold.

It only meows sometimes,
But only in glum times.

My cat is harmless,
I think it's just too weak to attack.

I'm sorry if I ever teased it,
Or if I ever sneezed on it.

Thomas Trexler, Grade 4
All Saints Catholic School

Soccer
It's about kicking a ball around
Passing and moving
Waiting for a loose ball

It's about a brilliant first touch
To get your team to the top
Helping your team start a possession

It's about getting ready to shoot
Having a man at the back post
And ripping a shot in the net

It's about celebrating
Getting some momentum,
So you can win

It's about a great sport, soccer

David Mercner, Grade 5
Pocopson Elementary School

Different
I'm different from you
You're different from me
But we still share
One BIG family tree
Small or tall
Stout or slim
He's different from her
She's different from him
In every little boy
And every little girl
There's hope we can share
One big world!

Grace Workman, Grade 5
Saint Theresa School

A Fall Walk
Crunch! What a bunch of crackling leaves falling down
Crash! What a laugh of kids falling down
Playing with the leaves in the wonderful breeze
Shhh! The teacher said don't push but listen
Drop, drop, a squirrel dropping his acorns preparing for hibernation
Eating that much must be a celebration.
A fall walk is where you talk
It is where you sing with the birds and dance with the trees
So next time I take a fall walk please come join me.

Liberty DeVenuto, Grade 6
Pennridge North Middle School

What Is Christmas?
White pearl snowflakes dancing in the air
Joyful children tumbling down shimmering crystal hills
Solid jagged icicles dangling
Snow covered fields shining like glitter.

Ruby red and white fluffy stockings gleaming
Fresh gumdrop gingerbread men smiling
Twinkling multicolored lights twirling
Sipping creamy sizzling hot chocolate.

Carley Davis, Grade 4
Fairview Elementary School

My Fish
My fish are as cool as a dog
They love to go swim in their tank
Their dinner's their treat, and me, they thank
It's easy as caring for dogs or cats.
At least they don't sniff each other's behinds
Another reason I'm glad their mine
They bobble their heads out of the water.
They're graceful to me; they're graceful in water
That's why I love them as much as a dog.

Kyle Raha, Grade 6
State Street Elementary School

Halloween
Halloween is a scary night.
Bats come out to fight.
Pumpkins laugh while witches cast spells.
The wolves roared like a dinosaur, as the wind whistles.
The monsters dance
As the werewolf catches his last chance.

Lucky Tasco, Grade 5
McKinley Elementary School

What I Do and Hear
A swan can swim
A butterfly can fly
It drizzles at dark
While I sleep through the night
Oh what beautiful things you can do and hear

Amanda Allen, Grade 5
Nether Providence Elementary School

Blue Is My World
Blue is the rooftop of my house that stares up into the clouds.
Blue is a soft jacket that I wear to keep myself warm.
Blue is a fairytale book that has many wonderful stories.
Blue is a sticky lollipop that is very tasty.
Blue is a blooming bluebell swaying from side to side in the wind.
Blue is tasty blueberry yogurt that I love.
Blue is a beautiful blue jay that soars through the blue sky.
Blue is a very blue sky that I always look up and admire.

Elizabeth Boyle, Grade 5
Holy Child Academy

Blue
Blue is the color of bluebells, blooming in a valley.
Blue is a ripe blueberry growing on a bush.
Blue is a blue jay soaring through the sky.
Blue is a blue fish jumping out of the ocean up in the air.
Blue is the color of the beautiful sky.
Blue is the rain falling from the sky.
Blue is the cool water we swim in on a hot summer day.
Blue is the color of the foaming sea, splashing.

Megan Zimmerman, Grade 5
Holy Child Academy

Thanksgiving Day
Thanksgiving Day is a wonderful holiday.
I sit at the table surrounded by friends and family.
We are going to give thanks on the day of Thanksgiving.
There's baskets of bread and a turkey the size of my head!
I can smell the sweet smell of potatoes and stuffing.
There are so many delicious things to eat!
I love Thanksgiving Day!

Bailey Marshall, Grade 6
Hopewell Memorial Jr High School

My Brother
My brother is kind.
My brother is sweet.
My brother is a fine young boy that is going to become a man.
My brother is the best brother I could ever ask for.
My brother is polite.
Why I don't know.
That's just the kind of brother he is.

Jerica Williams, Grade 5
Foster Elementary School

A Hartman Thanksgiving
H ere's my great Aunt Dee she's always first over.
A ll of my uncles and aunts come to my house for Thanksgiving.
R eally crazy uncles that are here till twelve,
T he favorite at Thanksgiving is Mom's stuffing balls.
M y mom makes amazing foods and pies.
A lways and forever in my heart,
N ice enough but they still tease me.

Abby Hartman, Grade 5
Foster Elementary School

My Family

I love my family. Oh! Yes, I do.
Sometimes, I don't show it, but it is true!
Sometimes, my mom is a pain
But it's a shame that I think of her like that,
My dad spanks like mad,
But consequences have to come for me
To learn what's wrong or right.
Brooke is a bugger.
She is always looking for a quarrel,
But she is my sister and I love her so!
My brother, Shay, is always excited.
He sometimes gets carried away.
We fight and we brawl.
Sometimes, it is not fair at all
When I get into trouble.
But I know I should not pout
Because he is only five.
I love my family. Oh! Yes, I do.
Sometimes, I don't show it, but it is true!

Sean O'Neill, Grade 4
Lincoln Elementary School

Features

We all have different features
If you think your features are better than others'
Try thinking other thoughts because you might be wrong
Even if you don't have wrinkles

Look at your nose in the mirror
Is it enormously huge, freakishly small,
Or just the right size?
The way you see it probably won't be the same way I see it.

Can your tongue touch your nose
Or just barely touch your lips?
Is your body straight and narrow
Or wider at the hips?

We all have special features
That make us who we are.
and if we see through God's eyes
We don't seem that bizarre.

Elie Robertshaw, Grade 5
St Joan of Arc School

Reason

Everything in life happens for a
reason even if it lasts for a season.
If someone comes in your life one season
and leaves the next season then they
were not there for a reason. So if someone
is in your life and you think they are not there
for a reason then kick them out the next season
and tell them it is for a reason.

Brian Allen, Grade 6
Colwyn Elementary School

Love

Love is like a mother rocking her sick baby to sleep
Love is like a baby saying its first words
Love is like a puppy's first bark
Love is a purple flower flying in the wind
Love tastes like creamy cool whip on hot chocolate
Love smells like roses and a box of chocolates
Love sounds like a violin playing on a wedding day
Love feels like a soft smooth blanket
Love looks like a mother and her daughter holding
hands while reading a scary book
Love makes me feel loved and cared for
Love is something everybody has in common

Sammy McDaniel, Grade 6
West Allegheny Middle School

A Swimming Race

Take your place behind the block
Step up, the race is about to start
The buzzer beeps
You spring off the edge
A perfect dive past the gutter's ledge
Feel the cool water rush past your skin
Your feet kick so hard you feel as if you have fins
A quick flip turn; a good start off the wall
You're ahead
Feeling like you are 10 ft. tall
Fast into the wall, the race won
You're very happy and you still had fun

Miranda Lapson, Grade 6
Hopewell Memorial Jr High School

A Great Day

I jumped out of bed
Today is going to be the best day ever I said
I got up and got ready for this beautiful day
I was ready to go out and play
My dad told me no, we have a party to go to
I was already in the car, it was hot in there whooo!
Arrived at the party, it went so quick
When my dad picked me up, I was out in a jif!
It was time to meet my mom at the pet store
My heart was pounding, I couldn't wait anymore!
My mom was already at the front desk
Finally I got my first dog, now my heart can rest!

Elizabeth Hribar, Grade 6
Hopewell Memorial Jr High School

As the Snow Falls

As the snow falls, children gaze out the window in awe.
As the snow falls, school starts to close.
As the snow falls, friends struggle to chase each other.
As the snow falls, a blizzard forms.
As the snow falls, kids sit inside sipping hot chocolate
As the snow ends, children have their last chance to enjoy it.

Henry Imgrund, Grade 6
St Joseph School

Doug the Dog
Doug the Dog
Was running around.
He went farther and farther,
He's making a sound.
Doug the Dog
Fell on the ground.
He yelled "Help!"
He was found.

Doug the Dog
Got a mouse.
He named it Mickey Mouse,
And took it to the house.
Doug the Dog
Played with his hair.
He pulled some of it out.
He sniffed the air.
Joseph Hochstein, Grade 4
St Andrew's School

Max the Monkey
Max the Monkey
Was jumping around.
He went to his house,
And fell on the ground.
He looked all around,
And lost his memory.
He heard a strange sound,
And realized he had an enemy.

He saw his enemy,
And thought he was dreaming.
He went to bed that night
And woke up screaming.
He went back to bed
And started dreaming again.
He played with his friend.
His name was Jonathan.
Katie Konieczny, Grade 4
St Andrew's School

Vacation
I love to go on vacation
with my family.
I like to go on rides
and going upside down too.
But when I go upside down too fast
I might start to feel sick.
When we have to leave
my brother and sister might start to cry.
So we ask our parents
for just one more try
to ride our favorite ride.
They agree we can ride our last ride.
Mary Kutschke, Grade 5
St Joan of Arc School

Faces
When I see
unfamiliar faces
in the beginning
I clutch onto my mother's arm.

But as years go on,
I see more
familiar faces.
I get to meet new people
on every year I go.

And I feel like a big family
on these very special
Thanksgiving days.
Anna Okada, Grade 5
Falk Laboratory School

One Great Summer Day
In the morning I went outside,
I knew it was going to be fun,
When I was out playing in the sun.
On this summer day.

I got my bathing-suit on,
We went in our pool,
The water felt very cool.
On this summer day.

I was outside gardening,
I smelled a rose,
It tickled my nose.
On this summer day.
Hannah D'Aquanno, Grade 4
Sacred Heart School

What Is Blue
Blue is the ocean
As blue as the sky.
Blue is the clouds
That form a shape that says hi!
Blue smells pure and sweet
It's as soft as a bird's tweet.
Blue is as light as merry weather.
Blue is as soft as a heron's feather.
Blue is my bed that warms my head.
Blue is the ice where people skate.
Blue is where there is no hate.
Blue is the dove that flies away.
Blue is the peace that flows my way.
To me blue makes my day.
Christopher Mitchell, Grade 6
St Hilary of Poitiers School

Nature
Nature is a wondrous thing
Just listen to the birds sing
The animals love to frolic and play
You can go look at the beautiful bay
All the oceans glisten in the sun
Nature is definitely second to none
All the beautiful plants surround you
Some plants are old and some are new
The mighty oak stands so high
It looks like it could touch the blue sky
Big puffy clouds up above
Near them I see a pretty white dove
Nature is big and interesting too
I hope you love it as much as I do
Arianna Gavatorta, Grade 5
Burgettstown Elementary Center

Jamaica
As I stepped off the plane,
I saw the colorful clear blue ocean.
To jump in it was my notion;
It looked as sweet as sugar cane.

The sun was brightly blinding
As I glanced up at the sky.
The jungle was an emerald green
So beautiful to my eyes.

The poor country was visible,
But the people were still happy.
I will always remember that trip
And be grateful for what I have.
Hannah Weaver, Grade 6
Linville Hill Mennonite School

School
How I feel about school?
It's really cool!
You can have so much fun.
I wish I got out at one.

What I do at school?
I learn many things so I'm not a fool.
I read and write.
I never fight.

What school does for me?
It brings out the best in me.
School gives me an education.
So I can reach my future destination.
Andrew Blaszczyk, Grade 6
St Jerome Elementary School

I Am Determined

I am determined,
To score a goal.

I sprint down the sideline,
Ball at my feet,
My numb cheeks are beaten up by the blasting cold air,
It's deadlocked like the sword in the stone,
With time running down,
Defender at my side,
Stabbing and jabbing at the ball,
I trip, I fall,
The whistle blows,
Still a long shot to take,
I run up ready to take a shot,

I am determined,
To score a goal.

Albin Wells, Grade 5
Falk Laboratory School

Soccer

It's about kicking balls
dribbling
and passing

It's about shooting
scoring
and booing

It's about celebrating when your team scores a goal
arguing with the referee
and being subbed in and subbed out

It's about speed and agility
power and muscle
it's about hostility

It's about an intense sport…Soccer!

Bradley Saunders, Grade 5
Pocopson Elementary School

Tasha

My cat Tasha is soft, fluffy and cute.
She looks like a giant snowball laying around.
Whenever I leave for school she is like a crying baby.
Tasha usually has her moods,
Sweet as sugar.
Dangerous as a lion.
Tasha has bright blue eyes.
Her fur coat that is bright white.
I don't know what I would do without her.
She is not just a friend to me,
She is family.
Anyone can see how precious she is to me!

Brenna McLaughlin, Grade 6
St Jerome Elementary School

The Christmas Season

Snow, little balls of fluff, falling from the sky,
Kids build snowmen really high.
Anxiety and excitement, like little anxious children
    waiting for the day,
For Santa to come with toys to play.

Snowball fights, long cold nights,
Looking at the rainbow lights.
Hot chocolate warm and yummy,
It's enough to fill our tummies.

Mama comes with cookies warm,
So we can sit and watch snowflakes form.
Listening to Christmas music everywhere,
Making sure our mittens are matched and in pairs.
Waiting to hear school is closed with joy and fear,
That's how we know the season's here.

Kylie Shortall, Grade 6
St Jerome Elementary School

The Door to the Left

It is mid December, and I have just moved.
I walk in my new home, looking around the first time.
Everything seemed fine, until I went upstairs.
I go past the attic door, when I feel I'm being watched.
I looked around, seeing nothing, I walked away.
That same night in bed, I get that feeling again.
I turn my light on and look around, but nothing is there
But as I look, I see the attic door is cracked open.
That whole night, I couldn't sleep.
Thinking I'm never going to wake up.
It felt like something nudged me, and there I was, awake.
I looked around to see the attic door opened, again.
The next day, I fell, almost head first down the stairs.
But it felt like something grabbed me, and I didn't fall.
Out of fear I screamed, "Leave me alone!"
And from then on, the attic remains closed.
Finally I walk to the attic, and open the door.

Zackary Cipolla, Grade 6
Hopewell Memorial Jr High School

A Mountain Dew Day

A Mountain Dew day is
Like misty mountains after a rainstorm
The roar of the fizzy waterfall
It's like licking a lemon-lime lollipop
Like a massive tastequake on my tongue
No dewy days have every tasted this good
The juicy lemon-lime taste exploding on my tongue
Mmm. Tastily delicious smell of your liquid
The taste of your mixed flavors going down my throat
My taste buds on their favorite day
Feel the drip drop of every sip
A Mountain Dew day

Matthew D. Kraynik, Grade 6
Pennridge North Middle School

Special Place
My place is in my mother's room
It is beautiful in there
It's a bright room
It is always peaceful
I relax in there
When I get tired
I lay down
Nothing but quietness fills
The air around me
I am happy and sad at the same time
Looking back on all the fun things
That happened in the past
And comparing them to now
Thinking about what's
Going to happen next
Lying on my mom's queen sized bed
Lying on that is like lying
On a big puffy cloud
Denise Lassiter, Grade 4
Wissahickon Charter School

Dewdrops
Dewdrops can be many things.
A crystal ball,
Or a diamond ring.
A swimming pool for a tiny bug,
Or a sweet drink for a thirsty pug.
A piece of the moon,
Or dust from the stars.
Or a rare gem to men from Mars.
Drops of sweat from the fairies above,
Or pieces of songs by the morning doves.
Drops of paint from an artist's brush,
Or an ocean, vast but lush.
It all depends on the point of view,
A tiny creature,
Or me and you.
Dewdrops can be many things.
A crystal ball,
Or a diamond ring.
Allison Love, Grade 6
McKinley Elementary School

Wet
Wet
Forest
Butterflies
Bright bold flowers
Mud
Damp
Tree frogs
Tropical
Insects crawling
Trees
Nicole Homanick, Grade 6
Nazareth Area Intermediate School

My Dog, Nemo
Nemo is my dog.
She is orange and white.
She is very hyper.

I love her,
She is fun to play with.
She loves to play,
Tug-a-War.

I give her really big treats,
When she's sad.
Nemo is so playful,
When she's wrestling with my cat.

I love my dog,
And my cat.
They both are big,
Fur balls of love.
Joanna McGinn, Grade 6
Chichester Middle School

Freckles
Freckles,
On your cheeks,
On your nose,
On your forehead,
On your toes.

Brown,
Red,
Dotted,
Sun-splashed,
Freckles.

Can you count them?
5, 10, 15, 20…
Like the stars,
The longer you look,
The more you see.
Freckles.
Alaina Duessel, Grade 6
Ross Elementary School

Fantastic Fall
Fantastic colors in fall.
Autumn is another meaning for fall.
Love to play outside.
Leaves fall from trees.

Terrific but cold weather.
Rapid winds blowing.
Everlasting evergreen trees.
Every fall is a little cold.
Soothing scents of fall.
Matthew Courtney, Grade 5
Clearview Elementary School

It's About…
It's about…
Children's excited faces
Presents in all places
Ho Ho Ho's and lots of bows

Snow from the sky falls
Each flake differently small
Ready to be turned into balls

Definitely not hot
More like cold and chilly
But everyone's acting silly

The sun is down
the day is done
And everyone had lots of fun
It's all about Christmas
Annie Klingenberg, Grade 5
Pocopson Elementary School

Rain Forest
Wet
Forest
Animals
Evaporate
Trees

Rain
Flowers
Tropical
Animals fly
Damp

Dark
Tropics
Insects crawling
Different birds
Cold
Madison DiFrancesco, Grade 6
Nazareth Area Intermediate School

Mystery Favorite
It can be light and maybe round
In the kitchen it can be found
Foil paper or maybe bagged
Dark or white
Summer or winter I don't care
I'll always find it there
I love it's taste
Plain or with nuts
In plain sight
I go right for a bite
Nice and sweet it's always right
As long as it is mine
Jacob Guiciardi, Grade 5
East Union Intermediate Center

The First Double Digits

10, it sounds amazing
the experience changes year by year
generation by generation
you'll wish to go back
you'll wish to go forward

life ahead will change
you're not a kid anymore
but, that's how you're treated
you're climbing the tree of adulthood
it is not a tree house
everyone wants to know what you're doing with life
you must be responsible
it's all down road from here
you used to pretend and have fun
you'd dress up and never clean up
playing with barbies and action figures
always playing and singing happy songs
like the world will never end…will it?
when you got sick you'd get better
it's time to turn a page in life
10, it sounds amazing but that can change.

Zoe Fox, Grade 5
Copper Beech Elementary School

It's a Hot Chocolate Day

Steamy cup of goodness on the table
Explosion of goodness meets my mouth
Cold breeze of autumn punches my cheeks
Soccer season has just begun and so has fall
Everybody is so relaxed and unstressed
Screech of the ref's whistle as soccer begins
As the mornings grow shorter and the nights come quickly
Parents cheering their kids on
Leaves are burning and leaving that pleasant smell
Flutter of snow in the sky
Because today is a hot chocolate day

James Colin Masgai, Grade 6
Pennridge North Middle School

Soccer

It's about slide tackling
screaming
and coaches losing tempers

It's about shouting
and scoring
and fans going wild

It's about kicking the ball away from the other team's player
goalies getting muddy when they save the ball

It's about scoring goals and winning the game
Soccer

Elizabeth Koehler, Grade 5
Pocopson Elementary School

Mother Nature

Her eyes were wet as the morning dew,
    The heart and mind were full of gloom.
Her heart ached of emptiness,
    When she unleashed the sadness.

Upon the world it rained and rained,
    The dim tides were hurled upon the shore.
Skies were black as charcoal dust,
    But then her sadness was no more.

She realized she was glad that we enjoyed her land,
    If only we could treat it more kindly than we did.

To show her joy and happiness,
    A good harvest was to come.

Mother Nature had no more worries of her precious land,
    She trusted that we would take care of it,
And do the best we can.

Claire Weisner, Grade 6
Milton Middle School

The Witch of Blackbird Pond

Why do they put me out?
Do they do it because I'm a flickering flame, yet they are water?
They burn me out since I am light
and they are darkness that closes all around me.
I'm then blinded and cut to shreds
because they are scissors snipping at me.
As a thin helpless cloth, I am ignored
And trampled
If I do or say something differently,
I am a statue that they crush and destroy
I am sky and they are land
I feel like I'm a huge mansion surrounded by tiny huts
They are twigs, but I am a beautiful tree
I try to run but they chain me down.
They are dull rocks, but I am a rare gem.
They are dark clouds that surround me
And block my sunlight from shining through.
Why do they try to make me the same?
How I long to escape these endless gray forests…

Callie Card, Grade 5
Boyce Middle School

What Is Green?

Green is the fresh leaves outside.
Green is as cold as a grape to your teeth.
Green is as fun as a Christmas tree.
Green is the feeling of money in your pocket.
Green is the sensation of a wet lawn on a cold morning.
Green is a tree fun and exciting.
Green is the sound of joy in the sky.
Green is a color that I enjoy.

Sean O'Hagan, Grade 6
St Hilary of Poitiers School

Soft Bird
Soft as a pillow.
All it really does is flies.
Whoosh! Whish! Flies like a fast plane
Big wings.
Nathan Fingerhood, Grade 4
McKinley Elementary School

Day and Night
Day is bright.
Night has light.
Day is play time.
Night is sleep time.
Derek Beach, Grade 4
W R Croman Elementary School

Fish
Small fish, peaceful and graceful
With a passion of love inside
Swimming in the cool mountain stream
Nothing but harmony in sight
Eli DePaulis, Grade 4
St Joseph School

Birds
Birds flying graceful and sweet,
when you fly I hear you tweet.
You like to fly more than me,
when you're done you rest in a tree.
Lauren Wewer, Grade 4
St Joseph School

Pumpkin Roll
Mix up the batter
Put the roll in the oven
A delicious treat
Trista Ikeler, Grade 4
Watsontown Elementary School

Falling Leaves
Red, yellow, and orange
Leaves falling on the soft ground
Chilly wind blowing
Elise Pertusio, Grade 4
Watsontown Elementary School

Candy
Candy is so sweet
I hope they let me eat some
Mmm, that was yummy
Breanna Hassinger, Grade 4
Watsontown Elementary School

Lost Love
Darkness sailed across the sky in the beautiful land of Zye.
A woman was there, her long flowing hair lingered in a question of why.
Why was she here? Whatever had happened? And why was she coming to Zye?
A man was strolling and the clouds were rolling, giving birth to rain.
Then the man stopped and suddenly hopped over to the woman in pain.
With that very woman he fell in love, he claimed she was an angel from above.
The man loved his future bride and once took her out to watch the tides.
In and out, the waves flowed about.
They went for a swim, but the man returned grim.
His love was nowhere to be found and the man was sure he had drowned.
At that very moment it began to pour, rain was falling like never before.
Then he stopped and turned around, and headed back toward the town.
That day was even more upsetting, since secretly he had made plans for a wedding.
He dreamt himself into a deep sleep, and suddenly felt a joyful leap.
He knew his love was out there, he thought she had a better life elsewhere.
Darkness sailed across the sky in the beautiful land of Zye.
A woman was there, her long flowing hair lingered in a question of why.
Aleah Alderson, Grade 5
Mount Carmel Area Elementary School

One Last Breath
One last breath and it's the end one last breath and I won't see you again
One last breath, my dear, I'm nearing my end
You say "I love you, please don't go!"
But it's not something I can control
11:58 as I say my last good-bye
"I love you, too, and we will meet again." 11:59 as you begin to cry
The clock strikes 12 as I drift off to sleep a sleep of which I will never awaken
You scream "No, don't leave me!" People look but don't dare to walk in
As my heart stops, yours starts to race
You cannot believe this is happening right here in this place
One last breath I took somewhere, somehow
But I will always be with you, as I am right now
As I look down upon you at the sight I hoped to never see
There I lie, there you cry helplessly
One last breath I took, but it's not quite good-bye
Until we meet again, I think, as I try not to cry
Kiersten Bohman, Grade 6
Mcclure Middle School

What Is Blue?
Blue is the feeling of rain, it brings you no pain.
Blue can be cold, its color can be very bold.
It can bring you joy, like a new toy.
You can feel blue in a breeze like the wind going through the trees.
You can smell blue too, in a hyacinth or in forget-me-nots.
Blue is like the twilight, it smiles in the night.
Blueberry pie is blue, like the color of the sky.
You can hear blue, like the crashing waves of the sea.
If you listen hard you can hear blue, like the sweet song of a blue jay.
Blue can smile at you, all through the day.
Blue is peace, it will never cease.
Blue is the ice that cools your drink,
Blue is the best color what do you think?
Meaghan Rossi, Grade 6
St Hilary of Poitiers School

Who Am I?
I'm cute and cuddly.
You cuddle me at night.
I'm as warm as your blanket on a cold dark winter night.
When you are little you love me just as if I were real.
But as you grow you ignore me and I get torn.
The more you grow the more you forget about me.
But still I am blue in your heart.
Just please remember me before I fall apart.

Jessica Cetorelli, Grade 4
Jefferson Elementary School

Skiing
Soft wooshing as you turn
Feels like you're flying
Cold wind in your face
Snow like powder

Wind in your hair
Riding the chair lift up the hill
The beautiful mountain as you look down skiing.

Morgan Pecuch, Grade 5
Maxwell Elementary School

Spring Is Near
When I step outside on a sunny morning,
I feel the warm sunlight on my face.
I know that spring is on its way,
to make us scream and play.
I like to see the fresh flowers blooming
and the rustle of the wind blowing against my body.
All I want to do is sit back, relax and enjoy
the beautiful spring time weather!

Rebecca Pietropaolo, Grade 6
Immaculate Conception School

Football Game
F ans are cheering
O ffsides on the Titans
O ffense scored a yard or two
T ouchdown! But we want more
B ring in an interception and drive it down the field
A ll the fans cheer for more
L et's go out there and score!
L ucky day because we won by four.

Nathaniel Gordon, Grade 5
Central Elementary School

Strong
S oldiers powerful as bears
T ry to encourage the soldiers
R emember they are fighting for us
O ld memories are streaming back into people's minds
N ever stop respecting the soldiers
G oing to end war

Brian Burzenski, Grade 4
Fairview Elementary School

The California Least Tern
The California Least Tern, have you heard?
Is one endangered and rare bird
It feeds on some fish
That makes a fine dish
I know I am right, trust my word.

This bird has a white and black head
Which looks like a crown, it is said
His bill is orange, not yellow
He's quite a nice fellow
Well, at least that's what I've read.

They are their own transportation
Who chat with their own nation
They live along the coast
And eat small fish the most
But they're endangered, and that's the frustration.

Michael Fishler, Grade 6
Nazareth Area Intermediate School

Darkness
Darkness…yes…it reminds me of a dark alley
Darkness is friends with light coming from the heights
But one without the other shall fall through the sky.

Even on Halloween, things may change
In the blazing sun,
Or in the haze of the moon.

For all things light may have a fright…
For all things extreme, it may seem…
Normal
Or abysmal.

Lying on a screen of shadows
"Rise, I say, Rise dark beings"
The light is not yet ready
For what lies ahead!

Shomari Holmes, Grade 6
Chichester Middle School

It's an Eggnog Day
It's an eggnog day.
The milky scent flows into your mouth.
It's beautiful thickness,
Sliding down your throat.
Its everlasting taste stays with you all day.
After one glass, you're ready for another.
The tasteful hint of cinnamon.
Coldness tickling your taste buds.
A waterfall of gold,
Swirling into your cup.
Large areas of gold with hints of brown.
Then you go to bed, praying for another eggnog day.

Zachariah Kracht, Grade 6
Pennridge North Middle School

There Was Never a Moment*

There was never a moment,
That I didn't want you,
When I didn't dream of you,
And imagine how you'd be.

You were always in my arms,
Holding you near,
Caressing your innocent brow.

There was never a moment,
I didn't think of you,
Your little arms around me,
Keeping you safe and warm.

Now that you're here,
You have gone beyond my expectations,
And my love for you was great and immediate.

There was never a moment,
You were away from my thoughts,
Now that you're here,
You'll never leave my heart!

Marlene Adelman, Grade 4
McKinley Elementary School
*Dedicated to my new sister Belle

A Math King

I read
As my finger slides over the problems
I digest
The questions at a speedy pace
Juggling the digits within my brain

I calculate
As my pencil scribbles down my thoughts
I apply
The Pemdas rules at every step
Extracting the numbers throughout my quest

I check
As my eyes sift through the process
I use
The skills I learn from you
Probing the answers at the end of my test

I smile
As my mind locks in the conclusion
I recognize
The powerful and logical training from you
Transforming me into a Math King

Michael Lu, Grade 6
Newtown Friends School

Softball

Single, double, triple, home run
No matter what you hit it's always fun
Coaches coaching, batters batting
The scores just keep on adding
Crack! The ball hit the bat
The ball flew out of the park and that was that
Running from base to base
The teams are face to face
Three strikes and you're out
That's what it's all about
The team is proud
The crowd is loud
In the end, when it's all done
We're happy whether lost or won.

Katie Kenney, Grade 6
St Jerome Elementary School

Christmas

Christmas makes me feel so good
It brings me lots of cheer
I'm overwhelmed with happiness
Nothing else makes me feel this way

Christmas is a special time for everyone
There's magic in the air
It's a joyful time that is spent with friends and family
And many memories are made

We sit in front of the fireplace
As the fire dances around the logs
We are so very tired after the long day
Like Santa, after delivering his gifts

Michael Murray, Grade 6
St Jerome Elementary School

To the Shore Once More

On a cold winter day I dream of the shore
Warm summer breezes to be once more
Seagulls skim waves while I search for shells
Funnel cake and caramel popcorn, Oh! those sweet smells

I could walk on the boardwalk morning and night
Souvenir shops and pinball arcades, Oh! what a sight
The thrill of the roller coaster and the merry-go-round
The children screaming with delight, how I love that sound

Soaking up sun; sitting by the salty sea
Waves roaring like a lion right in front of me
How I wish I could be there with my toes in the sand
On a blistering summer day, it would be so grand!

Kerianne Kistner, Grade 6
St Jerome Elementary School

High Merit Poems – Grades 4, 5 and 6

My Dog Saw a Frog

My dog saw a frog
There was tons of fog
I don't know how he saw the amphibian
We were in the Caribbean there was a Libyan right next to us
There were a lot of African people here in the Caribbean.

Andrew Young, Grade 4
St Anne School

Ocean

The sand and the ocean surrounding me
The waves crashing on the shore and seagulls screeching in the air
The refreshing scent of the ocean
The bitter salt water
The soft, inviting sand and serene ocean

Sarah Heise, Grade 5
St Anne School

Love

Love can start in many ways
you're just standing on the corner and in a second,
you see her standing there
it's like a replay in slow motion
she swings her hair back, looking beautiful.

Peyton Grant, Grade 6
John G Whittier School

Thanksgiving Means

Going to Rhode Island to spend Thanksgiving with family.
Having the most wonderful food in the world!!!
Playing with my cousins.
Seeing who can get the bigger half of the wishbone.
A time to be thankful for what you have.

Ben Ahmad, Grade 6
Moravian Academy Middle School

Kitty Kat

There once was a kitty named Kat,
Who always laid on her pink mat.
But Kat was not lazy,
Just a little crazy,
Because she laid next to the bat.

Emily Sniechoski, Grade 4
Sacred Heart School

Christmas

Christmas is a decorative holiday.
Christmas smells like gingerbread in the oven.
Christmas tastes like hot cocoa and marshmallows.
Christmas sounds like joyful cries of children.
Christmas feels like a warm sweater.

Tim Azizkhan, Grade 6
St Joseph School

Left and Lost, But Loved

Lost tiny puppy left in the cold.
The blistering wind and blundering snow.
If help doesn't come anytime soon.
Surely the creature will face great doom!
Shivering harshly from cold and fear.
Hope is lost, but help is near.
A blinding light shines past her eyes.
Lying there tranquil so still in disguise.
The little infant minute and weak.
Lets out a wail quiet and meek.
A creature walks toward her in a calming way.
Gentle hands saving the day.
If the dog could say just a mere two words.
"Thank you," would be the ones that were heard.

Mikhaila Layshock, Grade 6
Delahunty Middle School

What Is Red?

Red is the color when Christmas is here.
The lights, Santa Claus, and the reindeer
Red is dangerous and loud,
When we hear sirens on the road
Lollipops and Twizzlers remind me of red,
So do roses and strawberries.
They are as red as fireworks.
Red is your face when you're embarrassed,
It resembles bright red peppers.
Red is the hotness of boiling pots.
Burning and sizzling like snakes.
Red is a hot color also primary one.
Red is my favorite color, changing so bright.
It brings happiness and laughter to everyone's face.

Cintia Camacho, Grade 6
St Hilary of Poitiers School

Growing Up

My hair is as wavy as the ocean
My smile is as bright as the sun
I'm as crazy as a circus clown
And I love to have fun

I've grown a lot in the last few years
And it's bringing my grandma to tears
She used to love biting chubby cheeks
And nibbling at small ears

She loved the way I giggled in a squeaky sort of way
But now that I'm getting older it's all going away
Now I'm almost as tall as her, I'm changing every day
But giggling still might occur — when there is a funny thing to say!

Desiree Egan, Grade 4
Anne Frank School

Tony the Turtle

Tony the Turtle was playing a game.
He was not winning, and said, "This is lame."
He finally lost and was very mad.
He said to himself, "I am very sad."

Tony the Turtle went home that night.
He went to sleep, but he left on the light.
He woke up that morning and was very tired.
Later that day he was very wired.

Tony the Turtle was hanging around.
He fell asleep and was on the ground.
Then he woke up and played with his friends.
And this would be how the story ends!

Shannon Booth, Grade 4
St Andrew's School

Countries Giving Thanks

Brazilian food
   Thanksgiving from another country
     All homemade
       Signaling a good harvest

American delicacies
   Food made from the heart
     Cooking in the oven
       Everything is ready

Taking the hands of different countries
   Wrapped around the world
     Holding a cherished moment
       A holiday we all celebrate: Thanksgiving

Olivia Ames, Grade 5
Falk Laboratory School

Chocolate

Hershey makes it delicious
Children taste it
Parents say it is not nutritious
But hey…it's chocolate!

It does not have much of a color
It's really just brown
But when you eat it you just can't put it down
Because hey…it's chocolate!

It comes in different types
Milk, Dark and White
It makes everything right
BECAUSE HEY…IT'S CHOCOLATE!

Caroline Kenton, Grade 5
Pocopson Elementary School

Grandparents Are…

A big part of my life.
Making delicious food to eat when we visit them.
Listening patiently when I need them.
Coming into my mind when I'm thinking about love.
Loving me no matter what.

Amy Lu, Grade 6
Moravian Academy Middle School

Grandparents Are…

The smell of fresh baked cookies.
The seagulls on the beach.
The warmth of the holidays
The happiness of a little puppy running around.
The excitement in my heart when I see them.

Morgan Hesse, Grade 6
Moravian Academy Middle School

Red Is My Favorite Color

You can see it on flags; you can smell it in roses;
You can taste it in apples; you can feel it on strawberries;
You can hear it with cardinals.
The only thing you can't do with red is
Eat a red blueberry.

Ashley Durbin, Grade 5
All Saints Catholic School

Candy Canes

Candy canes are sweet, delicious with delight
You hang them on Christmas trees it's a pretty sight
But if you're not careful your sister will take a bite
It's not a pretty sight
But if she does it's not her fault it's the candy cane's delight.

Mira Newman, Grade 5
McKinley Elementary School

Freedom

Freedom is a lovely thing that doesn't bring pain or sorrow
it's a gift worth saving
freedom is like a door of opportunities
a ball of happiness
but some don't treat freedom with care until it's taken away

Jala Bullock, Grade 6
John G Whittier School

Friends

There was a young kitten who lived in a house.
She once had a friend who was a mouse.
They went out for a nice walk
They had a nice talk on their way.
Then the friends went to kitten's place to play together.

Megan Coval, Grade 4
West Branch Area Elementary School

Happiness

Happiness is winning a competition that you've been preparing for
Happiness is getting an A on a test that you studied really hard for
Happiness is eating delicious birthday cake on your birthday with your friends
Happiness is blue like a big blue sky on a sunny summer day
Happiness tastes like warm buttered popcorn melting in your mouth at the movie theater
Happiness smells like a fresh baked gingerbread house getting put on the dinner table on Christmas Day
Happiness sounds like the sizzle of fresh pancakes on the stove almost ready to eat
Happiness feels like cuddling with your furry dog on a cold winter day
Happiness looks like a fresh gingerbread cookie looking back at me with a nice smile on his face
Happiness makes me feel like I'm the luckiest person in the world
Happiness makes the world a better place for everyone
Happiness is the greatest thing you could ever have

Emily Zeigler, Grade 6
West Allegheny Middle School

Imagination

Imagination is a thousand elephants charging in an endless field.
Imagination is ball lightning Ka-Booming down on a dark red sunset.
Imagination is a transparent globe, full of ideas that build up inside you.
Imagination is pitch black, yet bright green.
Imagination tastes like pumpkin pie piled and piled with whipped cream.
Imagination smells like fresh cotton candy right after it is made in the machine.
Imagination sounds like a guinea pig singing with great passion any song it learns.
Imagination feels like a humongous vat of Jell-O.
Imagination looks like a cave spray-painted with every color you can think of.
Imagination makes me want to illustrate it in any way, shape, or form.
Imagination exists in all people of any shape or size.
Imagination is the mystical force that brings you to your very own world of peril, mystery, and adventure.

Jarod William Seibel, Grade 6
West Allegheny Middle School

Competition

Competition is the amazing game winner
Competition is accomplished by wining a trophy or the gain of pride
Competition is like the cameras clicking like a cricket on a hot summer's eve
Competition is red like the color of hard work
Competition tastes like a big swordfish you caught after a long battle
Competition smells like the fear of the other team when they faced the undefeated team
Competition sounds like my heart going thump-thump-thump when I was taking the free throw shot to win the game
Competition feels like the stinky, smelly, sweat soaring off my face like raging rapids
Competition looks like a hungry cheetah chasing an ostrich
Competition makes me like an eagle soaring over trees looking for its prey
Competition looks like a feeding frenzy of fish looking for food
Competition is me playing video games against my friends

Justin Baker, Grade 6
West Allegheny Middle School

Love

Love is ruby red like a beating heart in school on Valentine's Day
Love looks like a fabulous little baby sitting in a red crib feeling cheerful on a Sunday morning.
Love tastes like chocolate candy when you eat it on a Monday afternoon.
It smells like a marvelous perfume when you spray it on your body before you go to a party on Saturday.
It sound like ringing church bells on Sundays and on holiday.
It feels like hopping happily around the whole school on a spring day.

Mateusz Czebatul, Grade 6
Our Lady of Ransom School

Birds
Birds are unique in many different ways,
If you train them well they will sing all day.

They have feathers not many animals do,
Yesterday all over the house my little bird flew.

They look so graceful while flying their big outstretched wings,
When they're flying they look as majestic as kings.

I've taught my bird tricks he is so tremendously smart,
He is a dear friend I hold extremely close to my heart.

Birds are the animals I love most of all,
I love listening to my bird and his funny little calls.
Gianni Fera, Grade 6
Ss Simon and Jude Elementary School

The Beach
My favorite place to go is the beach,
I go there every summer; it's the place I can't wait to reach.

Playing in the sand is fun,
But there is more you can do, there's a ton.

Boarding is a total blast,
But don't go too far or you'll fall very fast.

The weather is warm, the beaches bright,
I even like to go to the beach at night.

Then suddenly it is so hard to believe,
It is time to go home, so we pack up and leave.
Nathan Bruce, Grade 6
Ss Simon and Jude Elementary School

The Grateful Sloth
Slinking slowly and sleepily,
I am thankful for the branch of the tree

My claws help me hang and my fur keeps me warm,
as I sleep away from harm

Harmful enemies? I have none,
when it comes to friends I have a ton!

In my opinion night is the best,
so in the dark and peace I can rest

I am thankful for the world that surrounds me,
with my forest friends, food and my tree!!
Amber Huddell, Grade 6
Interboro GATE Program

Halloween Night
I cannot wait for Halloween night,
but the only bad part is it usually gives me a fright.

Gray wolves are howling,
black dogs are growling.

Haunted houses have all the ghouls,
while all the ghosts are in the schools.

I went to a party and dressed up as a zombie,
but a little kid got scared and went crying to his mommy.

Witches flying into the moonlight,
riding their broomsticks out of sight.
Bobby McMaster, Grade 5
Ss Simon and Jude Elementary School

A Fall Day
What a beautiful fall day,
All the chirping blue jays.

All you hear is a crunching sound,
From all the leaves now lying on the ground.

There are so many leaves to rake,
It doesn't take long before I break.

I love to pile the leaves really high,
As I rake them they seem to multiply.

Jumping into them is so much fun,
I only get to do it when my job is done.
Garrett Berner, Grade 5
Ss Simon and Jude Elementary School

Nature
Nature is such a wonderful thing,
I love to stand by and hear the birds sing

When I get up in the morning, the first thing I see,
Is a baby deer, looking straight at me.

Sometimes I enjoy the shade of a tree,
As long as I don't get stung by a bee!

But sadly some people simply don't agree with me,
At least not until I show them the old oak tree

But the best part of nature is when the seasons turn to spring
And experience all the new life that it brings!
Tyler Mosher, Grade 6
Ss Simon and Jude Elementary School

High Merit Poems – Grades 4, 5 and 6

Ice Cream
Ice cream, ice cream, ice cream
Different flavors
Chocolate, vanilla, strawberry and more
With sprinkles, hot fudge galore!
Dairy Queen, Brusters
So many places to go
I want, I want, I want some more!

The ice cream truck goes beep, beep, beep
Go tell mom, ice cream is cheap, cheap, cheap
Your mom says yes
Yeah, yoo hoo!
Thank you!

Erin Pfeffer, Grade 5
Saint Theresa School

I Don't Care
As I was walking across the ocean floor,
stepping on seashells as it numbed my feet,
as the pain of the crabs biting my toes crossed my mind,
but I didn't care.

As I fell in the water because of the strong wind,
my eyes burning of the salt water,
as the jelly fish float around me hoping that I do not get stung,
but I don't care.

All these things hurt so bad,
but make me feel good inside.

Emma Cusick, Grade 5
Foster Elementary School

The Earth
Every day more life comes to Earth.
Peace is regained and war starts again.
Flowers grow, trees sprout,
Then winter comes and leaves fall out.
This is natural nature it always has been.
But some people find it a sin.
I disagree with this statement.
I say let the Earth have its natural balance.
Let the sky be blue and black when it's night.
Since Earth has life it has the right.
Love
The Earth

Madeline Longstreth, Grade 4
McKinley Elementary School

Thanksgiving Is…
A whole lot of turkey on your dinner plate.
Sharing time with your relatives in New York.
Enjoying the break from school.
Going over to your friends' houses.
Giving thanks!

Dillon Memon, Grade 6
Moravian Academy Middle School

Remembering Veterans
For those who have died we show great appreciation
Our veterans have risked their lives for this nation
Because of you, I am here
Because of you we no longer hide in fear

People come and people go, is there hope do we know
I sure hope so
Loved ones here lost and some are spared,
yet we live freely without despair

You face fear and death each day
This is no time to fool and play
For the battle wages on, 24 hours a day,
and leaves behind an image called history

With the turn of time the battle is gone,
The roar of war moves on,
War comes and war goes, war slips beneath your toes

Julia Foster, Grade 6
Pennridge North Middle School

When I Play Basketball
When I play basketball
I feel strong.
I dribble, dribble down the court
I bust a move,
I love the sport.
I shoot, I score,
The fans want more.
My heart is going crazy.
It's half time now,
I need a break.
But I can't stop thinking about what it will take,
To win this game,
And have a name,
To be the champions,
Who won their last game.
So you see when I play basketball
It's like a whole other me,
That is because when I play basketball it is key.

Andrea McCormick, Grade 5
St Peter Cathedral School

Beautiful Nature
Beautiful nature looks like:

Grass as green as a caterpillar
Trees as tall as a mountain
Butterflies as colorful as a rainbow in the sky

Bears climb up trees
To get honey from bees.

That's why nature is beautiful to me.

Toni Smith, Grade 4
Fairview Elementary School

Cardinal

Fiery red cardinal perched on a violet rose bush,
Whistling with the warm wind,
While the rain clouds travel by,
With a soft sprinkle.

Duncan Claerbaut, Grade 4
Fairview Elementary School

The Beach

Is so peaceful
When you need a place to go.
The roaring waves
Crashing and relaxing at the same time.

The beach
Lovely, amazing
Beautiful and still
The beach is serenely tranquil.

The beach, the sand
Squeezing between your toes
As the crashing waves
Roaringly go, go, go.

The thundering of the waves
Seem to be saying
"I am king of the ocean.
Come swim with me."

Time for the day
To come to an end.
Goodbye soothing beach.
I will come again!

Brooke Dienner, Grade 6
Linville Hill Mennonite School

My Mother Loves Me

M y mother's cooking is the best
Y ells at me when I misbehave

M y mother's love
O ther moms can't be compared
T he greatest
H ates when I misbehave
E very time I sin she forgives me
R eady for anything

L oves me always
O ne of a kind
V ery generous and kind
E veryone likes her
S he is wonderful

M akes my family happy
E stablished the recipe for happiness

Zachary Mangus, Grade 4
St Joseph School

Foods

Tart lemon juice,
Sour sweet tarts,
Red hot peppers,
Sour purple grapes,
Super spicy sausages,
Bitter pineapples,

Creamy pumpkin pies,
Freezing peach slushies,
Juicy green apples,
Minty chocolate peppermints,
Zesty orange oranges,
Icy ice cream,
Delicious sweet peppers,

Warm cinnamon buns,
Colorful lollipops,
Sugary candy,
Juicy red strawberries,
Chocolaty pop-tarts,
Strawberry red apples,
Sticky apple dumplings,

Mmmm!!!! Now I'm really hungry.

Marie Zimmerman, Grade 6
Linville Hill Mennonite School

About Me

My name is Yasmine,
Some say that I'm mean,
But, I am not mean,
I'm as cool as a bean.

I like to sing and dance,
Do you like my Hannah Montana pants?
I like to go to the country,
It reminds me of peace.

I am pretty tall,
And I look like a Barbie doll.
I have long, black hair,
In the morning, it causes quiet a scare.

I have many friends,
We fuss and fight but always make amends.
We like to go skating,
But never do any hating.

I'm only eleven,
But I hope I go to Heaven
Goodbye for now; I'm going to play a game,
Aren't you glad you know my name?

Yasmine Thurston, Grade 6
Chichester Middle School

What Nobody Thinks on Halloween

There are plenty of explanations why things happen on Halloween, well…this is what I think.
When a wisp of air rushes past your face, it might be just a breeze.
But it could also be a ghost trying to be silent but just barely touching you as you walk to the next house.
If you see some bushes trembling in the moonlight, it might just be a small animal.
But it could also be a bloodsucking vampire looking to see who his next victim might be.
If you're going to a haunted house with your friends you might see a door open just a little,
it might be a worker.
But it could also be a gremlin, sneaking up trying to scare you in a creepy way.
If you're counting your candy after a great night of trick-or-treating and there is an open piece of candy,
it could be just an accident.
But it could be a crazed scientist putting a potion in trying to turn you into a monster!
If you go out and nothing like this happens to you,
you know that they are just waiting, waiting until next year.
Happy Halloween!

Julia Davis, Grade 6
Hillcrest Elementary School

Contentment

Contentment is a sunny hot summer day at Topsail Beach with my family.
Contentment is chirping blue jays in the morning on a spring day.
Contentment is the sun smiling down at you while floating on a big comfy raft,
   floating on your pool.
Contentment is baby blue sweet cotton candy that melts in your mouth.
Contentment tastes like my favorite piece of tasty dark chocolate, savoring every bite.
Contentment smells like cinnamon muffins baking in the oven on a cold winter day.
Contentment sounds like raindrops hitting my window at night while I am trying sleep,
   hearing boom, boom, boom!
Contentment feels like my favorite fuzzy slippers I put on my feet after my warm shower.
Contentment looks like me enjoying the best ice cream ever, cappuccino crunch, at the beach.
Contentment makes me feel relaxed and happy to be myself.
Contentment is a great trait that everyone should aspire.
Contentment is about having inner peace and loving the way you are!

Abby Walls, Grade 6
West Allegheny Middle School

Sadness

Sadness is getting hurt and no one will help you.
Sadness is no one to care for you.
Sadness is the black sky raining down on you.
Sadness is the color midnight blue for the sound of nothing but the owls at midnight saying hoot…hoot…hoot.
Sadness tastes like the bitter bite of a sour apple.
Sadness smells like rotten eggs decomposing on the moldy ground.
Sadness feels like the sting of a thousand bees stinging over and over again.
Sadness looks like a lonely orphan with no purpose in life.
Sadness makes me feel lonely and down.
Sadness is a black cloud that stalks you in life and in your dreams.

Ronnie Schubert, Grade 6
West Allegheny Middle School

Halloween Jack-o'-Lanterns

Halloween pumpkins give quite a scare, cool and gross and icky.
You'll see pumpkins on Halloween night, cool costumes on strangers, and spiders everywhere.
Witches fly on that moonlit night, with their magic potions every Halloween night.
Kids go trick-or-treating and when they open the door you get quite a scare!

Nicole Vebelun, Grade 4
Burgettstown Elementary Center

Sharks
Gray with large, sharp teeth,
Eating almost anything,
Ocean predators.
Damon Peluchette, Grade 5
East Union Intermediate Center

Rontu
Bright, glistening eyes,
Long, brown, rough and aged fur,
Very strong, a friend.
Noah Darsie, Grade 5
East Union Intermediate Center

Frogs
I love watching frogs
Jump and splash in the cool pond
During the summer
Jordan Palmer, Grade 5
Burgettstown Elementary Center

Sea Turtles
Swimming through the kelp,
Gliding through the ocean blue,
Looking for dinner.
Tyler Zagorski, Grade 5
East Union Intermediate Center

Sting Rays
Swimming with such grace,
Floating on the ocean floor,
In the deep, blue sea.
Joshua Cendrowski, Grade 5
East Union Intermediate Center

Dolphins
Swimming in the sea,
Up and down through the blue waves,
As a ship goes by.
Alyssa Scoccia, Grade 5
East Union Intermediate Center

Dolphins
Dolphins swim freely,
In the deep, bright blue ocean,
Jumping playfully.
Destiny Ordean, Grade 5
East Union Intermediate Center

Sea Turtles
Sea turtles are cute,
Sea turtles have nice green shells,
Sea turtles lay eggs.
Kelsie Urbanek, Grade 5
East Union Intermediate Center

Caroline
I love my daughter Caroline with long black hair and bright blue eyes.
Her presence brings me total joy, even though I wanted a boy.

I brush her hair every night. It fills her face with great delight.
She's very smart and pretty too, and does so very well in school.
She's not my only child though, I also have a son named Joe.
He's much older than Caroline and isn't home most of the time.

Caroline got sick one day, and at the house she had to stay.
When she got hot her head got wetter, but after three hours she got better.
I was worried it was flu, but don't blame me 'cause you would too.
She's never gotten sick before, only cuts and then no more.

She says she feels like she is dying, I really hope that she is lying.
She lies in bed from day to day, it's June and this began in May.
I called the doctor right away, and over he came the next day.
"She's breathing slow," said Dr. Night, the thought of this turned my face white.

The doctor stayed with us that night, the things he said gave me a fright.
"Breathing slow," he said while sighing, "Means Caroline just might be dying."
And so my daughter Caroline, with long black hair and bright blue eyes,
And every day she lies in bed, my daughter Caroline is dead.
Baily Smith, Grade 5
Bedminster Elementary School

The Moon
As Artemis runs, bounds and leaps I lay in bed falling asleep
In my dreams she's coming near with her sacred pack of deer
Do I run, jump, sprint or scream? This is only a joyous dream
She and I take a jog through the weird and greenish fog
I can see Mount Olympus drawing near. I twitch with loathing, dread and fear
Will I meet Zeus and Hera? This is like a different era
As I come closer and closer, do I see Ares or just a poser?
Such beauty, grace, and elegance soon I sprint and run the distance
I hope, I pray that I can go in. My face spreads to a grin
Will I ever wake from this? Or will it stay this wonderful bliss
I feel a sudden surge of warm as I wake to a silver storm.
Sydney Towell, Grade 5
East Goshen Elementary School

Excitement
Excitement is a million dollars that you won in the lottery.
Excitement is an A+ on a huge test in your worst subject.
Excitement is an amazing animal that let you pet it.
Excitement is an ocean of colors like aquamarine and emerald waves.
Excitement tastes like a chilly, fresh strawberry on a hot summer day.
Excitement smells like hot, fresh baked cookies straight from the oven.
Excitement sounds like buttery popcorn cooking in the microwave. Pop! Pop!
Excitement feels like a soft, fuzzy blanket wrapped around you.
Excitement looks like little kids jumping and laughing in the summer.
Excitement makes me feel as happy as a butterfly flying high in the sky.
Excitement dances across the floor to the beat of the music.
Excitement is scoring the game winning goal of the Stanley Cup championship game
with only 10 seconds left on the buzzer.
Erin Smith, Grade 6
West Allegheny Middle School

High Merit Poems – Grades 4, 5 and 6

Fall

Fall
is fun
nothing gets done
Looking at the bees
jumping in leaves
Fall is
fun.

David Nguyen, Grade 5
Hamilton Elementary School

Thanksgiving

Thanksgiving
Fun, awesome
Playing, play fighting, playing ball
Fall, fun, family, games
Falling, fighting, jumping
Fun, colorful
Leaves

Kyla Stretz, Grade 5
Hamilton Elementary School

Leaves

Leaves
leaves crunch
leaves are falling
down, down, down, down
yellow, red, and orange
jump on it
Leaves.

Tamara Cabrera, Grade 5
Hamilton Elementary School

Fall

fall
colorful season
not so cold
with no blazing sun
with Thanksgiving fun
many leaves
blow

Jovanny Collado Cruz, Grade 5
Hamilton Elementary School

Leaves

Leaves
fall…fall…fall
Leaves turn orange, yellow,
Also purple weee…
Weee…Leaves
fall…fall
down

Kiara Mealing, Grade 5
Hamilton Elementary School

Speed

Speed is a blazing light coming to extinguish the darkness.
Speed is a fierce cheetah stalking his prey, ready to pounce.
Speed is a boom from a cannonball catapulting out of its cannon.
Speed is yellow like the lightning racing to the ground.
Speed tastes like sweet frosting on a warm cupcake.
Speed smells like the gasoline of a jet about to fuel up for its flight.
Speed sounds like the roar of the car's engine revving up for the race.
Speed feels like the smooth sleek speedboat's edges skimming the water.
Speed looks like a runner's footsteps crossing before the rest.
Speed makes me determined to win at any cost.
Speed is the waves running along the water to crash against the shore.
Speed is a blazing light coming to extinguish the darkness.

Felicia Mackey, Grade 6
West Allegheny Middle School

Your Imagination

Imagination is something that will take you anywhere.
Imagination will take you from fairy tales to nightmares.
Imaginations can be fun and creative or just terrible!
Imaginations are amazing!
If we didn't have our imaginations,
We wouldn't have any of our mechanical inventions, like cellphones.
Imagine love that is grateful, peaceful, or just heartbreaking.
Imagine you can be far away in a world of wonder.
Imaginations can take you anywhere without even leaving the room.
Imagine if you do something bad and what might happen.
Imagination can do anything, it can even change your future.
Your imagination is amazing!!!

Madison Nudd, Grade 5
Oswayo Valley Elementary School

Friendship

Friendship is the sound of laughter at a sleepover
Friendship is long walks and private talks
Friendship is eating Easy-Mac and texting friends
Friendship is yellow like the sun looking down on me
Friendship tastes like sweet, chocolaty brownies from the bakery
Friendship smells like flowery perfume flowing through the house
Friendship sounds like the soft chirp of birds in the morning
Friendship feels like the soft, silky fur of a kitten brushing against your leg
Friendship looks like bright pink, flowers blooming in a cold dreary meadow
Friendship makes me comfortable and cared about
Friendship is the warm glow inside you when friends surround you
Friendship is a true gift in life

Kaitlyn Kariman, Grade 6
West Allegheny Middle School

Excitement

Excitement is mint green like a tall tree in Penny Pack Park on a cool crisp day.
It looks like a big mint green tree in an enchanted forest on a spooky summer night.
It tastes like a piece of mint green gum on a drafty day down the shore.
It smells like mint tea cooking on the stove on a brisk November day.
It sounds like a whistle in the wind when the storm is just around the corner.
It feels like a cold frosty day outside at the last inning of the Phillies World Series game.

Christopher Campbell, Grade 6
Our Lady of Ransom School

Imagination

Imagination is an adventurous butterfly flying through my brain.
Imagination is an open field inviting me to sit down and write a new wonderful creative story.
Imagination is my way of escaping out of my regular life and into the new.
Imagination is like neon colored fireworks filling the air with energy.
Imagination tastes like all the different colored jelly beans.
Imagination smells like a sweet aroma of wild flowers and roses.
Imagination sounds like proud playful puppies playing in a valley.
Imagination feels like fur on a bunny when it lays at rest curled up like a tiny ball.
Imagination looks like an empty world begging for you to fill it with creative things.
Imagination makes me feel like there is a spark of enjoyment moving through my body.
Imagination is a big part of my life.

Alexis Smith, Grade 6
West Allegheny Middle School

Happiness

Happiness is spending time with my friends at the mall.
Happiness is seeing my new puppy Pepper when I come home from school
Happiness is having no homework over the weekend
Happiness is a giant green growing gladiolus flower in the fields
Happiness tastes like a freshly poured Coke over crackling ice
Happiness smells like freshly baked hot chocolate chip cookies
Happiness sounds like a large bag of Doritos being opened for the very first time
Happiness feels like a new white soft cuddly harp seal Beanie baby
Happiness looks like Christmas morning when we walk downstairs to open all of our presents
Happiness makes me smile
Happiness is a beautiful butterfly fluttering by

Megan McElhany, Grade 6
West Allegheny Middle School

Happiness

Happiness is the feeling of when you hit the game-winning home run in the championship softball game.
Happiness is when you go for a walk in the park and hear all of the woodland creatures like soft singing songbirds.
Happiness is when the Penguins won the Stanley Cup for the first time in 17 years.
Happiness is the yellow sun shining on you in the park on a summer day.
Happiness tastes like freshly made milk chocolate.
Happiness smells like 5 dozen fresh cut yellow roses.
Happiness sounds like the laugh of a child.
Happiness feels like the soft skin of a newborn baby.
Happiness looks like 2 little children playing in a meadow on a warm spring afternoon.
Happiness makes me feel that everyone should smile at least 5 times a day.
Happiness is when it sounds like you hear all of the colorful leaves singing in the autumn.

Kayla Stevens, Grade 6
West Allegheny Middle School

My Song of Life

Falling. I'm in a colorful tunnel falling. Down, down into warm oceanic waters below. Splash. I feel my body plunge into peace and serenity. I relax my muscles and look up at the welcoming sun through the waters beginning. I begin to sing. Floating a top a vast sea. I hum as I pull myself onto the silky sand of a windy island. The wind wraps me up in its cold and chilling presence. "Don't be angry!" I sing softly to the aggravated wind. He begins to sing along and many majestic notes fill the atmosphere. The soft beat spins me around and the slow notes tickle my skin. But I must watch out for the high and sharp notes, for they will prick my skin. I wrap myself in bliss around the notes and sure enough I get pinched by a high note. A small drop of blood falls down, down to the sun set, turning the whole island bright maroon. Suddenly I stop singing. I realize that my perfect life song has ended with much joy and tranquility.

Carmen Fisher, Grade 6
Hopewell Memorial Jr High School

Happiness

Happiness is a bike you ride all day.
Happiness is a day that I don't have to go to school.
Happiness is a day where I can go anywhere I want.
Happiness is as blue as the sky.
Happiness tastes like a delicious five star meal.
Happiness smells like a fresh apple.
Happiness sounds like a quiet flower garden.
Happiness feels like a smooth piece of glass.
Happiness looks like a colorful rainbow.
Happiness makes me feel relaxed.
Happiness is like a kid.

Randy Doehre, Grade 6
West Allegheny Middle School

Happiness

Happiness is a newborn puppy
Happiness is the blue summer sky
Happiness is everyone you love
Happiness is a bright bouncy blue
Happiness tastes like a big box of gourmet chocolates
Happiness smells like fresh baked cookies straight from the oven
Happiness sounds like best friends laughing together ha-ha-ha
Happiness feels like a chinchilla's fur
Happiness looks like a baby smiling at you
Happiness makes me cheerful and pleasant
Happiness is getting an awesome grade on my poem

Maria Kindy, Grade 6
West Allegheny Middle School

Happiness

Happiness is a good thing
Happiness is winning the lottery
Happiness is being a fantastic friend
Happiness is the color pink
Happiness tastes like a Jolly Rancher
Happiness smells like a big bowl of chocolate chip cookies
Happiness sounds like a loud bird chirping happily
Happiness feels like a soft silk blanket
Happiness looks like a very colorful rainbow
Happiness makes me like the sunshine on a warm summer day
Happiness is like a big flat screen TV

Devin Selinsky, Grade 6
West Allegheny Middle School

Two Paths

I came to this fork in the road.
Two paths ahead of me.
Which way should I go?
Should I follow the crowd?
Or go down the road only wise men go down?
I realized that if I want to be great
I should go down the road not many go down
It is a long road ahead if I want to succeed
But this is my choice if I want to be the best I can be.

Hope Bowden, Grade 6
Hopewell Memorial Jr High School

What Is Christmas?

Backyard snowball fights
Igloos glistening in the sunlight
Snow covered branches
Carolers sweetly singing.

Fuzzy red and white stockings as fat as can be
Juicy tender ham sizzling
Fluffy, sugary lady locks
Mirrored Santas reflecting peace.

That is Christmas!

Adriana Halulko, Grade 4
Fairview Elementary School

Fear

Fear is a big rottweiler chasing you
Fear is a flame catching your house on fire
Fear is someone being locked in a dark room without any lights
Fear is the color ebony on a dark and stormy night
Fear tastes like the hottest jalapeno pepper in the world
Fear smells like a dead skunk that just got run over by a car
Fear sounds like a girl screaming as loud as she can for help
Fear feels like someone getting bit by a tiger
Fear looks like a burglar busting through the window
Fear makes the grass shiver as if it were cold
Fear is someone telling you not to talk or you'll die

Allyssa Tome, Grade 6
West Allegheny Middle School

Happiness

Happiness is the birds singing in the morning.
Happiness is the thing that keeps me going through the day.
Happiness is the smile on my face every day.
Happiness is the bright yellow star in the dark sky.
Happiness tastes like chocolate chip cookies fresh out of the oven.
Happiness smells like daffodils blooming in the meadow.
Happiness sounds like popcorn popping over the hot stove.
Happiness feels like the gentle breeze brushing against my face.
Happiness looks like my mom smiling in the morning.
Happiness makes me want to never stop trying.
Happiness is a new adventure starting every day.

Austin Garcia, Grade 6
West Allegheny Middle School

Miss Lutz

M erry and joyful.
I ntelligent when it comes to teaching.
S o nice, pretty and beautiful.
S o happy and never sad.

L oves to teach and to be nice to others.
U ses vivid and precise words.
T eaches Language Arts, Science and Poetry.
Z ebra is not her favorite animal, but an elephant is.

Riley Napoleon, Grade 5
Foster Elementary School

Write What?
I'm staring at this blank, blank page.
This is a terrible plight!
I'm guessing that I'll start to age
Before I have something to write.

I'm thinking of writing about the fall
With all its leaves red and yellow.
Fall certainly isn't the worst thing at all,
Though better I think is its fellow,

Which is winter, with all its white, white snow,
That has the sun glistening off it.
But I don't like that theme. I know
I could write on something with wit!

A poem on a book that I have read?
Or math could be a topic?
Even something that I've heard said?
Perhaps on being sick?

I guess I could write about my pets
Or about my family.
Maybe even about my house!
Oh dear, what's wrong with me?

Molly Harnish, Grade 5
The American Academy

Internet Adventure
Interesting facts are everywhere;
All day long at the Internet I stare.
I can tell you that it is very rare
That I'd give up the computer just to share.

The Internet is an amazing thing,
Just search what you want, and it will come up — bing!
You can look at a picture or place or thing.
The Internet has…basically everything!

I click on the link and it blows my mind
A whole library of websites all combined!
I am quite amazed at what I can find,
But the Internet sites are making me blind.

Games are the thing I'm most interested in,
And when you're on the Internet, you have a whole bin.
Looking at them all, I make a slight grin.
"I think that I'll take one of these games for a spin!"

The Internet gives lots of help, you can see.
It hands out information, and most for free.
The Internet is a guarantee
That for up-to-date evidence, it's the key!

Rachel Meell, Grade 6
The American Academy

Christmas Day
I love Christmas day
Everyone is out to play
I always have so much fun
But all of my clothing makes me hot like the sun

Rebecca Morris, Grade 4
McKinley Elementary School

Cardinal
Blazing red cardinal perched on a black Trans Am,
Nestling her tiny babies,
Dark blue rain pours from the stormy heavens,
Mother cardinal whistles and protects.

Chad Plumley, Grade 4
Fairview Elementary School

Dancing Gardens
I love luscious, lacy dancing gardens,
Dancing in the whirling, whipping wind.
Water your dancing gardens, see what happens.
My tale is done, see you in the garden!

Rachel Hickok, Grade 4
W R Croman Elementary School

Teacher of the Piano
How your hands move
With such grace, so light, so tender,
Making the beautiful music dance across the pages.
Only the best can do so.

Christine S. Malek, Grade 6
Moravian Academy Middle School

Freedom
Life before freedom was bad
but now life is wonderful like a rainstorm
life before freedom was nothing but darkness
but now we get to see the light

Joshua Glover, Grade 6
John G Whittier School

The Night Sky
Last night I went out to look at the night sky,
all the stars above so high,
they glistened as I looked at them,
they are as sparkly as a gem.

Ally Conrad, Grade 4
St Joseph School

Cardinal
Apple red cardinal perched on a pine tree tip,
Glances at a school bus in the empty lot.
Thinking about her winter home,
During a frostbitten wintry blizzard.

Marina Fink, Grade 4
Fairview Elementary School

High Merit Poems – Grades 4, 5 and 6

Thanksgiving Is
Hanging out with family.
Watching the big game.
Looking at coupons in the newspaper.
Playing in the snow.
Eating my aunt's great cooking.
Thomas Lantz, Grade 6
Moravian Academy Middle School

Basketball
I love that feeling dribbling
down the court shooting
for the win
swish we
won!
Nickolo Lima, Grade 6
Notre Dame School

Breezy Days
The blue and green ocean
swooshes by as we
sit on the
tan colored
beach.
Kristina David, Grade 6
Notre Dame School

Basketball
Basketball is my favorite sport
Especially when I shoot
At the hoop
Swish it,
Score!
Kelsey Cromie, Grade 6
Notre Dame School

The Wind
I really love the wind
flowing through my hair
it feels great
then suddenly
quiet
Tony Bianco, Grade 6
Notre Dame School

Family
Family
Funny jokes
Laughing, playing, snuggling
Happy, funny, athletic, music
Friends
Kate McGarry, Grade 4
McKinley Elementary School

Joy
Joy is like moving up a level in dance.
Joy is like getting a good grade on a test that you study really hard for.
Joy is like getting another belt in karate.
Joy is the color of purple like a plump grape on a vine.
Joy smells like warm vanilla candles from a Yankee candle.
Joy looks like lovely lollipops lying inside Sweets in Heaven.
Joy sounds like birds outside on a warm summer day singing "chirp, chirp."
Joy makes me feel like I have a good day every day because I have joy in my life.
Joy is also like making a new friend when you have none.
Joy is like doing something good for someone you love or just a friend or
maybe even for someone you think just needs it.
And that is all of my sentences for Joy.
Taylor Britton, Grade 6
West Allegheny Middle School

Happiness
Happiness is a dog taking a walk in the park
Happiness is a child eating a chocolate ice cream cone
Happiness is a cat taking a long nap on a sunny porch
Happiness is a very soft pink
Happiness tastes like a fresh glass of lemonade on a hot day
Happiness smells like fresh chocolate chip cookies straight form the oven
Happiness sounds like the boom of fireworks on the Fourth of July
Happiness feels like the petals of a daisy in the springtime air
Happiness looks like the smile on a baby's face when it sees its parents
Happiness makes me want to jump around on a trampoline
Happiness makes the world go around
Emma Burke, Grade 6
West Allegheny Middle School

Joy
Joy is a trophy you get for winning the playoff game.
Joy is fluffy marshmallow in the center of a s'more.
Joy is a little puppy you get on your birthday.
Joy is a midnight blue sky in the middle of winter.
Joy tastes like a delicious popsicle straight from the freezer.
Joy smells like a fresh baked cookie straight from the oven.
Joy sounds like the last seconds dribbling the basketball in the big game.
Joy feels like a cozy warm blanket at night.
Joy looks like a sunny day in the middle of spring.
Joy makes me feel like I won the championship game.
Joy is being around friends and family all the time.
Breanna Reed, Grade 6
West Allegheny Middle School

Ode to Mrs. Neugebauer
Oh Mrs. Neugebauer you make me laugh when I am glum
You and me are alike we both like blue we like animals, too
You are important to me because you are my teacher
You get so tall when you get confident
You can have a mood sometimes, but mostly you are happy and loving
You are very hopeful for all the students
Every day you dress so pretty
Oh, Mrs. Neugebauer, you adore me.
Alyssa Novak, Grade 4
All Saints Catholic School

Trustful

T o be my hero
R everence for the flag
U nder the hands of God
S aved us from danger
T rained to be our soldier
F ull of love, care, and joy
U nite to family
L et them return
Amber Murphy, Grade 4
Fairview Elementary School

Cheering

Cheering is my favorite thing to do
It makes me happy even when I'm blue
We run, we chant, hop, and skip
We even got to run and flip!
Every Sunday we get ready to play
Even if our skies are grey
It's halftime now, time to hit the green
Let's go girls, let's support our team
Kayley Bittinger, Grade 4
Burgettstown Elementary Center

Winter Is…

Winter is as cold as an ice cube.
It tastes like warm hot chocolate
and smells like peppermint candy canes.
Winter reminds me of sitting by
the fire on a cold snowy night.
It sounds of neighbors playing
outside in the snow.
Winter feels like cold snow on bare skin.
Emily Yourish, Grade 5
East Union Intermediate Center

Fall

You can tell when fall is near
when kids run and shout with cheer.
The leaves turn red and orange and brown
when fall comes a rollin' into town.
The children rake up leaves
until the pile reaches their knees.
Then they will jump out of a tree
and land in the leaves with a WEEEEEEE!!!
Peter Hippert, Grade 6
Hopewell Memorial Jr High School

Parents

I love my parents oh yes, I do!
I think they're awesome how about you?
They're always there, when I am sad
And they correct me when I am bad
You should love your parents too.
And I'm sure they'll love you too.
Bryce Underwood, Grade 6
State Street Elementary School

Christmas

Lights everywhere glimmer,
The sunlight gets dimmer.
Carolers sing with joy,
Snow fights with girls and boys.

Presents under the tree,
Fill up my heart with glee.
A feast for all to share,
With love filling the air.
Olivia Barner, Grade 5
East Union Intermediate Center

Democracy

D elivers freedom
E quality for all
M ajority rules
O pinions count
C onstitutional rights
R epresents our country
A ll Americans count
C ommitment by all
Y ou can make a difference
James Campbell, Grade 5
East Union Intermediate Center

Our Beautiful World

Walking through the warm valley,
The orange leaves rustle and sing.

Eagles fly,
The wind howls,
Waterfalls thunder,
And wild flowers paint the world,
Going there calms you.
Dylan Davis, Grade 4
Fairview Elementary School

My Dogs

My dogs are weird —
My dogs are crazy.
One's named Max —
One's named Daisy.
When they go crazy —
You had better bail.
If having awesome dogs is a crime —
Then throw me in jail.
Cameron Brown, Grade 4
W R Croman Elementary School

Ghost

Creepy, spooky
Flying, scaring, sneaking
Scares lots of people
Boo!
Sean Cusick, Grade 5
St Anselm School

Football Mania!!!

F ootball is a complicated sport.
O ffense you have to know several plays.
O ffsides causes five yard penalty
T ouchdowns make you win
B esides field goals.
A ll of the football players will play
L eague referees keep the game fair.
L inemen keep the quarterback safe.
Chris Pierce, Grade 5
Central Elementary School

Work

Please, oh please won't you help me?
I have to make my whole desk neat.
Why my boss won't just let me be.
I wish I could just eat meat.
Now I'm home for dinner,
But I still have to do the taxes.
I still don't feel like a winner,
While everybody relaxes.
Carolyn McKnight, Grade 5
Foster Elementary School

Dear Little Bradley!

Dear little Bradley,
Why are you so sad?
You seem so sadly,
It makes me feel bad.
Just write me a letter.
Just please dear please,
And make me feel better,
I'll even get on my knees.
Hannah Roddy, Grade 5
Foster Elementary School

My Silly Dad

My silly dad is funny,
He always makes me laugh.
I giggle until my side hurts,
and my face almost splits in half.
My dad might be silly,
but he's like a prayer sent from above,
and I'm thankful every day,
that I have him to love.
Ashley Rock, Grade 4
Middle Smithfield Elementary School

Leaves

Red, yellow, orange, and brown
All the leaves are falling down
Rake them up into a bunch
Jump on them and they go crunch
The wind blows them all around
Spreading color throughout the town
Payton Whyne, Grade 5
Saint Theresa School

Thanksgiving Is
Going to see relatives in Connecticut,
Turkey, pumpkin pie, and mashed potatoes, of course.
Grandparent's Love feast — a card from my grandparents.
Smile and laughter — lots of it!
Being thankful for many things,
A fun-filled Thanksgiving once again.

Erin Danaher, Grade 6
Moravian Academy Middle School

Soccer Ball
I'm a soccer ball.
I roll fast.
I can talk to people, but no one knows.
I talk and talk all day and roll around and play.
As fun as it is to talk, no one can know.
If you're a soccer ball who knows how to talk, give me a knock!

Lillye Kuhn, Grade 4
McKinley Elementary School

Excited
Excited is yellow
It sounds like someone jumping and saying "Yeah!"
It smells like firecrackers burning on the Fourth of July
It tastes like a chocolate cake covered with birthday candles
It looks like kids having fun at the playground
Excited feels like publishing my first book and everyone likes it

Emily Frumento, Grade 4
Anne Frank School

Angry
Angry is flaming red
It sounds like someone screaming downstairs
It smells like the cinder of a burning fire
It tastes like burned fish covered with ash
It looks like a really mad bull attacking a really helpless person
Angry feels like a fire is burning you

Olesea Romanovich, Grade 4
Anne Frank School

The Sun
I awoke and all I see is the sun smiling at me
I am amazed at what all I see
it is a great world.
I can see the sky is blue
and I could take a nice dip in the pool
what a great world in front of me.

Ben Lane, Grade 5
McKinley Elementary School

When the Lights Go Out
When the lights go out on Halloween,
The ghosts come out with shrieks and screams.
The leaves in the wind try to run away.
Then the sun rises up and scares the goons away.

Byron Crawford, Grade 5
McKinley Elementary School

If I Had a Million Dollars
If a million dollars I did receive,
I'd have lots of ideas, you'd better believe.
I'd order a great, huge bowling alley
To liven up the dead who live in Death Valley.
I would order a baseball stadium
And also request some caladium.*

I would build an arcade with stores so grand
That they would love it in Thailand.
I would buy a garage so very tall
That in it you would put a waterfall.
I would also get a great, long hall
So we could play some flag football.

My friend's backyard is so very small
I'd buy some land as big as Gaul.
Not all of this would be for me.
I'd share these things with the world, you see.
A million dollars is wishful thinking,
So into my dream I'm slowly sinking.

*caladium: a tropical plant

David Matej, Grade 4
The American Academy

Christmas Is My Favorite Holiday
Christmas is my favorite holiday;
I get so excited to see
My dad stumbling in with a tree
Filling the house with pine, like a forest
We decorate the tree
I get to put the big sparkling star on top
Shining as bright as the North Star.
Hush! Is that the sound of Christmas carolers at my door?
I greet them with a cup of hot chocolate and warm,
Sugar cookies tasty and sweet.
They sing a Christmas melody and hand me a candy cane
Mmmmmm! sticky against my lips.
On Christmas Eve I jump into bed feeling anxious and excited
It's hard to fall asleep knowing
Christmas is tomorrow morning.
As soon as I open my eyes, I run downstairs and WOW!
There are so many presents under the tree for me!
We share the holiday with family and friends
Enjoy family tradition.
When the day is over I say to my mom, "Christmas will be back
  before you know it."

Nicole Faraldo, Grade 6
St Jerome Elementary School

Shining Air
The fingers on my hand dance in the morning air
My soul is the breath of the shining air
The angels help me when I'm in a scare

Chris Douglas, Grade 5
Nether Providence Elementary School

Football
Crowd yelling "Go team"
The players score a touchdown
The game is over
Bryce Woland, Grade 4
Watsontown Elementary School

Snowflakes
Snowflakes are crystals
Fall from the sky in winter
They're cold on my face
Harriet Tyler, Grade 4
McKinley Elementary School

The Stream
The trickling stream
Shining in the burning sun
While fish swim silently
Warren Wilson, Grade 5
Pocopson Elementary School

The Traveler's Spirit
The traveler's spirit is on our street
Its ghost body shimmers in the dull light
The traveler's spirit travels at night
Gracein Hoyle, Grade 5
Nether Providence Elementary School

Run
In the green grass I run barefoot
Words are dancing in my head while I sing
Then the sunrise bursts with light
Victoria Salah, Grade 5
Nether Providence Elementary School

The Whale
Lob tailing freely
Blowhole spurting out water
Oceanic beast.
Peter Rinehart, Grade 6
Trinity Middle School

Whales
An ocean breeze blows.
A whale is lonely but bold,
Swimming to catch up.
Joshua Coatsworth, Grade 6
Trinity Middle School

What I Am Thankful For
family and friends
shelter, food, drink and freedom
my teachers and school
Justin Karli, Grade 4
St Joseph School

Loneliness
Loneliness is an empty school on a Saturday morning with no one there but you
Loneliness is a dark, drastic dream waking you up at midnight
Loneliness is a mirror's reflection with only your figure in it, nothing else
Loneliness is the color white, blank and empty
Loneliness tastes like water from the faucet — tasteless
Loneliness smells like the fragrance of a single red rose posed in a bud vase
Loneliness sounds like the air racing past you, WHOOSH!
Loneliness feels like a smooth sheet of paper with no writing, no folds, nothing on it
Loneliness is a perched pirate's bird frantically flying away from his shoulder
Loneliness makes me feel like a torn hole has formed in my chest
Loneliness sounds like a loud silence
Loneliness is a shadow leaving, walking away from you
Onshea Floyd, Grade 6
West Allegheny Middle School

Football
Football is fun but rough
If you want to play you have to be tough
Football players fly like birds on the field
They only stop when the referees blow the whistle and the play is on yield
Football players are really good
Especially when they're playing in their own neighborhood
The football has wings when the quarterback throws
The wide receiver catches but to stay in bounds he uses his toes
I think that playing defense is the best part of the game
If they win they will probably get fame
The offense earns the points
When they get hit, they really hurt their joints.
Tommy Penko, Grade 6
St Jerome Elementary School

Basketball
Basketballs are big round balls
You can find them at most malls
They are like baseballs hard and round
Only basketballs can bounce on the ground
You dribble the ball down the court
It doesn't matter if you're tall or short
The winner makes the most points
Make sure you stretch or you will hurt your joints
When the referee calls a foul on me for being pushed on the ground
    and I go to the foul line and shoot the ball I like the whooshing sound
Basketball is my favorite sport
I'm really good at it I'm happy to report
Noelia Ramirez, Grade 6
St Jerome Elementary School

Joy
Joy is elegant blue like a wonderful waterfall with waving waters in an island jungle.
It looks like lovely, little lavender lilacs laying lazily like lily pads on a pond in spring.
It tastes like sweet apples off the tree of God's great creation.
Joy smells like strong lemons grown from California citrus in La Quinta.
Joy sounds like quiet breezes at wintertime in a forest.
It feels like soft snow in the slippery slopes of Big Bear Mountain.
Giovanni Marrero, Grade 6
Our Lady of Ransom School

Dolphins
They swim in the sea,
Moonlight shining on the beach,
Those graceful creatures.
Joshua Cravener, Grade 5
East Union Intermediate Center

Rainbow
What a rainbow day
A sunny nice joyful day
A fun rainbow day
Justin Beck, Grade 4
Fishing Creek Elementary School

A Snake!
A snake a snake a baby
Black snake with white and
Black. In a tree stump.
Asjia Price, Grade 4
Fishing Creek Elementary School

Stripes
Stripes stripes stripes
Stripes are straight and cool
Stripes stripes stripes
Zach Silvio, Grade 4
Fishing Creek Elementary School

Forks and Spoons
Useful kitchen tools
they help you eat food a lot
Morning and afternoon
Wyatt Park, Grade 4
Fishing Creek Elementary School

The Manta Ray
Manta Rays are big,
Graceful, swimming sea creatures,
Floating on great wings.
Jacob Potter, Grade 5
East Union Intermediate Center

The Recession
In a large crisis,
Where we have no money,
Loved ones get us through.
David Happe, Grade 5
Foster Elementary School

Ocean
Miles of blue water,
Dolphins glide out of the sea,
Waves burst on the shore.
Joshua Bechtold, Grade 5
East Union Intermediate Center

Friends
Friends are people who care for you,
They'd do anything to protect you,
Friends are powerful people, who are there for you from life to death,
When you struggle,
They struggle
They are the ones that help you in your times of need
They are the person whose shoulders you cry on,
When you are sad, they are the people you confide your feelings to,
They are the people you talk on the phone with all night long,
Friends are people who know your feelings before you do,
Friends are people you count on like a sunrise, every day,
Friends are people who mean the world to you.
Natalie Flores, Grade 6
St Jerome Elementary School

Guess Who?
You toss and turn me all about
I'm jingling in your pocket
You have a happy smile on your face
As you pass me down from person to place
And soon as I know it I end up on the ground
The very next day I am found
you carry me in wallets and in glass jars
And better yet someone's been replacing me by the name of the cash card
You can count me but more of us are made each day
But some of you save me in big metal banks
And that's how we like it each and every day
Answer: Money
Spencer Serrano, Grade 4
Jefferson Elementary School

Happiness
Happiness is vanilla cupcakes with pink frosting.
Happiness is winning the championship game of a basketball tournament.
Happiness is spending time with family and friends.
Happiness is the color blue like the sky in late May.
Happiness tastes like blazing hot chocolate with whipped cream on a cold winter's day.
Happiness smells like delicious chocolate chip cookies straight from the oven.
Happiness sounds like the chirp, chirp of a baby blue bird.
Happiness feels as soft as the fur on a cute chubby little kitten.
Happiness looks like a colossal vanilla ice cream sundae with hot fudge and sticky caramel.
Happiness makes me feel as if joy is jumping around inside of me.
Happiness is swimming in a pool on a sizzling summer day.
Happiness is the warm feeling you get when you do something great.
Angela Martelli, Grade 6
West Allegheny Middle School

Happy
Happy is pink
It sounds like people cheering
It smells like rows of roses
It tastes like some chocolate chip cookies
It looks like children playing outside
Happy feels like someone jumping up in the air and saying "Hooray!"
Wida Kakar, Grade 4
Anne Frank School

Exhilaration

Exhilaration is like a trip to Hawaii won at a game show.
Exhilaration is high diving into a swimming pool.
Exhilaration is like the feeling of riding down a water slide.
Exhilaration is a blur, running down the stairs on Christmas morning.
Exhilaration tastes like the wind blowing in your mouth, riding the Cosmic Chaos at Kennywood.
Exhilaration smells like your first chocolate bar.
Exhilaration sounds like my heart pumping, driving in a race car.
Exhilaration feels like the Vince Lombardi Trophy, smooth and shiny.
Exhilaration looks like your first home run ball, flying over the fence.
Exhilaration makes me scream, AHH! walking through a haunted house.
Exhilaration is reaching the summit of Mt. Everest.
Exhilaration is the wind catching you when you skydive.
Exhilaration is like skateboarding, shooting into the air.

Anthony Dominick, Grade 6
West Allegheny Middle School

Fantasy

Fantasy is the start of eternity
Fantasy is the glimmer in a knight's sword as he shouts over the horizon
Fantasy is the magic concealed in a story of pure value
Fantasy is purple, blue, and turquoise like a majestic sapphire
Fantasy tastes like victory, sweet, yet delightful
Fantasy smells like thousands of diverse scented candles all combined into one fragrant audacious candle with the wick burning gradually
Fantasy sounds like the "Pring" from a lonely musician's lyre as he sits on a stool rendering a slow, daunting hum
Fantasy looks like an eerie overpowering feeling as if you being controlled, but you know it is a great feeling and that you are safe
Fantasy looks like the ominous frost, devouring every plant in sight in the grim winter chill
Fantasy makes me wonder how far it can go without breaking reality's rules
Fantasy is where flowers reach to the sky amidst the radiant sun running rapidly down the flowers stalk
Fantasy is the perfect getaway for proving the impossible, possible

Brad Custer, Grade 6
West Allegheny Middle School

Love

Love is the pop to my tart and the peanut to my butter.
Love is like skydiving onto 300 feather pillows, but even if you miss the target, the ground will always break your fall!
Love is the most powerful thing in the world!
Love is the color dark pink splattering up against the whitest wall.
Love tastes like freshly baked cookies that are crunchy and creamy on the outside and soft and moist on the inside.
Love smells like 100 red roses growing on sizzling summer days.
Love sounds like FIREWORKS courageously crashing so cheerfully in the nighttime sky!
Love feels like a chinchilla's fur so soft it feels like air!
Love looks like a cuddly cheetah cub playing with her mother.
Love makes me want to EXPLODE with happiness and joy!
Love is sweet and never to be forgotten.
Love is powerful and should never be proud.

Kelly Diskin, Grade 6
West Allegheny Middle School

Basketball

The beat of the basketball dribbling down the floor. The sound of players hustling up and down the floor. The crowd going crazy at the buzzer. The coach gives an order. The players obey just like soldiers. Referees blow their whistle to control the game. An upset player gets fouled out then thrown out. At last the game is over, the score 99 to 1. Then the gym quiets down, waiting for the next one.

Austin Zuppe, Grade 6
Hopewell Memorial Jr High School

High Merit Poems – Grades 4, 5 and 6

I Have Heard of a Girl
I have heard of a girl who planted lilies in her garden
which shown the beauty of life in her hands.

I have heard of a girl who gave pioneers supplies
to give hope and faith for the truth to come.

I have heard of a girl whose eyes shone in the moonlight
with care in her arms and life that comes forth with her.

I have heard of a girl who came from far away lands
in her dreams her imagination is wide as an eye can see.

I have heard of a girl who made promises with her heart
her love and care for the wildlife changes forever in her soul.

I have heard of a girl whose singing is a gentle lullaby
it lulls the coyotes asleep who howls in the moonlit sky.

I have heard of a girl who drank from a cactus when she was thirsty.
I have heard of a girl whose love is as strong as steel
who never lets go of a bond with her and wildlife.
Sierra Blystone, Grade 5
Chicora Elementary School

A Great Winter
Every year I just can't wait.
To see the great snowfall in the yard.
When I see one drop of snow.
I know it is going to be great.
Winter always starts off strong.
When Christmas comes along.
When everybody is happy and good.
Doesn't winter start off so great?
Next, is the school closings.
When there is snow we are off.
Off to the hill that's what I'll say!
Where people go down it is always a thrill.
Or maybe a game of hockey where everyone has fun.
After the game I would like to know who won.
Lastly, there are winter sports.
Like skiing, snowboarding, and sledding.
It is always a thrill when I go up the hill.
When I go down I have a thrill.
Even though it is a chill outside.
Now you can see my point.
Of why winter is so great.
Luke Janicki, Grade 6
Hopewell Memorial Jr High School

Thanksgiving Day
Thanksgiving dinner is so good
Apples, cherries, stuffing, and turkey is like candy
On a hot summer day
On Thanksgiving Day never eat less than the best
Benny Smith, Grade 5
Central Elementary School

Happiness
Happiness is the sun rising on a new day.
Happiness is a football player making an amazing touchdown.
Happiness is someone getting a new puppy.
Happiness is golden lemonade on a hot summer day
Happiness tastes like a chocolate cake right out of the bakery.
Happiness smells like cookies sizzling out of the oven.
Happiness sounds like birds singing a beautiful morning melody.
Happiness feels like cuddling a teddy bear.
Happiness looks like a cloudless day in the middle of July.
Happiness makes me feel like a million dollars.
Happiness is a touchdown at a Penn State game.
Luke Kadlecik, Grade 6
West Allegheny Middle School

The Awesomest Christmas
Ah, Christmas is a time for family.
Also, time for happiness for the kids.
Get by the fireplace and get warmed up.
But most of all get the Wii out and play Wii Sports!
Get your radio-controlled truck.
Build a ramp and go as fast as you can go!
Get your new playhouse and play with your Barbies or Bratz.
You can also donate some of your toys.
To sent to kids that don't have any.
That would make you feel good.
And the kid that got your toy would not be gloomy.
Ricardo Hernandez, Grade 5
Lincoln Elementary School

Why I Like Fall
L eaves falling to the ground
E very leaf turning colors
A nimals getting ready to hibernate
V ery small amount of green leaves
E nergetic kids playing with leaves
S mells like leaves

R ough leaves on the ground
A lot of leaves on the ground
K ids jumping in leaves
E very teacher putting leaves or pumpkins on the calendar
Shysaun Whitlow, Grade 5
Clearview Elementary School

The Artist Within Me
When I want to be creative, I let my mind be free,
My picture fills with lots of colors that you can plainly see.
What I thought was my imagination, forms before my eyes.
When it molds its shape on paper, it takes my by surprise!

When I'm finished with my project, I may look like a mess.
But when you lay your eyes on it, you will be quite impressed!
Many artists start out like me, they aren't very well known.
I can only hope I am, when I am fully grown.
Sydney Rusek, Grade 5
East Union Intermediate Center

Softball
Softball is fun
Especially when you win.
My favorite thing is when
you hit a home run.
Keiley Lloyd, Grade 5
Hamilton Elementary School

Thanksgiving Is…
Spending time with family.
Eating plump turkeys.
Making pies.
Being thankful.
Nancy Hart, Grade 6
Moravian Academy Middle School

Thanksgiving Is…
Giving thanks to God.
Spending time with your family.
Eating my aunt's famous turkey.
Having a good time.
Mercedes Y. Smith, Grade 6
Moravian Academy Middle School

Thanksgiving Is…
Eating turkey and other great foods.
Playing football with my dad.
Watching Thanksgiving Day parades.
Seeing family and being thankful.
Sophie Kitch-Peck, Grade 6
Moravian Academy Middle School

Fall Leaves
F all
A utumn
L aughing
L ove
Cheyanne Higgins, Grade 4
West Branch Area Elementary School

Thanksgiving Is…
Eating Turkey and orange juice.
Going to the Outer Banks.
Walking along the beach.
Playing football on the street.
Tom Bloxam, Grade 6
Moravian Academy Middle School

Bike
B est thing to do
I love to feel the wind in my hair.
K ills when you get hit in the shin
E nding tricks clean feels so good.
Henry Downs, Grade 4
McKinley Elementary School

A Wonderful Time of Year
Strolling down the sidewalk, I hear the crunch of leaves beneath my feet.
I feel a chilly wind nipping at my nose, telling me that the summer is over.
I see the leaves on the trees, turning brilliant yellows, oranges, and reds,
contrasting against the branches of the trees and blue sky.
I jump in a pile of leaves, listening to them crackle and crunch under me,
staring in awe at the world's beautiful transformation.

The land lays barren, waiting for a blanket of white to embellish it.
Foggy mist arises from a not yet frozen river, awaiting the cold to conceal it.
All these are signs of the seasons changing, their Maker's handiwork
showing in each small element of nature's beauty.
The lovely time of year that our Lord has created, the wonderful,
magnificent season of fall!
Heather Johnston, Grade 6
Portersville Christian School

A Fall Walk
When I took my first step outside of the school, a great sensation raced through my body.
Everywhere I walked I kept seeing little wind tornadoes made out of leaves.
I saw the janitor as he trimmed the grass with the tractor.
I smelled the aroma of gasoline burning as I walked.
I heard "Crunch" "Snap!"
I looked down and saw millions of beautiful leaves looking up at me as if I were their master.
I was walking and I could hear the wind whistle,
but he silence was soon broken by the sound of a woodpecker.
When I reached this one spot leaves were falling on my head along with acorns.
I saw a seagull soar over the top of the twisted and mixed looking sunrise.
Unfortunately, when it was time to go back inside the school
my last vision was a blue wildflower that looked as if it was a beautiful rose.
Now do you know what I did during the fall walk?
Jeffrey Rastetter, Grade 6
Pennridge North Middle School

Strength
Strength is power surging through my veins.
Strength is defeating an enemy ten times stronger than you.
Strength is the power to take on the whole world at once.
Strength is yellow like lightning bolting across the world in a split-second.
Strength tastes like a bowl of ice cream on a blazing summer day.
Strength smells like flowers in the endless garden of ultimate power.
Strength sounds like thunder booming across the valley of weakness, bringing it back to life.
Strength feels like a brick, strong enough to endure anything.
Strength looks like a wolf, bravely battling beastly enemies.
Strength is a lion, dominating its opponent.
Strength is what I have to prove that I am the best.
Derek Clontz, Grade 6
West Allegheny Middle School

Bonfire
Looks like red, yellow, orange, blue, and white leaves jumping up and down
Sounds like 1,000 fire crackers exploding.
Smells like burning wood.
Tastes like delicious s'mores.
Feels like the warmth is going through your veins.
Brandon Mercier, Grade 6
Portersville Christian School

Best Friend

A best friend is a treasured gift.
A prize beyond compare
Someone who is loyal.
That you know will always be there.
Through thick and thin.
Through sun and rain.
They'll share your joy,
as well as your pain.
A best friend listens
patiently to every word you say
But most of all a best friend
is like you in every way.

Ciani Blackmon, Grade 6
Colwyn Elementary School

Maxwell

Maxwell is my hairy friend
He will protect me to the very end
He jumps, he barks, he has brown hair
He's always happy when I'm there
I love to take him for a walk each day
Because he loves to run and play
I love to sleep with him each night
He wakes me up when it gets light
Even though his size is small
Maxwell acts like a king, ruler of all
"Yip, yip, yip," is the sound
Every morning from my little Yorkie hound

Logan Zadroga, Grade 6
St Jerome Elementary School

Thanksgiving

T hankful day
H oliday
A mazing food
N o limits
K indness
S aving peace
G iving people
I nviting
V ery many exciting things
I ndians and pilgrims
N ever ending food
G ratitude.

Alaisa Davis, Grade 5
East Union Intermediate Center

My Grandmother Is

A wonderful person to be around.
A source of wisdom and knowledge.
A smile of delight.
Maker of wonderful meals.
A master of card games.
Always happy to chat.

Joren Husic, Grade 6
Moravian Academy Middle School

Curious Visitor

A tiny little person sits
On my window sill.
She stares up in wonder
Looking intently at me.
Her delicate wings flutter.
I open up the glass window pane
Inviting her in.
And in she flies
Her twinkling wings
Shining in the moonlight.
She settles down into my lap
And emits a tiny snore.
Then as she drifts away
Into the realm of sleep
I whisper into her small, little ear,
"Good night and sweet dreams, little fairy."

Maddy Hopkins, Grade 6
Hopewell Memorial Jr High School

Life

One day life formed on Earth
Like fruit growing on a tree
Gradually the life took many forms
Spreading out like a family tree
Life grew and grew
As though it couldn't stop
Old life died,
New life became,
Just as if it doesn't have a weakness
Life was, will be, and is everywhere
There is no way to diminish life
When you try,
New life comes,
It is as hard to destroy as plastic
So what I'm trying to say is life is
FOREVER.

Nicholas Cerdera, Grade 5
Copper Beech Elementary School

Friends

Friends are as nice as a summer day
So what are they?
They are special people in our heart
My friends top the chart

Friends are loving and incredible
Time with them will always be memorable
We talk on the phone all night and day
The phone we will never put away

Everyone should have good friends
To have fun with until the ends
My friends and I laugh together
My friends and I are friends forever

Taylor Benussi, Grade 6
St Jerome Elementary School

I Am a Bird

I am a bird.

Soaring high in the sky,
with the sun beating down on me.

The rain is falling,
From a height it feels
like metal on my delicate feathers.

I walk on the street.
People walk, bike, drive by,
unaware of me.

I am a bird.

Hanna Wells, Grade 5
Falk Laboratory School

Autumn

The colors of all
The wind is in call
Yellows, browns, reds
The leaves are soft beds

Little children running
Having tricks that are very cunning
Can we all join,
When they flip the coin?

The four seasons
There are reasons
Can we love all?
Of course we can love fall

Monty Helfst, Grade 6
Moravian Academy Middle School

Christmas Time

There is something in the air
That nothing can compare
Bringing families together
In all kinds of weather

We know the feeling is right
As Santa takes off on his flight
Spreading peace and joy
To every girl and boy

As we put our Christmas tree up high
We hear our Savior cry
A bright star in the sky
That has guided us to not tell a lie

Allyson Chalmers, Grade 6
St Jerome Elementary School

Soccer

Soccer is my favorite sport
It gives me real great joy
I like to play on weekends
Just like any boy

The sport is played around the world
By countries far and wide
They come together every 4 years
To show their country's pride

The U.S.A. is my favorite team
They surely show
That they are ready to face the world
And help the sport to grow

John Teesdale, Grade 6
St Jerome Elementary School

Life

Life leads to many a path
Some bring honor, some bring wrath
The good path you should follow
Because the other's dark and hollow

Life is long to the young
But to the old it is hung
By a thread of silk and twine
To break, when it is their time

Life's a cloth that God has sewn
By His hands and His alone
Satan tries to make it fray
But God resews it every day

William Reil, Grade 6
St Jerome Elementary School

What the World Is

What a beautiful world…

All the birds are singing.
My puppy is running and bells are ringing.

What a spectacular world…

My mom and I are swinging
My dad and brother are swimming

What a wonderful world…

The leaves are blowing in the air.
The flowers are going in my hair.

Leigha Ours, Grade 4
Fairview Elementary School

Octopus

Octopus is large,
Floating in the deep, dark sea,
With red tentacles.

Robbie Yodanis, Grade 5
East Union Intermediate Center

Dolphins

Their bodies are sleek,
Their fins flap nice and graceful,
Then they swim along.

Shea Zetwo, Grade 5
East Union Intermediate Center

Index

Abbott, Richard 62
Adelbock, Devon 42
Adelman, Marlene 114
Adler, Austin 27
Affinito, Calvin 71
Aguirre, Domenique 65
Ahmad, Ben 115
Alderson, Aleah 112
Alejo, Allison 24
Allen, Amanda 106
Allen, Brian 107
Allen, Marcus 25
Alley, Gabrielle 32
Alvarado, Diana 92
Amadore, Alyssa 75
Ames, Olivia 116
Anastasi, Nic 50
Ancrum-Lowery, Dymeere .. 39
Anderson, Griffin 40
Anderson, Melanie 97
Andrews, Danielle 67
Anewalt, Erica 52
Anzulavich, Gage 45
Archambo, Bryan 16
Argiro, Anthony 100
Arias, Norah 78
Arias, Nyrell 38
Arnone, Deanna 27
Arnone, Samantha 80
Artuso, Ben 52
Ashmore, Jessica 52
Atoo, Jessica 26
Austin, Jack 91
Ayala, Declan 86
Azcona, Gianna 72
Azizkhan, Tim 115
Babyak, Daniel 14
Backer, Owen 42
Baddick, Hannah Gabrielle .. 22
Bailey, Hannah 28
Bair, Aron 81
Bajgoric, Emil 30
Baker, Justin 117
Baker, Madison 77
Banas, Allison 90
Banaszak, Madison 47
Baranowski, Angela 66
Baranowski, Aubrey 66
Barbacane, Leah 19
Barbacane, Olivia 92
Barcza, Jake 54
Barkman, Adam 33

Barner, Olivia 128
Barnick, Tyler 99
Barry, Bridget 103
Barry, Sean 54
Beach, Derek 112
Bechtold, BreAnna 52
Bechtold, Joshua 131
Beck, Justin 131
Becker, Tahjae 38
Bejjani, Adelyne 31
Belmont, Joey 33
Benasutti, Paige 74
Bence, Brianna 59
Benjamin, Hunter 99
Benussi, Taylor 135
Bergman, Marlie 41
Berner, Garrett 118
Berrios, Alyssa 80
Berzins, Rudy Mikus 13
Bianco, Tony 127
Bigley, Emily 64
Biksey, Michelle 46
Bittinger, Kayley 128
Blackmon, Ciani 135
Blank, Julianne 36
Blaszczyk, Andrew 108
Blosky, Andrew 25
Bloxam, Tom 134
Blystone, Sierra 133
Bock, Chloe 84
Bohatch, Jaimie 56
Bohman, Kiersten 112
Bond, Anthony 95
Bonicky, Alayna 19
Bonomo, Gino 97
Boone, Alexander 33
Booth, Shannon 116
Borne, Kevin 18
Boronsky, Gabrielle 57
Bowden, Hope 125
Bowman, Andrew 69
Boyd, Julia 101
Boyer, Tariq 55
Boyle, Elizabeth 106
Boyle, Shannon 41
Boyle, Sophie 63
Bradley, Mazie 102
Bradley, Ricky 30
Brazukas, Elizabeth 13
Brener, Mya 8
Brennan, Hannah 8
Brennan, Kaelin 23

Britt, Alexander 82
Britton, Taylor 127
Brock, Sienna 66
Brooks, Ahyanna 33
Brooks, Ashlin 79
Brooks, Eniya 68
Brosky, Katie 102
Brown, Cameron 128
Brown, Dylan 90
Brown, Jelissa 89
Brown, Kaila 96
Brown, Kalina 41
Brown, Steven 43
Brown, Taylor 90
Brown-Hunt, Maya 40
Bruce, Ben 93
Bruce, Nathan 118
Bucher, Andrew 36
Buck, Alyssa 12
Buck, Gabrielle 92
Bullock, Jala 116
Burgan, Callie 35
Burke, Emma 127
Burke, Tommy 68
Burner, Eileen 56
Burns, Juliana 30
Burroughs, Justin 51
Burrows, Emma 45
Burrows, Luke 58
Burzenski, Brian 113
Buterbaugh, Julianne 74
Bynum, Mason 77
Cabrera, Tamara 123
Caldwell, Jordyn 54
Camacho, Cintia 115
Camarote, Ashlee 8
Cammarota, Joel 81
Campbell, Christopher 123
Campbell, Grace 37
Campbell, James 128
Campbell, Pryclynn 8
Campos-Santos, Bruno 93
Cannon, Maya 8
Cantando, Anthony 94
Cantrell, Emily 91
Cao, Eric (Yu) 42
Carabajal, Ashley 12
Card, Callie 111
Carlin, Sydney 56
Carne, Annie 103
Carpenter, Claire 39
Carter, Robert 96

Caruso, Abby 24	Curry, Griffin 29	Donson, Hailey 9
Castelluci, Josh 45	Cusano, Chloe 21	Dorcon, Tyler 81
Castilloveitia, Karina 103	Cusick, Emma 119	Dougher, Molly 40
Casturo, Kay I 34	Cusick, Sean 128	Douglas, Chris 129
Caubel, Greg 41	Custer, Brad 132	Downs, Henry 134
Cecchine, Kevin 66	Czebatul, Mateusz 117	Dracup, Josh 58
Cecil, Jordan 37	Czopek, Sumir 35	Dro, Felton 47
Cendrowski, Joshua 122	D'Alesandro, Nico 93	DuBree, Olivia 18
Cerdera, Nicholas 135	D'Amore, Marissa 58	Duessel, Alaina 110
Cetorelli, Jessica 113	D'Angelo, Lily 30	Duff, Erika 103
Chachoute, Brianna 75	D'Aquanno, Hannah 108	Duff, Kaitlyn 44
Chalmers, Allyson 135	Damjanovic, Alex 74	Duncker, Trinity 63
Cherry, Sylvie 16	Damon, Mackenzie 21	Dunmyer, Cameron 46
Chesson, Theodore 11	Danaher, Erin 129	DuPlessis, Lauren 9
Chestnut, Gillian 88	Dano, Megan 88	Duquette, Alec 92
Chhor, Victoria 49	Darsie, Noah 122	Durbin, Ashley 116
Chmura, Calvin 42	Daukaus, Lauren 35	Dych, Allie 31
Choi, Amanda 23	David, Kristina 127	Dyer, Hunter Joseph 77
Ciccarelli, Joshua 80	Davis, Alaisa 135	Ecker, Jeffrey 43
Cipolla, Zackary 109	Davis, Carley 106	Ecker, Zachary 33
Claerbaut, Duncan 120	Davis, Dylan 128	Edwards, Jessica 22
Claerbaut, Megan 71	Davis, Jake 18	Egan, Desiree 115
Clark, Dillon 28	Davis, Julia 121	Elghatit, Tory 68
Clegg, Maria 97	Davis, Paige 14	Ender, Ashley 11
Clements, Max 53	Dean, Jayson 63	Ennis, Steven 10
Clontz, Derek 134	Debes, Nolan 12	Escott, Elizabeth 33
Coatsworth, Joshua 130	DeCarlo, Alli 18	Esposito, Nicole 87
Coble, Tristan 15	Defuria, Dylan 66	Evans, Aeneus 44
Cogar, Trevor 100	Delgado, Janessa 50	Evans, Emily 43
Cogis, Lexi 45	Dellaporta, Julia 30	Everdale, Erin 73
Colbert, Jared 68	DeLuca, Isabella 9	Ewing, Emily 21
Coleman, Gabriel 27	Dengel, Samantha 60	Facer, Trevor 11
Coleman, Samantha 39	Dengler, Brittany 89	Faller, Mark 9
Collado Cruz, Jovanny 123	Denish, Jordan 99	Faraldo, Nicole 129
Collins, Kaitlin 78	Deorah, Manasi 72	Farrell, Sean Patrick 30
Colon, Ross 53	DePaulis, Eli 112	Faust, Abigail 35
Colville, Robert 46	Derosa, Serena 39	Fedel, Mike 79
Conover, Anna 47	Derr, Isaiah 45	Fenstermacher, Alexis 35
Conrad, Ally 126	DeVenuto, Liberty 106	Fera, Gianni 118
Conroy, Devon 9	Devers, Kiera 40	Figliolia, Emily Susan 26
Corson, Hannah 91	Diaz, Elio 38	Figueroa, Alexis 16
Costacurta, Julia 28	Diaz, Jeryka S. 31	Fingerhood, Nathan 112
Costlow, Emily 47	DiBiase, Samantha 44	Fink, Marina 126
Cottage, Alaina 71	DiCandilo, Stacy 85	Firuta, Matt 20
Council, Theresa 88	Dienner, Brooke 120	Fisher, Carmen 124
Courtney, Matthew 110	DiFrancesco, Madison 110	Fishler, Michael 113
Coval, Megan 116	DiLoreto, Serena 105	Fleming, David L. 76
Cowder, Jenna 14	Dimes, Maura 101	Flor, Samantha 80
Coyle, Trevor 64	Dinkfelt, Cory 105	Flores, Gabriela 50
Cranmer, Jennifer 55	DiRosa, Murphy 10	Flores, Natalie 131
Cravener, Joshua 131	DiSanti, Maria 8	Flowers, Kelcey 69
Crawford, Byron 129	Diskin, Kelly 132	Floyd, Onshea 130
Crider, Jessica 48	Dodds, Kaylor 41	Forchielli, Sarah 70
Cromie, Kelsey 127	Doehre, Randy 125	Ford, Donovan 104
Crowe, Jarrett 28	Dojcak, Ashley 59	Forgie, Amanda 78
Cudahy, Maura 69	Dolan, Shelby 71	Foster, Julia 119
Cumming, Cassidy 11	Dolata, Ethan 36	Fox, Casey 90
Cunnard, Jarret 53	Dominick, Anthony 132	Fox, Kayla 67
Cunningham, Lisa 18	Donatelli, Christina 57	Fox, Zoe 111

Index

Franklin, Leah 84
Franzini, Michael 38
Fredley, Abby 46
Freeman, Noah 89
Frey, Katy 19
Friedel, Mia 9
Fritch, Debbie 96
Frumento, Emily 129
Fry, Oceanne 63
Fugaro-Thompson, Ben 75
Fullerton, Lindsay 91
Fuss, Erica 79
Galbraith, Julia 25
Gall, Aubrey 31
Gallagher, Judy 64
Gallagher, Timmy 69
Gallo, Andrew 22
Galvis, Nicole 87
Gandhi, Avani 82
Gannon, Katie 60
Gao, Chenlang 10
Garcia, Austin 125
Gardiner, Trevor 9
Garis, Christine 9
Gartenmayer, Ryan 47
Gavatorta, Arianna 108
Gawronski, Zach 62
George, Christina 14
Gery, Briana Paige 24
Giampa, Matthew 34
Giblin, Brody B. 52
Gilligan, Erin 53
Girod, Alberto 27
Girvin, Tyler 81
Gist, Ryan 103
Giura, Chris 103
Gladden, Lizzie 11
Glover, Joshua 126
Glover, Joshua Randall 68
Gmys, Megan 28
Gnegy, Eva 20
Gold, Amir 87
Goldfarb, Emily 11
Golovin, Ilya 99
Goodman, Jill 32
Goodwald, Benjamin 37
Gordon, Nathaniel 113
Govachini, Emma 32
Gow, Grant 35
Graef, Alexis 87
Graham, Ayanna 69
Graham, Emma A. 39
Graham, Jonathan 95
Grant, Peyton 115
Greegus, Justin 35
Green, Daniel 11
Green, Garrett 90
Greenleaf, Jennifer 75
Greenway, Gabriel 64

Gregoire, Catherine 69
Grencer, JJ 82
Griess, Alexis 40
Grimm, Nicole 77
Grogan, Haley 30
Grubb, Brennon 37
Guiciardi, Jacob 110
Gwardzinski, Tiffany 54
Haag, Ryan 9
Hackert, Abby 17
Hager, Brandon 71
Haldeman, Cory 82
Hallman, Tess 92
Halulko, Adriana 125
Halvin, Alexis 89
Hamel, Peter 31
Hamilton, Kara 16
Hamm, Bryanna 81
Haniman, Samantha 9
Hannah-Lee, Toriah Morea 89
Happe, David 131
Harding, Jayna Ray 13
Harnish, Molly 126
Harrar, Allyah 43
Harrison, Matthew 55
Hart, Nancy 134
Hartman, Abby 106
Hassinger, Breanna 112
Hawkins, Tamaiya 29
Hays, Makenzie 59
Heastings, Spencer 32
Heffelfinger, Jessica 44
Hefferin, Sarah 13
Heise, Sarah 115
Helfst, Monty 135
Heller, Elizabeth 80
Heller, Nichole 88
Heller, Sarah 71
Henderson, Ava 25
Hermann, Sierra 49
Hernandez, Jessica 49
Hernandez, Kaylani 96
Hernandez, Ricardo 133
Hernandez Rivera, Kevin 67
Herzberger, Leighan Patricia .. 98
Herzig, Marissa 91
Hesse, Morgan 116
Hessler, Alex 39
Hickok, Rachel 126
Higgins, Cheyanne 134
Hill, Lexi 23
Hines, Jacob 25
Hinkle, Max 22
Hippert, Peter 128
Hite, Dominic 71
Hite, Olivia 71
Hiteshew, Sean 36
Hochstein, Joseph 108
Hogg, Katie 43

Holdcraft, Wesley 41
Holland, Dominique 47
Hollenbach, Brodie 68
Holmes, Shomari 113
Holt, Emily 74
Holzheimer, Jordan 51
Homanick, Nicole 110
Hooper, Nicholas 10
Hopkins, Maddy 135
Hotovec, Tyler 54
Hovanec, Zachary 48
Howard, Pacey 58
Howe, Maria 60
Hoy, Allison 25
Hoy, Shawn 35
Hoyle, Gracein 130
Hribar, Elizabeth 107
Huddell, Amber 118
Huddell, Amy 104
Hummert, Hanna 50
Hunsberger, Dalton Wayne 93
Hunsiker, Skylar 24
Husic, Joren 135
Iams, Erin 33
Iannarelli, Victoria 73
Iezzi, Annie 92
Ikeler, Trista 112
Imgrund, Henry 107
Imredy, Andrew 16
Inyang, Sylvester 96
Itri, Nino 34
Izzo, Kayleigh 34
Jachimowicz, Kelsey 57
Jacobs, Drake 19
Jacoby, Kylee 21
Janicki, Luke 133
Jarman, Lance 8
Jarrett, Sean 63
Jefferson, Jada 13
Jeffrey, Greer 53
Jenkins, Julianne 23
Jimenez, Jenna 102
Johnson, Amy 15
Johnson, Jason 31
Johnston, Heather 134
Johnston, Timothy 38
Jones, Bobby 38
Jones, Madeline 49
Josey, Jenna 29
Jukic, Ana 23
Kadlecik, Luke 133
Kakar, Wida 131
Kariman, Kaitlyn 123
Karli, Justin 130
Karolski, Justin 21
Kasper, Gillian 33
Katara, Vivek 11
Kebede, Feben 96
Keenan, Aimee 40

Kelly, Ally 8	Lawless, Bobby 29	Marrero, Giovanni 130
Kelly, Grace 99	Lawryk, Brandon 86	Marricone, Frank 15
Kendra, Colin 43	Layshock, Mikhaila 115	Marshall, Bailey 106
Kenney, Katie 114	Lazo, Christopher 49	Marshall, Lindsey 10
Kenny, Marty 71	Le, Victoria 11	Martelli, Angela 131
Kenton, Caroline 116	Lee, Becky 68	Martin, Jimmy 67
Kenyon, Lanaya 81	Lemashane, Quintin 53	Martinazzi, Alyssa 27
Kern, Douglas 64	Leng, Olivia 24	Marzolf, Mallory 64
Keyser, Luke 91	Lerda, Sydney 31	Masgai, James Colin 111
Khalifa, Malek 10	Lesko, Isabelle 53	Mason, Skyler 99
Kindy, Maria 125	Levitus, Ricki 78	Master, Nathan 56
King, Tiffany 18	Lewis, Krys 42	Matej, David 129
Kirkwood, Madeline 92	Lewis, Nia 58	Matesic, John 42
Kirstein, Justin 49	Lewis, Sebastian 20	Mathew, Ashley Elizabeth 101
Kistler, Allura 8	Li, Cindy 71	Matos, Danielle I. 27
Kistner, Kerianne 114	Lima, Nickolo 127	Matthews, Barbara 34
Kitch-Peck, Sophie 134	Lin, Ken 85	Matthews, J'Lynn 34
Klingenberg, Annie 110	Lindinger, Bernard 83	Mattiace, Jessica 40
Kobb, Emma 10	Lisco, Gia 31	Mayer, Maggie 89
Koehler, Elizabeth 111	Liu, Irene 56	McBride, Sabrina 21
Komorowski, Chelsea 43	Liu, Jessica 28	McCarry, Samantha 39
Konieczny, Katie 108	Lloyd, Keiley 134	McCormick, Andrea 119
Kopchik, Parkar 12	Lo, Michael 88	McDaniel, Sammy 107
Korzuch, Sara 25	Locante, Kelsey 9	McDaniel, Zoe 14
Kothe, Alexandra 62	Lock, Dylan 21	McDonnell, Norah 28
Kotwica, Victoria 40	Lomas, Brett 54	McDonough, Anna 81
Kowalski, Jimmy 46	Long, Lauryn 37	Mcelhaney, Robert 45
Kozlowski, David 41	Longstreth, Madeline 119	McElhany, Megan 124
Krachie, Andrew 27	Loomis, Courtney Ray 65	McFadden, Evan 12
Kracht, Zachariah 113	Lora, Nathaly 21	McGarry, Kate 127
Kraynik, Matthew D. 109	Lorimer, Emily 76	McGee, Daniel 42
Kreeger, Austin 61	Losco, Briana 104	McGinn, Jimmy 69
Krisovenski, Karly 8	Love, Allison 110	McGinn, Joanna 110
Kriznik, Anthony 94	Loyer, Joshua 67	McGlade, Nick 54
Krotec, Jocelyn 24	Lozito, Joseph 30	McGlinn, Kaitlyn 38
Krouse, Carter 101	Lu, Amy 116	McGonigle, Lauren 56
Krull, Joshua 56	Lu, Michael 114	McGough, Stephen 64
Kuhn, Lillye 129	Ludlum, Samantha 51	McGrath, Gregory 14
Kurlander, Campbell 49	Luna Raposo, Lessly 81	McGrath, Taylor 77
Kurtz, Kylan 58	Luther, Emma 54	McGuckin, Aidan 32
Kutos, Shannon 92	Lutz, Jonathon 13	McKimpson, Casey 104
Kutschke, Mary 108	Lytle, Hayley 9	McKinney, Quaintesha 68
Labritz, Courtney 43	Macasek, Brandon 55	McKissick, Jeffrey 35
Lamendola, Mark 95	Mackey, Felicia 123	McKnight, Carolyn 128
Lamure, Ruhama 81	Mahlandt, Taylor 17	McLaughlin, Brenna 109
Landis, Matt 16	Mahoney, Sean 17	McLaughlin, Laurel 24
Lane, Ben 129	Mahoney, Sean 74	Mclendon, Kira 20
Lane, John David 81	Main, Josh 52	McMaster, Bobby 118
Lang, Eric 16	Majercsik, Mary 105	McMullen, Brigid 15
Lantz, Merideth 18	Malek, Christine S. 126	McNavish, Sophia 20
Lantz, Thomas 127	Malone, Liam 60	McNeely, Shannon 80
Lapson, Miranda 107	Manchini, Noelle 31	McNeill, Grace 28
Large, Justice 59	Mancini, Emily 17	McQueen, Colin 64
Larkin, Rachel 85	Mangus, Zachary 120	Mealing, Kiara 123
LaRusso, Sami 97	Mannino, Carrie 37	Meell, Rachel 126
Laskowski, Chris 74	Marchese, Clare 9	Mejia, Larice 59
Lassiter, Denise 110	Markham, Erin 30	Melvin, Tanner 17
Laughery, Brenna Marie 20	Marks, Ryan 33	Memon, Dillon 119
Lavery, Corey 83	Marmaras, Grace 82	Mercier, Brandon 134

Index

Mercner, David 105
Mercurio, Reilly 20
Mertz, Brenna 81
Messner, Michael 59
Metcalf, Hannah 55
Metz, Emily 103
Metzger, Mike 12
Miazio Jr., David 54
Mihaljevic, Emily 94
Milhimes, Luke 82
Millan, Alexandra 67
Miller, Haley 25
Miller, Joella 28
Miller, Rayna 97
Mininall, Paige 40
Missry, Julie 78
Mitchell, Christopher 108
Molinari, Olivia 52
Monaghan, Cecilia 20
Mondragon, Haley 31
Monteforte, Megan 88
Montenegro, Elena Isabelle 61
Moore, Jaelyn 22
Morales, Jason 104
Morgan-White, Trae 47
Morris, Rebecca 126
Morris, Ty 104
Moschgat, Nick 57
Mosher, Tyler 118
Moss, Da'Jour 74
Mosser, Juliana 14
Mravintz, Hunter 27
Mull, Keira 45
Mullen, Casandra 61
Muriceak, E.J 17
Murphy, Amber 128
Murphy, Conall 62
Murray, Maria 36
Murray, Matt 101
Murray, Michael 114
Musselman, Erik 105
Myers, Kylie 56
Nace, Joe 99
Nadonley, Jacob 99
Nadorlik, Jake 95
Namukwana, Jeaninah 59
Napoleon, Riley 125
Naticchia, Nicole 57
Navarro, Tanner 47
Naylor, Robert 95
Nemesch, Taryn 78
Nero, Gregory 26
Newman, Lainey 75
Newman, Leo 99
Newman, Mira 116
Nguyen, David 123
Nikolos, Zoe 16
Nissley, Brooke Lyn 80
Niven, Maya 61

Noble, Madeline 100
Nolan, Emily 48
Novak, Alyssa 127
Nudd, Madison 123
Null, Sarah 60
O'Brien, Alex 93
O'Brien, Margaret-Mary 75
O'Brien, Olivia 58
O'Connor, Sabrina 72
O'Hagan, Sean 111
O'Hare, Brooke 51
O'Neill, Sean 107
O'Rourke, Lance 11
Oakes, Donovan 37
Oberholtzer, Megan 18
Ojeda, Lianis 34
Ojeda, Sebastian 18
Okada, Anna 108
Olash, Collin 91
Oliphant, Anthony 34
Oliver, Monique 86
Ordean, Destiny 122
Ours, Leigha 136
Owens, Melina 24
Owings, Yrsa 38
Pacheco, Andrew 60
Padgett, Kne'aja 59
Palandro, Sarah 57
Palmer, Jordan 122
Palmiere, William 64
Palumbo, Bennett 58
Parekh, Nilay 46
Parisi, Alexandra 47
Park, Wyatt 131
Parsons, Isabel 34
Patel, Hiren 50
Paul, Brian 44
Pawling, Samuel Reed 33
Pecuch, Morgan 113
Peluchette, Damon 122
Peng, Angeline 48
Penko, Tommy 130
Perdue, Natalie 104
Perez, Thannushka 56
Perry, Alyssa 83
Perry, Valerie 41
Persin, Katie 23
Pertusio, Elise 112
Peters, Katherine 49
Petito, Armand W 84
Petrone, Mara 95
Petruccelli, Michael 92
Pfeffer, Erin 119
Phan, Nhi 69
Phillips, Asia 46
Pichi, Alex 96
Pickering, Alexis 23
Pickering, James 61
Pierce, Chris 128

Pietropaolo, Rebecca 113
Pigoni, Michael 10
Pipes, Jarret 103
Pirl, Alison 19
Pirrone, Jaime 27
Placha, Alyssa 74
Plotnick, Alyssa 58
Plumley, Chad 126
Poillon, Ricky 81
Pokora, Francheska 105
Polovoy, Allison 21
Popp, Joseph 85
Portner, Nikolai 39
Potter, Jacob 131
Powers, Kate 18
Preux, Taniyah 51
Price, Asjia 131
Priddy, Jordin 19
Przybylinski, Erin 10
Puchalski, Kellyn Nicole 89
Pugh, Alana 63
Qually, Simone 100
Quasey, Katie 55
Quinn, Joseph 83
Rachko, Lindsay 9
Radich, Luke 78
Raha, Kyle 106
Ramesh, Aish 44
Ramirez, Herminio 32
Ramirez, Noelia 130
Rastetter, Jeffrey 134
Reading, Caitlyn 61
Ready, Matt 36
Rebuck, Madison 66
Reddy, Mahima 71
Reed, Breanna 127
Reedy, Catherine 67
Reedy, Julia 56
Reese, Kelsey 49
Regan, Madison 83
Rehfuss, Michela 52
Reil, William 136
Remshard, Kayla 82
Renda, Zack 92
Renner, Savannah 99
Reyes, Jorge 88
Riccardi, Alexander 25
Richason, Noah 69
Ricketts, Zoe 28
Riehl, Lenéa 49
Rightmyer, Jillian 63
Rinehart, Peter 130
Rivera, Mayra 46
Roberto, Ally 54
Robertshaw, Elie 107
Robinson, Peirce 69
Robinson, Tom 29
Robinson, Zha'Keirah 97
Roces, Mark 100

Name	Page
Rock, Ashley	128
Roddy, Hannah	128
Rodriguez, Carmen	50
Roese, Connor	16
Rogliano, Ashley	45
Rohm, Ryan	30
Roll, Isabella	91
Roma, Jacob	104
Romanovich, Olesea	129
Rombach, Victoria	24
Rosado, Yaridis	49
Rose, Amirah	68
Rossi, Meaghan	112
Roteman, Meredith	66
Rowlands, Sara	50
Rowles, Curtis	17
Rubenstein, Josea	66
Rudy, Kristin	81
Rudzinski, Michael	26
Ruebeck, Noah	11
Rusek, Sydney	133
Russell, Hunter	13
Rutkauskas, J.R.	60
Rutkowski, Anna	99
Ryan, Jessa	76
Salah, Victoria	130
Saleem, Jonah	16
Salivonchik, Steven	13
Sam, Eileen	75
Sammartino, Vincent	91
Sanchez, Ashley	98
Sanchez, Elijsha	81
Sanchez, Elyja	97
Sandt, Ally	42
Santana, Joseph	28
Santana, Mariah	91
Santiago, Hiram	31
Santry, Nicole	51
Saunders, Bradley	109
Saunders, Micah	61
Savage, Hannah	35
Scaccia, Jeremy	93
Scalen, Jessica	15
Scarpone, Sophia	65
Schatten, Samantha	72
Scheers, Abigail	85
Schiavo, Michael	103
Schmac, Taylor	58
Schoener, Kyle	13
Schroeder, Mason	24
Schubert, Ronnie	121
Schule, Elizabeth	76
Schultz, Noah	96
Schumann, Claire	82
Scoccia, Alyssa	122
Scott, Michael	95
Sebastian, Erin	50
Seibel, Jarod William	117
Seitz, Kayla	31
Selinsky, Devin	125
Sellers, Megan	27
Sellinger, Rebecca	25
Serafini, Olivia	23
Seroka, Jordan	103
Serrano, Spencer	131
Sessoms, Jamil	86
Seybold, Forrest	19
Shank, Connor	63
Sharp, Danielle	102
Shawgo, Shannon	89
Shipley, Abigail	58
Shoop, Anna	25
Shortall, Kylie	109
Shoup, Kayla P.	82
Silvio, Zach	131
Simmer, Caroline	41
Sinclair, Spencer	94
Siwula, Michael	77
Skirda, Justin	35
Skiviat, Avery	34
Slagel, Katelyn	34
Slaugenhaupt, Aislinn	70
Slavicek, Alexis	59
Smink, Alyssa Taylor	58
Smith, Alexis	124
Smith, Alison	43
Smith, Baily	122
Smith, Benny	133
Smith, Erin	122
Smith, Kendall	81
Smith, Lauren	38
Smith, Mercedes Y.	134
Smith, Toni	119
Smoker, Victoria	38
Sniechoski, Emily	115
Snopkowski, Alina	51
Snyder, Chad	45
Sobczuk, Basia	26
Sorbello, Zachary	15
Soveral, Rachel	13
Spagnoletti, Alyssa	36
Spirnock, Jacob	9
Spisak, Tiffany	38
Spyropoulos, Dina	85
Stahl, Lauren	19
Staley, Alexis	68
Stephens, Alexa	46
Stepp, Nicole	91
Stevens, Kayla	124
Stiffy, Sarah	14
Stillwagon, Julie	10
Stipe, Ryan	43
Stocku, Ryan	14
Stoltzfus, Jared	99
Stopyra, Samantha	80
Storm, Cole	67
Stott, C.J.	57
Stout, Carolyn	23
Stowman, Allison	97
Strahan, Theo	62
Strati, Christina	19
Stretz, Kyla	123
Strohl, Julia	53
Strohl, Kaleigh	56
Subah, Monqualine	67
Suder, Valerie	21
Sundgaard, Alyssa	61
Swaray, Mohamed	97
Taramelli-Dickinson, Mallory	23
Tarnoff, Ashley	85
Tasco, Lucky	106
Taylor, Tatiana	28
Teesdale, John	136
Thomas, Blake	86
Thomas, Devonte	75
Thurston, Yasmine	120
Timar, Angelica	69
Tipton, Grace	11
Todd, Kody	89
Toledo, Adrian	90
Tome, Allyssa	125
Tomlinson, Alexus	43
Torrence, Ahmier	69
Torres, Emmanuel N.	12
Torres, Kayana	37
Torres, Tiyananonsion	96
Towell, Sydney	122
Tracey, John	13
Traczek, Camille	97
Tran, Jennifer	40
Trebicka, Sarah	70
Tremblay, Alice	87
Trexler, Thomas	105
Trimber, Lauren	72
Trotter, Elijah S.	24
Trout, Eliza	95
Truxon, Isis	100
Tucci, Matthew	50
Tull, Tynetta	69
Turchan, Ashley	67
Turner, Dana	102
Turner, Madysen	17
Turner, Reanna	55
Tutsock, Matt	102
Tyler, Harriet	130
Umbaugh, Cailin	65
Underwood, Bryce	128
Updegraff, Nolan	83
Urbanek, Kelsie	122
Valenti, Kayla	97
Vas, Jacque	103
Vasquez, Miguel	29
Vebelun, Nicole	121
Vega, Kaylee	79
Vicente, Sabrina	83
Violi, Julia	12
Visan, Alex	71

Vivio, Tyler 56
Vizcaino, Jesenia 62
Vizza, Julia 80
Vogt, Connor 76
Volk, Tori 82
Vukelich, Jack 45
Waddell, Rachel 55
Wagner, Morgan 83
Wahlgren, Emily 21
Walker, Austin 26
Walker, Lydia 59
Walker, William 97
Wallace, Hope 83
Walls, Abby 121
Walsh, Jack 45
Wamser, Calvin Isaac 54
Wang, Vicki 79
Ward, Braden 69
Warner, Serena 102
Wasekanes, Joseph 66
Wattenmaker, Rick 39
Watters, Keri 12
Wayman, Erin 41
Waynar, Parker 86
Wayne, Devin 87
Weaver, Hannah 108
Weaver, Olivia 76
Weaver, Tess 47
Webster, Savannah 23
Weichel, Mark 98
Weisner, Claire 111
Weiss, Adam 102
Weiss, Laura 25
Weller, Emily 45
Wells, Albin 109
Wells, Hanna 135
Wells, Molly 89
Welsh, Nicole 42
Werynski, John 86
Wessel, Ali 100
Westhoff, Rachel 79
Weston, Natalie 88
Wewer, Lauren 112
Wheeler, Jackie 74
Whelan, Billy 88
White, Cameron 20
White, Cassandra 39
White, Christopher 18
Whitlow, Shysaun 133
Whitmore, Madeleine 90
Whyne, Payton 128
Wicklund, Danielle 20
Williams, Jerica 106
Williams, Tatiana 96
Williamson, Ali 74
Wilson, Johnathan 14
Wilson, Sedona Sowell 77
Wilson, Warren 130
Wilson-Ussack, Alexis 91

Wingate, Carley Ann 72
Wingert, Jarod 84
Wirth, Lydia 24
Witherow, Sarah Kathryn 36
Witherspoon-McClam, Tinijia 89
Wlodarczyk, Michael 41
Woland, Bryce 130
Wolfe, Timothy 29
Woodson, Marina 38
Workman, Grace 105
Wright, Emily 22
Wurst, Megan 8
Yanovich, Arianna 80
Yarow, Ibrahim 71
Yodanis, Robbie 136
Yoder, John 46
Young, Andrew 115
Young, Jeddy 52
Young, Kelsey 36
Yourish, Emily 128
Yujanova, Victoria 92
Zaborowski, Laurel 22
Zacharias, Elizabeth 101
Zadroga, Logan 135
Zagorski, Tyler 122
Zanella, Nicole 97
Zaremski, Megan 39
Zawalnicki, Brooke 35
Zawycky, Peter 93
Zeigler, Emily 117
Zemaitis, Alexander 27
Zetwo, Shea 136
Zhang, Yang 105
Zhitnitsky, Brandon 34
Zimmerman, Marie 120
Zimmerman, Megan 106
Zimmerman, Reilly 29
Zmuda, Lawrence 99
Zuppe, Austin 132
Zvyagelsky, Aaron 28

Author Autograph Page

Author Autograph Page

Author Autograph Page

Author Autograph Page

Author Autograph Page

Author Autograph Page

Author Autograph Page

Author Autograph Page

Author Autograph Page

Author Autograph Page

Author Autograph Page

Author Autograph Page

Author Autograph Page

Author Autograph Page

Author Autograph Page

Author Autograph Page

Author Autograph Page

Author Autograph Page